LEVEL 1
AWARD IN
BUSINESS SKILLS

STUDY TEXT

Qualifications and Credit Framework

AAT Level 1

Q2022

It belongs to

KAPLAN PUBLISHING'S STATEMENT OF PRINCIPLES

LINGUISTIC DIVERSITY, EQUALITY AND INCLUSION

We are committed to diversity, equality and inclusion and strive to deliver content that all users can relate to.

We are here to make a difference to the success of every learner.

Clarity, accessibility and ease of use for our learners are key to our approach.

We will use contemporary examples that are rich, engaging and representative of a diverse workplace.

We will include a representative mix of race and gender at the various levels of seniority within the businesses in our examples to support all our learners in aspiring to achieve their potential within their chosen careers.

Roles played by characters in our examples will demonstrate richness and diversity by the use of different names, backgrounds, ethnicity and gender, with a mix of sexuality, relationships and beliefs where these are relevant to the syllabus.

It must always be obvious who is being referred to in each stage of any example so that we do not detract from clarity and ease of use for each of our learners.

We will actively seek feedback from our learners on our approach and keep our policy under continuous review. If you would like to provide any feedback on our linguistic approach, please use this form (you will need to enter the link below into your browser).

https://forms.gle/U8oR3abiPpGRDY158

We will seek to devise simple measures that can be used by independent assessors to randomly check our success in the implementation of our Linguistic Equality, Diversity and Inclusion Policy.

British Library Cataloguing-in-Publication Data

A catalogue record for this book is available from the British Library.

Published by
Kaplan Publishing UK
Unit 2, The Business Centre
Molly Millars Lane
Wokingham
Berkshire
RG41 2QZ

ISBN 978 1 83996 295 0

The text in this material and any others made available by any Kaplan Group company does not amount to advice on a particular matter and should not be taken as such. No reliance should be placed on the content as the basis for any investment or other decision or in connection with any advice given to third parties. Please consult your appropriate professional adviser as necessary. Kaplan Publishing Limited and all other Kaplan group companies expressly disclaim all liability to any person in respect of any losses or other claims, whether direct, indirect, incidental, consequential or otherwise arising in relation to the use of such materials.

CONTENTS

INTRODUCTION

HOW TO USE THESE MATERIALS

These Kaplan Publishing learning materials have been carefully designed to make your learning experience as easy as possible and to give you the best chance of success in your AAT assessments.

They contain a number of features to help you in the study process.

The sections on the Unit Guide, the Assessment and Study Skills should be read before you commence your studies.

They are designed to familiarise you with the nature and content of the assessment and to give you tips on how best to approach your studies.

STUDY TEXT

This Study Text has been specially prepared for the revised AAT Level 1 qualification introduced in 2022, based on the specification published in June 2022.

It is written in a practical and interactive style by expert classroom tutors.

In this Study Text:

- key terms and concepts are clearly defined

- all topics are illustrated with practical examples with clearly worked solutions based on sample tasks provided by the AAT in the new assessment style

- frequent activities throughout and at the end of the chapters ensure that what you have learnt is regularly reinforced

- 'Test your understanding' activities are included within each chapter to apply your learning and develop your understanding

- a 'Case Study' brings the subject to life and puts the content covered into a real life context

- Mock Assessments and end of chapter activities reinforce understanding to prepare you for the assessment.

ICONS

The chapters include the following icons throughout.

They are designed to assist you in your studies by identifying key definitions and the points at which you can test yourself on the knowledge gained.

 Definition

These sections explain important areas of Knowledge which must be understood and reproduced in an assessment

 Example

The illustrative examples can be used to help develop an understanding of topics before attempting the activity exercises

 Test your understanding

These are exercises which give the opportunity to assess your understanding of all the assessment areas.

 Case study

These examples put the chapter content into a real life context, using the case study of Jessica and her role at How Two Ltd.

 Case study activities

Following the chapter summary, these questions enable further practice using the real life context of the above case study.

UNIT GUIDE

Introduction

The AAT Level 1 Award in Business Skills offers students the opportunity to develop key practical skills used in every business as a route into employment. On completion of this qualification, students will also be equipped with a strong foundation from which to progress to further study with AAT in either accountancy or bookkeeping if they would like to do so.

Students should choose to study the AAT Level 1 Award in Business Skills to help them develop their employability skills and prepare for the workplace. Students will develop their basic numeracy skills to support everyday business activities, which will also be of use in their activities outside work. Students will also gain a practical understanding of how money moves in business and the processes and procedures that control the sales and purchases processes.

The Award in Business Skills introduces students to the world of work and develops their employability skills. The qualification covers a range of skills and the relevant supporting knowledge in two mandatory units:

- Working in the business environment
- Using numbers in business

A student completing this qualification will develop an understanding of how different organisations operate, across both the public and private sectors. They will learn how to contribute effectively in the workplace by working with others, managing their time, behaving professionally and maintaining security of data. Students will gain an understanding of the ways in which businesses process sales and purchases and the documentation and procedures used to move goods and services between businesses.

Studying this qualification will also equip students with the basic numerical skills needed in the workplace, and in life outside work. These numerical skills range from simple calculations that are used most often in business to working with decimals, percentages and fractions, and applying proportions and ratios. Students will also learn tools and techniques to enhance the presentation of numerical data.

The skills developed in this qualification can lead to employment in junior or supporting administrative roles in companies, for example, as:

- a data entry clerk
- an accounts administrator
- an administrative assistant
- a receptionist
- a retail assistant
- a customer service advisor.

Mandatory units – overview and learning outcomes

Working in the business environment

Overview

This unit provides students with an introduction to the business environment. Students will the skills needed to contribute effectively in the workplace, including team working, communication, effective time management and the need for professional behaviour. They will explore workplace communications and the use of software for different business tasks, while understanding the need for data security and learning how to keep data secure. This unit will also look at the different methods of communication and the characteristics of effective information.

Students will explore the key features of different types of organisations and the sectors in which they operate. They will learn the purpose of different organisations and how they operate, and also how organisations are commonly structured.

Students will learn the importance of sales, purchases and expenses, and the procedures that support them, to the success of the business. Students will discover that businesses need to make more sales (income) than purchases (expenses) to operate profitably. Students will become familiar with the relevant terminology and common documents used. They will gain the skills necessary to perform practical finance-related tasks while following business procedures.

Students will understand the different types of organisation that exist, including profit and not for profit. They will also understand that businesses make money by selling goods and services and not for profit organisations provide services to the public and generate income to support their purpose. They will understand that businesses have to use their income to pay for the costs of running the business. They will know the processes involved in making both sales and purchases and will understand how they can contribute to the success of a business by following business procedures accurately and on time.

Learning outcomes

1. Develop skills for the workplace
2. Understand how organisations operate
3. Understand how sales and purchases support business
4. Apply business procedures to sales and purchases

Using Numbers in Business

Overview

Numeracy is an essential business skill and helps an employee to operate more effectively in any workplace. However, students will also encounter many situations outside work where basic numeracy is required. Completing this unit will help students to develop their confidence and their ability to use numbers in a wide range of situations.

On completion of this unit, students will have the skills to practically apply a range of common numerical methods to everyday business situations, whatever their role and regardless of the type of organisation in which they might work. They will be able to record and sort numbers, to identify differences between figures and to complete simple calculations. Students will be able to work out averages, use time and currency in calculations that support everyday business activities and work with more complex calculations, including those involving common decimals, fractions, percentages and proportions.

Basic formulas and formatting will also be taught in order to enhance the presentation of numerical data.

Learning outcomes

1. Perform simple business calculations

2. Calculate decimals, fractions, percentages, proportions and ratios

3. Use tools and techniques to present numerical data

The skills developed in this qualification may also underpin those developed further in the following Level 2 qualifications:

- Level 1 Award in Bookkeeping
- Level 2 Certificate in Bookkeeping
- Level 2 Certificate in Accounting

Scope of content and assessment criteria

Working in the business environment

Develop skills for the workplace (Chapters 4, 5 & 8)

1.1 The responsibilities of the employee and employer

Learners need to understand:

1.1.1 the responsibilities of the employee:

- follow workplace policies and procedures
- report any health and safety risks

1.1.2 the responsibilities of the employer:

- provide induction to new staff that includes organisation policies and procedures
- provide a safe working environment

1.2 Working and communicating with others

Learners need to understand:

1.2.1 the characteristics of effective team working:

- clear roles and responsibilities
- respect
- trust
- co-operation
- common goals
- realistic deadlines
- good communication
- timekeeping
- reliability
- professionalism

1.2.2 the benefit of working in teams:

- collaboration
- sharing ideas
- team morale
- achieving goals
- utilising individuals' skills and expertise
- shared learning

1.2.3 why different methods of communication are used in the workplace:
- emails
- business letters
- online meetings
- reports
- spreadsheets
- telephone calls
- face-to-face
- instant messaging
- intranet
- shared communication channels

1.2.4 the characteristics of effective written communication:
- free from spelling and grammatical errors
- key information is included
- appropriate salutations are included
- content is clear and can be understood by the reader.

1.2.5 how software is used in workplace communications:
- word processing
- spreadsheet
- email
- presentation.

Learners need to be able to:
1.26 identify effective and ineffective communication:
- business letters
- emails.

1.3 Time management

Learners need to know:
1.3.1 how to use planning aids to manage their time:
- online calendars
- work schedules
- online collaborations tools
- to-do lists (including digital to-do-lists)

1.3.2 the effect on others of failing to meet a deadline

- others may be replying on work produced by the team
- impact on other deadlines of the team

1.3.3 that work might be allocated based on how urgent and important it is.

1.4   Professional behaviour

Learners need to understand:

1.4.1 the principle of confidentiality:

- Compliance with General Data Protection Regulations

1.4.2 how to follow policies and procedures:

- sustainability (environmental awareness)
- use of social media
- use of personal phones
- dress codes
- answering and making business phone calls

1.4.3 principles of good time keeping:

- being at work on time
- keeping to break times
- not leaving early
- discussing workloads with supervisor
- agreeing time off with manager

1.4.4 principles of polite communication with colleagues and customers:

- using correct names
- listening to the other person
- avoiding slang, swearing and offensive humour

1.4.5 personal qualities required for employment:

- honesty
- adaptability
- trustworthiness
- commitment.

1.5   The importance of keeping data and information secure

Learners need to understand:

1.5.1   why it is important to make sure that data and information is secure:

- prevents loss and unauthorised sharing of information
- protects against computer failure or viruses
- maintains confidentiality
- protects customer information
- complies with any legal requirements
- loss of business / personal reputation

1.5.2   how data and information is kept secure:

- use of strong passwords / not sharing passwords
- screensavers
- encryption
- firewalls
- use of secure network: remote / hybrid working
- storage of hard-copy records, physical access restrictions
- storage of soft-copy records: cloud-storage, archives, secure back-ups, restricted access, cybersecurity
- authentication required to access cloud-based information
- not sharing laptops/computers with others
- not leaving confidential information where non-authorised personnel may see/not working in a public space
- not discussing confidential information where non-authorised personnel may hear
- anti-virus software
- cookies and privacy settings
- the importance of only sharing information with authorised personnel
- checking correct recipient before sending required information

1.5.5 threats to data security:

- viruses
- hacking
- phishing
- system crashes
- employee fraud

- corrupt files
- natural disasters
- accidental deletion.

Understand how organisations operate (Chapters 1 & 4)

2.1   Key features of different sectors

Learners need to know:

2.1.1 the key features of the retail sector:
- sells goods to the public
- may have a number of branches, franchises or online

2.1.2 the key features of the manufacturing sector:
- makes products either for sale or as components for further manufacturing

2.1.3 the key features of the service sector:
- provides services rather than manufacturing or selling goods

2.1.4 the key features of the charity and voluntary sector:
- generates income to support its purpose

2.1.5   the key features of the public sector:
- provides services to the public
- funded by the government

2.1.6 businesses can operate from a physical location and/or online.

2.2   Purpose of different types of organisations

Learners need to understand:

2.2.1   that some organisations are run for profit:
- sole trader
- partnership
- private limited company (Ltd
- public limited company (PLC)

2.2.2   that some organisations are run not for profit:
- charities
- community and voluntary organisations
- public sector
- social enterprises
- community interest companies (CICs)

2.2.3 additional considerations:
- sustainability
- ethics
- diversity and equal opportunities.

2.3 Structure of an organisation

Learners need to understand:

2.3.1 different organisations of different sizes have different structures

2.3.2 typical departments within an organisation and what they do:
- finance
- human resources
- information technology
- sales and marketing
- production
- distribution

2.3.3 the structure of a three-level organisation chart:
- directors
- department managers
- department staff

2.3.4 levels of responsibility in an organisation and who each level reports to:
- director
- manager
- staff.

Understand how sales and purchases support businesses (Chapters 6, 7 & 8)

3.1 Purpose of sales and purchases

Learners need to understand:

3.3.1 the importance of sales and purchases:
- businesses need money to operate
- selling goods and services makes money (income)
- buying goods and services costs money (expenses)
- businesses need more income than expenses to run profitably
- the meaning of profit and loss: income minus expenses
- the meaning of surplus and deficit for not-for-profit organisations

3.1.2 possible problems when there is more expenditure than income:
- not enough money to pay for purchases
- bank account may become overdrawn
- suppliers may withdraw credit
- business could fail

3.1.3 possible opportunities when there is more income than expenditure:
- saving opportunity
- business growth
- repay loans
- provide return to owners.

3.2   Principles of sales

Learners need to understand:

3.2.1 who goods or services are sold to:
- customs   *What is the difference between them?*
- clients

3.2.2 that some sales are made on a cash basis

3.2.3 that some sales are made on a credit basis

3.3   Principles of purchases

Learners need to understand:

3.3.1 who goods or services are bought from: suppliers

3.3.2 that some purchases are made on a cash basis

3.3.3 that some purchases are made on a credit basis

3.3.4 that businesses may have a list of approved suppliers.

3.4   Payment terms

Learners need to understand:

3.4.1 the purpose of payment terms:
- to ensure that customers know when to pay their invoices
- to ensure that suppliers are paid at the agreed time.

3.4.2 common terminology:

- payment in advance
- payment on delivery
- payment 10, 14, 30 or 60 days after invoice date
- payment at end of the month of invoice

3.4.3 how payment terms offered to customers/clients and received from suppliers affect the bank balance.

Apply business procedures to sales and purchases (Chapters 7 & 8)

4.1 Importance of business procedures

Learners need to understand:

4.1.1 why it is important to follow business procedures:

- to avoid errors
- to avoid missing internal and external deadlines
- to ensure processes are completed as required by the business
- to maintain good business relationships with customers and suppliers

4.1.2 how to follow procedures:

- completing documents fully and accurately
- completing documents on time
- obtaining authorisation
- ensuring procedures being followed are up-to-date

4.2 Business procedures for sales

Learners need to understand:

4.2.1 documents used in the sales process:

- customer order
- delivery note
- sales invoice

4.2.2 the process of making sales:

- customer places order
- business delivers goods or provides services to customer
- business invoices for goods or services
- business receives and records the income.

4.3 Business procedures for purchases

Learners need to understand:

4.3.1 documents used in the purchase process:

- approved supplier list
- purchase order
- delivery note
- goods received note (GRN)
- purchase invoice

4.3.2 the process of purchasing goods or services:

- business selects supplier
- business raises purchase order
- business receives goods or services from supplier
- business checks delivery note against goods received
- business completes goods received note (GRN)
- business makes a note of any differences and queries them with supplier
- business checks purchase invoice against purchase order and delivery note/goods received note (GRN)
- business makes payment and records expenditure

4.4 Procedures

Learners need to be able to:

4.4.1 select an approved supplier for specified goods or services

4.4.2 check for differences between documents in the purchase process (purchase order, goods received note (GRN), delivery note):

- incorrect items or quantity of goods
- items missing from delivery
- incorrect item price
- incorrect calculations.

Using numbers in business

Perform simple business calculations (Chapters 2 & 3)

1.1 Record and sort whole numbers

Learners need to be able to:

1.1.1 record numbers in words and figures

1.1.2 arrange numbers, including positive and negative numbers, in ascending and descending order
- identify highest number
- identify lowest number

1.1.3 calculate range

1.1.4 identify most frequently occurring number or numbers (mode).

1.2 Check results of calculations

Learners need to be able to:

1.2.1 estimate figures

1.2.2 round figures

1.2.3 estimate highest and lowest possible results

1.2.4 cross-check calculations

1.3 Identify differences between figures over time

Learners need to be able to:

1.3.1 identify increases

1.3.2 identify decreases.

1.4 Complete calculations

Learners need to be able to:

1.4.1 use numerical functions:
- addition
- subtraction
- multiplication
- division
- calculate average (mean)

1.4.2 work with common units of time.

Calculate decimals, fractions, percentages, proportions and ratios (Chapter 2)

2.1 Calculate decimals, fractions and percentages of numbers

Learners need to be able to:

2.1.1 calculate decimals

2.1.2 calculate simple fractions

2.1.3 calculate whole percentages

2.1.4 calculate figures using whole percentages

2.1.5 express a number as a fraction or percentage of another.

2.2 Calculate equivalent fractions, percentages and decimals

Learners need to be able to:

2.2.1 convert fractions into percentages and decimals

2.2.2 convert percentages into fractions and decimals

2.2.3 convert decimals into percentages and fractions.

2.3 Calculate and apply simple proportions and ratios

Learners need to be able to:

2.3.1 express two numbers as a ratio

2.3.2 apply a proportion or ratio to a number.

Use tools and techniques to present numerical data (Chapter 3)

3.1 Formulas

Learners need to be able to:

3.1.1 use formulas when completing calculations:

- addition
- subtraction
- multiplication
- division.

3.2 Formatting

Learners need to be able to:

3.2.1 use formatting to enhance presentation of information:

- bold
- italics
- underline
- change font colour / size
- fill cell
- accounting
- thousands
- percentages
- decimal places

KAPLAN PUBLISHING

The assessment

Students must successfully pass one combined mandatory unit assessment to achieve this qualification.

The proportion of this qualification assessed by externally marked assessment is 100%.

The assessment in this qualification:

- is set and marked by AAT

- is computer based

- is time-limited

- is scheduled by training providers or assessment venues

- takes place at approved training providers and assessment venues under controlled conditions.

This qualification is not graded.

Assessment for this award will be by Computer based assessment (CBA), under timed conditions. The time allowed for the assessment is 90 minutes.

The weighting of the learning outcomes is as follows:

Working in the business environment

1. Develop skills for the workplace	20%
2. Understand how organisations operate	15%
3. Understand how sales and purchases support businesses	15%
4. Apply business procedures to sales and purchases	15%

Using Numbers in Business

1. Perform simple business calculations	15%
2. Calculate decimals, fractions, percentages, proportions & ratios	10%
3. Use tools and techniques to present numerical data	10%

Total   **100%**

STUDY SKILLS

Preparing to study

Devise a study plan

Determine which times of the week you will study.

Split these times into sessions of at least one hour for study of new material. Any shorter periods could be used for revision or practice.

Put the times you plan to study onto a study plan for the weeks from now until the assessment and set yourself targets for each period of study – in your sessions make sure you cover the whole course, activities and the associated questions with answers at the back of the Study Text.

When working through your course, compare your progress with your plan and, if necessary, re-plan your work (perhaps including extra sessions) or, if you are ahead, do some extra revision/practice questions.

Effective studying

Active reading

You are not expected to learn the text by rote, rather, you must understand what you are reading and be able to use it to pass the assessment and develop good practice.

A good technique is to use SQ3Rs – Survey, Question, Read, Recall, Review:

1   **Survey the chapter**

    Look at the headings and read the introduction, knowledge, skills and content, so as to get an overview of what the chapter deals with.

2   **Question**

    Whilst undertaking the survey ask yourself the questions you hope the chapter will answer for you.

3   **Read**

    Read through the chapter thoroughly working through the activities and, at the end, making sure that you can meet the learning objectives shown within the summary.

4   **Recall**

    At the end of each chapter, try to recall the main ideas of the section/chapter without referring to the text. This is best done after short break of a couple of minutes after the reading stage.

5   **Review**

    Check that your recall notes are correct.

KAPLAN PUBLISHING

You may also find it helpful to re-read the chapter to try and see the topic(s) it deals with as a whole.

Note taking

Taking notes is a useful way of learning, but do not simply copy out the text. The notes must:

- be in your own words
- be concise
- cover the key points
- be well organised
- be modified as you study further chapters in this text or in related ones.

Trying to summarise a chapter without referring to the text can be a useful way of determining which areas you know and which you don't.

Three ways of taking notes

1   Summarise the key points of a chapter

2   Make linear notes

A list of headings, subdivided with sub-headings listing the key points.

If you use linear notes, you can use different colours to highlight key points and keep topic areas together.

Use plenty of space to make your notes easy to use.

3   Try a diagrammatic form

The most common of which is a mind map.

To make a mind map, put the main heading in the centre of the paper and put a circle around it.

Draw lines radiating from this to the main sub-headings which again have circles around them.

Continue the process from the sub-headings to sub-sub-headings.

Highlighting and underlining

You may find it useful to underline or highlight key points in your study text – but do be selective.

You may also wish to make notes in the margins.

Further reading

In addition to this text, you should also read the 'Student section' of the 'Accounting Technician' magazine every month to keep abreast of any guidance from the examiners.

KAPLAN PUBLISHING

How organisations operate

1

Introduction

There are different types of business organisations, each having their own agenda and objectives. To understand the business environment, it is crucial to understand the different sectors and the types of organisations which operate in each.

In this chapter you will learn about the various types of business organisations and how they are structured.

KNOWLEDGE	CONTENTS
Working in the business environment	1 The key features of an organisation
2 Understand how organisations operate	2 The structure of an organisation
2.1 Key features of different sectors	3 Summary and further questions
2.2 Purpose of different types of organisation	
2.3 Structure of organisations	

1 The key features of an organisation

1.1 Case study: an introduction

 Case study

Jessica has decided that she has had enough of full time education.

She wants a career and at the same time she needs to earn some money. After careful consideration and following discussions with a careers advisor, Jessica thinks that an apprenticeship would be the best way forward for her.

As Jessica is unsure of the type of career that she would like to start training for, she has decided to investigate different kinds of organisations to gain an insight into how they worked and possibly identify something that she would enjoy.

Jessica is aware that there are many different business sectors and starts by looking at each in turn.

1.2 The different sectors within business

There are many different sectors in the world of business. You need to know what these are and how to differentiate between them.

 Definitions

The retail sector sells goods to the public.

The manufacturing sector makes products to sell to the public or as components for further manufacturing.

The service sector provides services rather than manufacturing or selling goods.

The charity sector generates income to support its purpose.

The public sector provides services to the public. These services are funded by the Government with money generated through taxes.

The private sector includes profit making organisations. This can be a sole trader working alone or they may have employees. There are also partnerships and limited companies in the private sector.

1.3 The retail sector

The retail sector includes any organisation (typically shops) selling goods to the general public.

On a local level, this includes any small shop (for example, a grocer or a newsagent).

Other retailers, such as some large supermarkets and retail outlets, have several branches throughout the country and many even have stores worldwide (for example, Tesco and Marks and Spencer).

There is an increasing trend towards buying goods online, including groceries and household essentials. The majority of large stores and supermarkets have an online shopping facility, including 'Click and Collect' services where a customer can order their products on a website and then go to a shop or collection point to obtain their purchases. Other companies specialise in online sales and have a minimal high street or physical presence (for example, Amazon and clothes retailers such as ASOS).

The retail sector also includes franchises. A franchise is where the owner of the business (franchisor) sells rights to a third party (franchisee). These rights include the ability to use their logo, sell their products or services and use their system of doing business. The franchisor receives ongoing royalties from the franchisee. Lots of well-known fast food companies are franchises (for example, Subway and McDonald's).

1.4 The manufacturing sector

The manufacturing sector includes businesses ranging from a small company with a few employees on the production line to large factories with hundreds of employees.

Their primary concern is manufacturing and they can produce anything, whether that is goods to go on sale to the public or components for further manufacture.

 Examples

For example, a clothing factory will produce completed garments to supply to retail outlets for direct sale to the general public.

Whereas, a car manufacturing company only actually has an assembly line. The components that go in to assembling a car will have been produced in different factories, therefore these would be classed as components for further manufacture.

1.5   The service sector

The service sector provides services that do not involve the manufacture or selling of goods.

These businesses do not focus on the supply of physical products and instead seek to provide advice or a service to the customer or user.

transporte

💡 Examples

Buses, trains and trams all provide the public with a transport service. Road haulage is another service, trucks transport goods around the country, some even travel abroad to export goods to retailers.

Banks provide a financial service.

advogados — Solicitors provide a legal service.

1.6   The voluntary sector

The voluntary sector comprises of organisations whose main objective is to generate income to support their purpose. Organisations within the voluntary sector are run not-for-profit, meaning that they use all funds earned or donated to fulfil their primary purpose and achieve their objectives.

Voluntary organisations engage with a huge range of issues from youth clubs to specialist research. The objectives of voluntary organisations include addressing topics such as climate change, providing affordable housing or protecting specific groups of people in society, such as the homeless.

There are many types of voluntary organisations, such as co-operatives, social enterprises or community interest companies (CIC's). Co-operatives are owned and controlled by members who may be customers, employees or local residents, all of whom may be using its services. Members work together to meet the objectives of the organisation, often to fulfil specific economic, social or cultural needs. Most importantly, all members have an equal say in how the business operates.

Social enterprises aim to change the world for the better. All profits are reinvested to create positive social change. A community interest company is a special type of limited company, which aims to benefit the community as opposed to private shareholders.

Charities form the largest single category in the voluntary sector. They are governed by specific legislation such as the Charities Act 2011 and Charities (Social and protection) Act 2016.

Some charities have high street shops selling goods donated by the public. Donations are all voluntary, as is the time given by most staff working in the charity shops. However, most charity shop managers are paid a wage.

Money is raised through a variety of methods in the charity sector: donations in envelopes from the public, television campaigns and collection boxes in stores are just some of the other ways this is achieved.

 Examples

Examples of co-operatives include football clubs which are run by the supporters, local childcare providers and farmer co-operatives such as ARLA foods. *is a global dairy company and cooperative owned by over 9000 dairy farmers, with over 2000 of whom are British.*

AIM: work together to create a sustainable long term future for the dairy industry.

Examples of social enterprises in our communities or on the high street include cinemas, leisure centres and coffee shops.

Examples of community interest companies (CIC's) include waste recycling businesses, day care centres and local transport providers.

enterprises = empreendimento.

There are many thousands of examples of charities helping various causes. These include: *RSCPA = Royal Society for the Prevention of cruelty to Animals.*

Animal welfare (RSCPA, Blue Cross) *United Nations Children's Fund*

Disaster relief and humanitarian causes (British Red Cross, UNICEF)

Health and age-related issues (Age UK, Cancer Research, Guide Dogs for the Blind) *Barnardo's Children's Charity.*

Young people at home and abroad (Barnardo's, Save the Children)

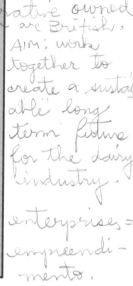

 Activity

Write down the names of as many charities you can think of. *Salvation Army.*

Then, write down what you think each charity does for the public or for the 'common good' of society.

Then check their websites to see if what they do is what you think they do.

The salvation Army helps victim of modern slavery, to nurseries, community choirs and food banks.

1.7   The public sector

The public sector provides services that are essential to the population, such as education and health care.

They are funded by the Government using monies raised through taxation and are not-for-profit organisations.

 Examples

Public sector organisations include the NHS (National Health Service), Police, Ambulance and Fire Brigade.

1.8   The private sector

The private sector is made up of organisations aiming to make profit for the owner/owners. *comerciantes individuais*

These may be sole traders, partnerships or private limited companies, all of which are described in the chart below.

Type of Business	Ownership
Sole Trader	A sole trader business is owned by one person.
	If the business makes a profit the owner will keep all the profits. However, if the business gets into financial difficulty, the sole trader is responsible for all the debts.
	A sole trader may work on their own or have several employees. The owner is in direct control of all elements and is legally accountable for the finances of the business.
	Sole traders may use a trade name or business name other than their own legal name.
Partnership	A partnership is similar to a sole trader business but is owned by between two and twenty people.
	Each partner will take a share of the profits of the business or be liable for the losses of the business.

Limited companies	When a limited company is set up it is given its own legal identity. The ownership of these companies is divided into shares of the business. Any profit made by the business is allocated to shareholders in the form of dividends, based on how many shares they hold.
	Shareholders have limited liability which means that they are not liable for the business's debts. If the business gets into financial difficulty, shareholders only lose the money they invested.
	The shares of private limited companies (Ltd) are usually given to the directors of the organisation or other private individuals.
	The shares of public limited companies (plc) are sold on the stock exchange which means that anyone from the general public can buy them.

Test your understanding 1

Match the different sectors to the key features of organisations within each. Put a tick in the correct box. *r defende a lei — fornece ajuda*

	Transports people	Makes products	Upholds the law	Provides aid	Sells goods	Makes profit
Retail					✓	✓
Manufacturing		✓			✓	✓
Service	✓		✓	✓		✓
Charity				✓ *		
Public	✓		✓	✓		
Private		✓	✓	✓	✓	✓

*LAW WORKS IS A CHARITY WORKING IN ENGLAND AND WALES TO CONNECT VOLUNTEER LAWYERS WITH PEOPLE IN NEED OF LEGAL ADVICE, WHO ARE NOT ELIGIBLE FOR LEGAL AID AND CANNOT AFFORD TO PAY AND WITH THE NOT-FOR-PROFIT ORGANISATIONS THAT SUPPORT THEM.

*LEGAL AID: IS A PUBLIC FUNDING GIVEN BY THE GOVERNMENT WHICH ALLOWS A PERSON LEGAL HELP IN CERTAIN ISSUES OR CASES.

PUBLIC SECTOR IS UPHOLDS THE LAW. COULD IT BE TRANSPORTS PEOPLE? UPHOLDS THE LAW COULD ASLO BE CONSIDERATED SERVICE?

Test your understanding 2

Are the following types of organisations profit or not-for-profit organisations? Tick the correct box for each.

	Profit	Not-for-profit
Retail	✓	
Manufacturing	✓	
Service	✓	✓
Charity		✓
Public		✓
Private	✓	

Test your understanding 3

Complete the sentences below using the pick list provided.

___PUBLIC___ sector organisations are normally concerned with the provision of basic government services.

___SOLE TRADERS___ are private businesses owned by one person.

___PRIVATE___ sector organisations are primarily concerned with making profit from the sale of goods or services. Where these businesses have shareholders they are known as _LIMITED COMPANIES_

accionistas

Pick list

Private   Public   Charity

Sole traders   Partnerships   Limited companies

Test your understanding 4

Identify the purpose of each sector by matching the sector in the first column with the purpose in the second column.

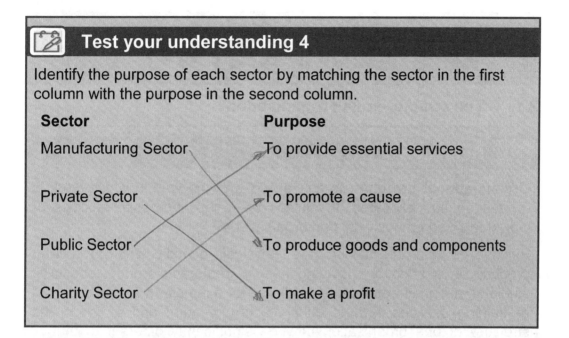

Sector	Purpose
Manufacturing Sector	To provide essential services
Private Sector	To promote a cause
Public Sector	To produce goods and components
Charity Sector	To make a profit

Test your understanding 5

Below are six descriptions of what different organisations do. Match the description to the relevant sector from those provided by placing a tick in the relevant box.

	Sells furniture	Is a sole trader	Animal welfare	Offers financial advice	Provides education	Makes zips for clothes
Retail	✓	✓				
Manufacturing	✓	✓				✓
Service		✓	✓	✓	✓	
Charity			✓	✓	✓	
Private	✓	✓	✓	✓	✓	✓
Public			✓	✓	✓	

2 The structure of an organisation

2.1 The structure of an organisation

 Definition

Organisational structure is concerned with the way in which work is divided up and allocated. It outlines the roles and responsibilities of individuals and groups within an organisation.

Businesses can operate from a physical location such as selling products in a shop or providing beauty treatments from a specialist studio on a high street, or solely online – for example, online counselling or training services. Others do a mixture of both, and as such, the structure of one organisation may be significantly different to that of another.

Within each organisation, there will be several different departments, all performing various functions and with separate areas of expertise and unique responsibilities.

The exact nature of these departments and the way they relate to each other and contribute to the organisation will vary for each sector, so we will consider each in turn before identifying common features for all sectors.

 Definition

Function – an activity carried out in an organisation. For example, the accounting function is carried out by the staff in the accounts department.

2.2 Typical departments in retail

In retail, the size of the store determines how many departments it has. A small store such as a speciality shop or newsagents does not have various departments (this will be explored later in the chapter).

Therefore, we are going to concentrate on the larger retail outlets. This would include any high street clothing or homeware shop with multiple sites, as well as supermarkets and department stores.

Key departments for these organisations typically include:

- Item-specific product areas – different sections relating to the type of goods on sale for example food, clothing, alcohol, tools etc.

- Cashiers – to collect money from the customer

- Shelf-stackers and stock controllers – to monitor and replenish stock sold

- Finance – to handle all accountancy services including the handling of all bookkeeping transactions and payables and receivables. Also usually responsible for payroll and the use of accounting software for the management of financial data and costing using spreadsheets.

  However, the cash flow of a large store is usually also monitored throughout the day. Cashiers have to sign into a cash register, making them responsible for any shortfall in takings while they are using that till. Any refunds or voiding of a transaction has to be authorised by a store supervisor. When there is a change in cashier the cash register can be emptied and the takings counted. Collectively at the end of the working day all cash register takings are added together giving the total sales figure for the day.

- Sales and marketing – to ensure retail sales through methods such as advertising and promotions including discounts on goods. Some product ranges (e.g. food and cosmetics) can be promoted in store where customers are invited to try small samples in an attempt to entice them to buy the product. Catalogues or leaflets are often used to promote sales. This department usually monitors consumer trends and aims to meet supply and demand.

- Despatch and receipt of goods – to arrange the delivery and storage of stock. Large stores have storage facilities that not only receive goods for sale but also have to despatch goods to customers buying from the internet or mail order.

- Administration – to sort documentation and maintain records, including filing to assist other departments such as finance and despatch. This department is also typically responsible for the ordering and allocation of supplies such as stationery and all tasks relating to the organisation of meetings within the business.

- I.T. – to monitor all daily operations in store, including stock, ordering and purchasing, wages, cash registers, supply chains, cross-company stock inventory, training needs of personnel and communication between departments. This department is of vital importance in the retail sector.

- Human Resources (H.R.) – responsible for recruitment, traditionally they screen, interview and place workers into suitable roles. However, in recent times the staff in this department are part of an interview panel whereby the manager/supervisor of a department may be involved with the interview. H.R may also be responsible for training, compensation, safety, benefits and payroll.

Note: While small retailers do not have different departments, and tend to self - manage the day to day running of the business, they usually employ an accountant to do their bookkeeping and ensure that all their finances are accurate and up to date.

2.3 Typical departments in manufacturing

Unlike the retail sector, the manufacturing sector relies heavily on the operating of equipment and therefore many of the departments within a typical manufacturing company relate to the production process.

- Production – where employees make the goods or components. This usually relies on the use of machinery.

- Maintenance – machines can develop faults. The maintenance department will have personnel such as engineers, fitters and electricians. Some machines are operated by computer systems rather than people and if these develop a fault an I.T. technician needs to diagnose and rectify the problem.

- Packaging – once the goods have been made they are packaged and stored ready to be delivered to the customer.

- Despatch – responsible for the timely distribution of goods. This is usually by road transport but can also be by rail (e.g. in quarries where products such as lime and aggregates are loaded into goods trains).

- Finance – as in the retail sector, this comprises of accountancy staff responsible for all bookkeeping, payroll, costing and the use of accounting software for the management of financial data.

- Sales and Marketing – promotes the sales of goods by advertising, telephone, the internet and visiting potential customers to show their product. Many manufacturers also use third party sales agencies or wholesalers/resellers to generate sales.

- I.T. – most companies in this sector have an internal computer program application, accessible to authorised personnel. All departments listed will have an authorised user. Computer systems can track productivity at every level and are a useful tool in communication between departments.

- Administration – as in the retail sector, this department is responsible for maintaining records, organising office supplies and other clerical support for other departments and senior management.

- Human Resources (H.R.) – as in the retail sector, this department is responsible for recruitment and staff training and welfare.

2.4 Typical departments in the service sector

The service sector by definition is a very broad group of organisations, from varied parts of the economy. Any organisation whose business relies on providing a service rather than the products supplied by the manufacturing sector, could be termed as providing a service. Given how vast the spectrum of this category is, it is impractical to list them all and their departments.

The following overview of some organisations should assist in identifying the structure of most service sectors.

Transport services

This includes buses, trains, trams and aeroplanes, all of which provide the transportation of passengers to a destination of their choice. The key departments include:

- Transport – not only to enable the customer to complete their journey, but also trucks, vans and planes to transport other goods

- Planning – the creation and monitoring of routes and timetables

- Maintenance – all transport needs to be maintained and repaired where necessary. Each area of transport has workshops where the maintenance/repairs can be carried out by personnel with the necessary skills to complete the work needed.

- Drivers/Pilots – to fulfil the requirements necessary of their chosen career in order to be able to transport passengers. Similarly, a special licence has to be obtained to transport goods or passengers.

- Ticket sales – Passengers can purchase tickets in various ways such as online, a ticket office, aboard the transport, or a seasonal pass.

- Transport office – to take orders for deliveries, plan drivers' work and allocate routes appropriately.

- I.T. – as in the other sectors above, but also to provide information to customers and drivers, including vehicle tracking and electronic timetables.

- Administration – as in the other sectors above.

- Human Resources – as in the other sectors above.

- Finance – as in the other sectors above.

Banks and financial services

Conversely, banks and financial service organisations are also part of the service sector, providing a variety of different services and advice to their customers.

Departments within a bank include:

- Lending

- Saving

- Investment

- Credit Cards

- Customer Service

- I.T – as in the other sectors above, but including online banking services.

- Administration – as in the other sectors above.

- Human Resources – as in the other sectors above.

2.5 Typical departments in the voluntary sector

Whilst the previous types of organisation considered are largely operated in order to generate profits, the charity sector and public sector often have different aims.

Although the nature of the charity's primary fundraising activities will to some extent determine the staff and departments it will have, the following functions would be common to most charities:

- Head Office – co-ordinates and allocates the income generated.

- Fund-raising – devise ways of generating income, often including telephone and e-mail campaigns, as well as shops, collection boxes and other specialist functions below.

- Shops – take in goods donated by the public and sell them back to customers to generate funds

- Collection boxes – these are distributed throughout the country usually in large stores for the public to donate cash. Their periodic collection and processing require co-ordination.

- Online – most charities offer various ways of donating online, including sponsored activities (e.g. mountain climbs), where all the proceeds go to a pre-chosen charity.

- Human Resources - as in the other sectors above.

- Finance – as in the other sectors above, including payroll for those who do receive a wage.

2.6 Typical departments in the public sector

There are many public services, all of which have one thing in common. They are controlled by the government.

They are given a specific budget and are expected to adhere to it. The government can impose penalties for overspending or contravening rules.

If we consider some of the main public sector organisations, each will have their own specialist departments, as follows:

- The N.H.S. – Providing healthcare

- Police – Upholding the law and protecting the public

- Fire Service – Extinguishing fires and rescuing people in various situations such as accidents

- Ambulance Service – Treating the sick and injured on scene and transporting them to hospital

Each of the public sector services mentioned above will have the following departments in addition to their main services:

- Finance – accountants responsible for bookkeeping, costing, payroll, etc.

- I.T. – each government department has internal I.T systems that can be accessed by staff. Most staff have access to specific areas of the system and have passwords that will allow them to access the area that they are authorised to use. The I.T department is usually large and employs many technicians to keep the system updated and running smoothly.

- Complaints - all government services have a complaints department.

2.7 Typical departments in the private sector

The departments present in private sector organisations will largely overlap with those in the retail, manufacturing or service sectors dependent on what the business does to make profit.

A large online retailer, a manufacturer of electrical components and an insurance company would all be considered to be in the private sector and although each would have specialist departments, most would share common departments such as administration, sales and marketing, product-specific groups, despatch/transportation, research/development, I.T., finance and human resources (H.R.).

Let us consider one type of business in the private sector which would not necessarily have as many specialist departments, sole traders. Returning to the overlap with the retail sector, most small shops are usually sole traders in business. Their primary aim, as with any organisation in the private sector, is to make a profit. However, unlike some of the earlier examples of private sector businesses and the previous illustration of a larger retail company, they do not have separate in-store departments.

 Example

The Cornwall Christmas Gift Emporium is a small shop selling a mixture of festive decorations, presents and cards. It is run by its owner, Bob, and has two part-time shop assistants, Olivia and Jade.

The organisational structure therefore does not include as many specialist departments as for the larger retailers on the high street, many of whom have national teams for functions such as finance, IT and HR.

The Cornwall Christmas Gift Emporium consists of:

- Owner – Bob works in the shop and is responsible for day-to-day operations, including acting as the principal cashier.

- Shop assistant(s) – Olivia and Jade, who also serve customers and act as cashier(s).

- Owner acquires own goods – Bob goes to trade events, suppliers and the cash and carry to collect goods to sell on to his customers.

- Owner sells and promotes own goods – Bob uses local advertising and social media.

- Owner performs most Human Resources tasks including conducting own interviews, recruitment and training.

- Finance – owner employs a local accountant to ensure finances are up to date and accurate, based on Bob's receipts; the accountant also works out Olivia and Jade's wages for Bob.

2.8 A common factor for all organisations

Accountancy is a service provided to anyone who requires expert financial assistance. It is apparent that all organisations in any sector need this service to ensure that their finances are in order and that they are complying with the necessary finance legislation.

Test your understanding 6

Show the purpose of each department by placing a tick in the relevant box.

	Sells to the consumer and advertises promotions	Responsible for the computer hardware and software in a business	Deals with the recording and processing of financial transactions	Packages and stores the goods before despatch	Makes components for further assembly
IT		✓			
Production					✓
Sales and marketing	✓				
Packaging				✓	
Finance			✓		

2.9 The hierarchy of an organisation

Definition

The hierarchy of an organisation describes the way that responsibility is distributed between different levels of an organisation, in terms of the status of the employee rather than their department or function.

The internal structure of an organisation, and the number of levels of responsibility, can therefore vary dependent on its size.

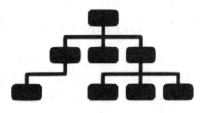

For example, every large organisation has a Chief Executive Officer (CEO) who has the responsibility for the overall success of an entire organisation. Their role within companies and public or private-sector organisations includes planning, directing and coordinating operational activities. They also devise policies and strategies to ensure that organisations meet their goals. For the purpose of this chapter we will look at the structure of an organisation below this level.

Smaller organisations have directors and managers who perform similar roles to a CEO. Let us then consider a three-level organisation, with directors, managers and employees.

Example

A three-level organisation:

Director(s)

Overall responsibility for the day to day running of an organisation, strategies, finances, decision making, planning, delegation, leadership, problem solving, overseeing other departments

Department Manager(s)

Delegation of duties, oversees staff, ensuring that employees are performing their duties correctly and in a timely manner, promotes productivity, problem solving, ensures that staff have all the tools/equipment necessary to fulfil their role, time management.

Reports any problems/issues that they are unable to solve to the Director unless it is a specific problem with a member of staff, in which circumstances, Human Resources may be asked to be involved.

Department Staff

Carry out all duties expected of them in a timely and efficient manner.

Pay attention to detail and deadlines.

Report any problems to their line manager.

2.10 The importance of responsibility within an organisation

Regardless of the size or type of organisation, the duties and responsibilities need to be shared out appropriately to ensure maximum productivity and output.

It is important that the responsibilities of individuals are fully understood so that individuals can be praised for good work or be held accountable if a task has not been completed correctly.

Directors and managers will employ staff and utilise their strengths to ensure maximum success. All businesses need to provide the relevant training and necessary resources to allow staff to complete their tasks to the required standard. Collaboratively, this will ensure a business is working productively to meet the organisation's objectives.

Test your understanding 7

Place these job titles in the correct order, with the most senior person at the top and the least senior person at the bottom.

Person	Hierarchy
Department staff	*Director*
Department manager	*Department manager*
Director	*Department Staff*

 Test your understanding 8

Place these job titles in the correct order, with the most senior person at the top and the least senior person at the bottom.

Person	Description
Department staff	Carry out all duties expected of them *Dept. staff*
Department manager	Overall responsibility for the day to day running of an organisation *director*
Director	Oversees staff, ensuring that employees are performing their duties correctly *Dept. manager*

3 Summary and further questions

You should now be able to identify different types of organisation, the sector in which they operate and the departments necessary to allow them to function effectively. You should also have an understanding of how these organisations may be organised internally and how responsibility is distributed between different types of employee.

You should also be able to identify which organisations are run to make a profit or those which are not-for-profit organisations.

Let us return to the case study for further questions relating to the topics covered.

 Case study activity 1

To help with her research, Jessica thinks about the local companies her friends and family work for.

- Her father is a financial advisor for the Owlsmoor Building Society
- Her mother is a fundraiser for the Cheshire Dogs Trust
- Her best friend is a sales assistant at TZMinz, a clothes shop
- Her sister has an admin role at Rainson & Sons, a producer of plumbing parts

For each organisation, select the correct sector from the options provided. Tick the box to show the correct answer.

	Retail	Manufacturing	Service	Charity
Owlsmoor Building Society			✓	✓
Cheshire Dogs Trust				✓
TZMinz	✓			
Rainson & Sons		✓		

Could any of these be considered to be public sector organisations? Tick the relevant box(es).

Owlsmoor Building Society	
Cheshire Dogs Trust	
TZMinz	
Rainson & Sons	

Case study activity 2

Jessica starts to look for jobs online.

To limit her search, she considers which department she would like to work in. Match the following definitions with the correct department to assist Jessica in her search.

Department	Definition
PRODUCTION	This department sells the company's goods and services to customers.
SALES	This department is responsible for typing, collecting and distributing mail, keeping & filing records, organising meetings and maintaining resources.
ADMINISTRATION	This department deals with the recruitment of new staff, the training of new and existing staff, pay negotiations and regular staff appraisals.
ACCOUNTING	This department is responsible for producing the goods or services that a business provides by making best use of the various inputs.
HUMAN RESOURCES	This department is responsible for keeping records and accounts, for giving advice on budgets to other departments, and for paying wages and salaries.

Handwritten annotations:
→ SALES
→ ADMINISTRATION
→ HUMAN RESOURCES — avaliações
→ PRODUCTION
→ ACCOUTING
orçamentos

Answers to chapter activities

Test your understanding 1

	Transports people	Makes products	Upholds the law	Animal welfare	Sells goods	Makes profit
Retail					✓	
Manufacturing		✓				
Service	✓					
Charity				✓		
Public			✓			
Private						✓

Test your understanding 2

	Profit	Not-for-profit
Retail	✓	
Manufacturing	✓	
Service	✓	
Charity		✓
Public		✓
Private	✓	

Test your understanding 3

Public sector organisations are normally concerned with the provision of basic government services.

Sole traders are private businesses owned by one person.

Private sector organisations are primarily concerned with making profit from the sale of goods or services. Where these businesses have shareholders they are known as **Limited companies.**

 Test your understanding 4

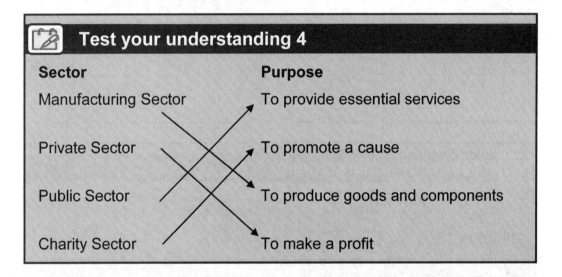

Sector   **Purpose**

Manufacturing Sector   To provide essential services

Private Sector   To promote a cause

Public Sector   To produce goods and components

Charity Sector   To make a profit

 Test your understanding 5

	Sells furniture	Is a sole trader	Animal welfare	Offers financial advice	Provides education	Makes zips for clothes
Retail	✓					
Manufacturing						✓
Service				✓		
Charity			✓			
Private		✓				
Public					✓	

Test your understanding 6

	Sells to the consumer and advertises promotions	Responsible for the computer hardware and software in a business	Deals with the recording and processing of financial transactions	Packages and stores the goods before despatch	Makes components for further assembly
IT		✓			
Production					✓
Sales and marketing	✓				
Packaging				✓	
Finance			✓		

Test your understanding 7

Hierarchy

Director
Department manager
Department staff

Test your understanding 8

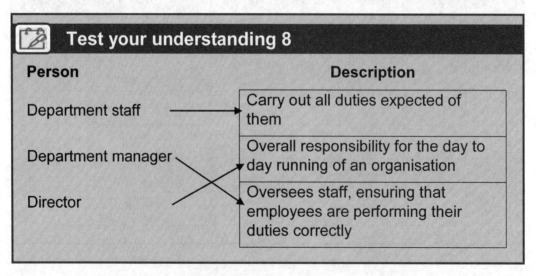

Person	Description
Department staff	Carry out all duties expected of them
Department manager	Overall responsibility for the day to day running of an organisation
Director	Oversees staff, ensuring that employees are performing their duties correctly

Case study activity 1

	Retail	Manufacturing	Service	Charity
Owlsmoor Building Society			✓	
Cheshire Dogs Trust				✓
TZMinz	✓			
Rainson & Sons		✓		

None of the organisations could be considered to be public sector.

 Case study activity 2

Department	Definition
PRODUCTION	This department is responsible for producing the goods or services that a business provides by making best use of the various inputs.
SALES	This department sells the company's goods and services to customers.
ADMINISTRATION	This department is responsible for typing, collecting and distributing mail, keeping & filing records, organising meetings and maintaining resources.
ACCOUNTING	This department is responsible for keeping records and accounts, for giving advice on budgets to other departments, and for paying wages and salaries.
HUMAN RESOURCES	This department deals with the recruitment of new staff, the training of new and existing staff, pay negotiations and regular staff appraisals.

Using numbers in business

Introduction

When you are working in an accounting department you will need to be confident in handling money and working with numbers. You will also be expected to be able to use a calculator effectively

This chapter covers the essential mathematical skills you will need to perform simple business calculations: addition and subtraction, multiplication and division, percentages, ratios and fractions, and calculating the average of a range of numbers.

KNOWLEDGE	CONTENTS
Using numbers in business	1 Mathematical symbols
1 Perform simple business calculations	2 Decimal places and rounding up and down
1.1 Record and sort whole numbers	3 Addition and subtraction
1.2 Check results of calculations	4 Multiplication and division
1.3 Identify differences between figures over time	5 Fractions and ratios
1.4 Complete calculations	6 Percentages
2 Calculate decimals, fractions, percentages, proportions and ratios	7 Calculating averages
	8 Identifying differences and checking results of calculations
2.1 Calculate decimals, fractions and percentages of numbers	9 Summary and Interview Assessment
2.2 Calculate equivalent fractions, percentages and decimals	
2.3 Calculate and apply simple proportions and ratios	

1 Mathematical symbols

1.1 Case study: an introduction

 Case study

Having thoroughly researched different types of organisations, their structure and roles within each department, Jessica realised that her avid interest in mathematics and her enjoyment of working with computers made **accountancy** her most favoured employment option.

She noticed that all organisations had one thing in common; they all need individuals to keep the financial side of the business in order. Having made her choice of career, Jessica started to apply for jobs that matched her skillset and academic ability.

Jessica was very excited to be invited for an interview. She was informed that as part of the interview process, she would have to complete an assessment. This would be in two parts, the first part being a mathematics assessment and the second part a basic spreadsheet assessment. Jessica was provided with a brief overview of what would be covered.

Despite Jessica being good at Maths (achieving a grade 7 at GCSE), the prospect of completing an assessment as part of an interview made her nervous. Jessica decided to undertake some revision ahead of the interview to give her the best chance of showcasing her abilities.

1.2 Common symbols

The following table shows the most common symbols you will see for the mathematical functions you will be using in this unit.

	Addition	Subtraction	Multiplication	Division
Calculator	+	-	X	÷
Computer keyboard	+	-	*	/
Written	+	- or ( )	X or @	$\frac{2}{3}$

Case study

As part of the interview assessment Jessica needs to know how to use the different numerical functions.

Using the figures 8 and 4, the following calculations would be performed:

	Addition	Subtraction	Multiplication	Division
Calculator	8 + 4	8 - 4	8 x 4	8 ÷ 4
Computer keyboard	8 + 4	8 - 4	8 * 4	8 / 4
Written	8 + 4	8 - 4	8 x 4	8 ÷ 4
Answer	**12**	**4**	**32**	**2**

1.3 Punctuation

In the UK a full stop [.] is used to separate pounds and pence and a comma [,] is used to separate thousands. For example, to make it easier to see the difference between £1000000, £100000 and £10000 count 3 zeros back from the right and put a comma, then count another 3 zeros back from the first comma and put another comma, and so on.

- £1000000 becomes £1,000,000 or one million pounds
- £100000 becomes £100,000 or one hundred thousand pounds
- £10000 becomes £10,000 or ten thousand pounds.

When you are dealing with a long list of numbers putting the commas in the right place makes the figures easier to read, and you will be able to perform the calculations more efficiently.

Note: Some countries use commas for the decimal point and the thousand separator is shown by a full stop. Always follow the convention of the country you are working in.

1.4 Currency

For numbers that represent money you should always show the relevant currency symbol. The currency symbol for UK sterling pounds is **£**. Euros are represented by **€,** and for US dollars the symbol is **$**. You can either write the symbol against each amount or the currency symbol can be shown at the top of the list.

Case study

How Two Ltd. is a multinational organisation, meaning that they have offices in several countries. As a result, they deal with currency in different forms including pounds, euros and US dollars.

As part of the interview assessment, Jessica needs to know how work with common units of currency. This will be important if dealing with Sales and Purchases from different countries.

The sales from last week are listed below:

	UK Sales	European Sales	American Sales
Monday	565484	235987	456987
Tuesday	897342	342565	432664
Wednesday	1018765	287900	473990
Thursday	542890	401389	489014
Friday	675989	307999	455555

Required:

Add up the sales for each country; make the figures easier to read and use the appropriate currency symbol for the totals.

 Case study

Solution:

	UK Sales		European Sales		American Sales	
Monday	565484	**565,484**	235987	**235,987**	456987	**456,987**
Tuesday	897342	**897,342**	342565	**342,565**	432664	**432,664**
Wednesday	1018765	**1,018,765**	287900	**287,900**	473990	**473,990**
Thursday	542890	**542,890**	401389	**401,389**	489014	**489,014**
Friday	675989	**675,989**	307999	**307,999**	455555	**455,555**
Total	**£3,700,470**		**€1,575,840**		**$2,308,210**	

Written in words:

UK Sales – Three million, seven hundred thousand, four hundred and seventy pounds.

European Sales – One million, five hundred and seventy-five thousand, eight hundred and forty euros.

American Sales – Two million, three hundred and eight thousand, two hundred and ten dollars.

2 Decimal places and rounding up and down

2.1 Decimal places

For the AAT assessment, the instructions will always tell you whether you should round your answer to the nearest pound (whole number), or to one or two decimal places.

Whole number: £500   Five hundred pounds

Two decimal places: £49.99   Forty nine pounds and ninety nine pence

One decimal place: £2.5 million Two and a half million pounds

Note: If you are using a calculator the display will not show the second decimal point if it is zero. When writing the answer down you should always include the missing zero.

📖 Case study

The job role that Jessica is applying for includes working with both sales and purchases. This means that Jessica must be able to round figures accurately when generating sales invoices or when checking purchase invoices.

When calculating amounts to be entered on a sales invoice, the following steps should be taken:

A customer buys 5 items costing £2.50 each. You enter 5 times £2.50 by keying 5 x 2.50 on the calculator. The display shows 12.5.

This answer should be written as £12.50 to show the pounds and pence.

In the workplace, always check how many decimal places you should show. If you are not sure, show your answers to two decimal places.

Monetary amounts should always be shown to one or two decimal places, or whole numbers. However, the calculator may show more figures after the decimal place than you need, so you will need to round your answer.

2.2 Showing pounds and pence to two decimal places

Calculations which require the answer to be shown in pounds and pence should always be given to two decimal places. If your calculator shows more than two decimal places, you will need to round the answer.

Look at the number in the third decimal place – if it is 5 or above, round the number in the second decimal place up. If it is below 5, the answer is rounded down – you do not need to change the number in the second decimal place.

2.3 Rounding up

 Case study

Jessica may also be asked to calculate the cost of a single item when a number of items have been charged for. The following steps should be taken:

If you are asked, for example, to calculate the cost of one box of a product when 3 boxes cost £500, you do the following:

- divide £500.00 by 3 by keying 500. ÷ 3 on the calculator.

The display shows 166.666666667.

As the third decimal place is larger than 5, you should round this answer **up** to the nearest penny - £166.67.

2.4 Rounding down

 Case study

Jessica may also be asked to calculate the cost of a single item when a number of items have been charged for. The following steps should be taken:

If you are told, for example, that a supplier has given you a price of £100.00 for 3 boxes of a product and you need to know the cost for one box you do the following:

- divide £100.00 by 3 by keying 100. ÷ 3 on the calculator.

The display shows 33.3333333333

			$100 \div 3 =$
		33.3333333333	
(	)	%	AC
7	8	9	÷
4	5	6	×
1	2	3	−
0	.	=	+

As the third decimal place is below 5, this answer should be rounded **down** to the nearest penny. This means you do not have to change the figure in the second decimal place, so the answer is £33.33.

2.5 Rounding answers to the nearest whole number

To round numbers to the nearest whole number, you need to look at the number in the first decimal place - if the number in the first decimal place is 5 or above, round up the pounds figure. If it is below 5, round down the pounds figure – you do not need to change the pounds figure.

 Example

You have been asked to round the following figures to the nearest whole pound.

Original figure	Rounded to the nearest whole pound	Notes
£49.99	£50	The number in the first decimal place is 9 – the pounds figure is rounded up.
£425.20	£425	The number in the first decimal place is 2 – the pounds figure is rounded down. You do not need to change the pounds figure.

KAPLAN PUBLISHING

3 Addition and subtraction

3.1 Addition and subtraction in accounting

There are many tasks in the accounting function where you will be required to add and subtract lists of numbers. You will need to complete these tasks confidently and efficiently. You should always add up lists of numbers twice to check that you get the same answer both times.

When you are writing down lists of numbers make sure that the decimal points are aligned, so that the figures are easier to read and calculate.

 Example - addition

You have been asked to add the weekly sales and you have written the following list.

Monday	£15,000.00
Tuesday	£14,500.50
Wednesday	£ 9,250.00
Thursday	£16,700.00
Friday	£18,000.00
Saturday	£25,000.00

Using a calculator effectively

When working with monetary numbers you should always key in the decimal point on the calculator. If you need to add a whole number you do not need to key in the zeros after the decimal place and if the pence are a multiple of 10 you do not need to key in the final zero.

Use this technique to add up the list of weekly sales.

The answer on your calculator will be:

15000. + 14500.5 + 9250. + 16700. + 18000. + 25000. =

$$98450.5$$

This answer should be written down as **£98,450.50**

Test your understanding 1

The Sales department have been given the following information for last week's sales.

Credit Sales	Monday	£ 22,399.00
	Tuesday	£ 23,210.50
	Wednesday	£ 22,225.20
	Thursday	£ 24,375.00
	Friday	£ 16,010.00

Cash Sales	Monday	£ 2,499.99
	Tuesday	£ 3,325.50
	Wednesday	£ 2,769.00
	Thursday	£ 2,005.00
	Friday	£ 2,047.20

You have been asked to:

a)   Calculate the weekly credit sales   £ 108,219.70

b)   Calculate the weekly cash sales   £ 12,646.69

c)   Calculate the total weekly sales   £ 120,866.39

 Definitions

Sales – the exchange of goods or services to an individual or organisation in exchange for money.

Cash sales – sales made where a payment is taken at the point of sale (immediately on the supply of the goods). The payment itself can be made by cash (currency), cheque, debit or credit card, or bank transfer. An example of a cash sale is when you go into a shop, choose the items you want to buy, and pay in the shop.

Credit sales – sales made where the goods or services will be paid later than the point of sale. Many organisations give credit to their regular trade customers so that one payment can be made for all the transactions made in each month.

3.2 Subtraction to calculate profit

As stated in Chapter 1, all private sector organisations' primary purpose is to make profit. Therefore it is important to know how to calculate the profit (or loss) a business has made.

Profit is the amount of money an organisation earns after expenditure has been deducted from income. If an organisation spends more money than it has earned, this is known as a loss. This will be covered in depth in Chapter 6.

 Definition

Cost of Sales – The direct cost of producing the goods and services that have been sold.

Gross profit – The profit (or amount of money left) from sales after the cost of sales has been deducted.

Net profit – The amount left from sales income (gross profit) after cost of sales and all other expenses (such as wages, electricity and marketing costs) have been deducted.

To calculate gross profit, cost of sales are subtracted from sales income.

To calculate net profit, all other expenditure is subtracted from gross profit.

Although for your assessment it is not necessary to distinguish between gross and net profit, the following examples show how both are calculated as both terms are widely used and both types of profit are calculated in business.

 Case study

How Two Ltd's sales income for the last month has been calculated to be £98,000. *gross profit*

The cost of sales came to £58,800 and other expenditure was £25,000.

Jessica is to calculate the gross profit and the net profit.

a) Calculate gross profit

She should:

Subtract the cost of sales, £58,800 from the sales income, £98,000.

To do so, key in 98000 − 58800 =

Therefore, the gross profit is £39,200.

b) Calculate net profit

Jessica should:

Subtract all other expenditure, £25,000 from the gross profit, £39,200.

To do so, key in 39200 – 25000 =

Therefore, the net profit is £14,200.

Example

You have been given the following financial information for a business:

Sales income	£259,258.75
Cost of sales	£156,540.00
Wages	£85,000.00
Marketing	£5,297.50
Premises costs	£3,200.00
Vehicle costs	£2,785.80

Required:

Calculate:

a)   Gross profit

b)   Net profit

Solution

a)   To calculate gross profit, subtract £156,540.00 from £259,258.75

259258.75 - 156540. =

102718.75

Gross profit is £102,718.75

b)   There are two methods for calculating net profit:

   i.   Subtract each expense from the gross profit figure:

102718.75 - 85000. - 5297.5 - 3200. - 2785.80 =

6435.45

Net profit is £6,435.45

   ii. First add up all the other expenditure, and then subtract that figure from your gross profit figure of £102,748.75

85000. + 5297.50 + 3200. + 2785.80 =

96283.3

102718.75 - 96283.3 =

6435.45

Net profit is £6,435.45

Test your understanding 2

For October, How Two Ltd. had credit sales of £258,956.50 and cash sales of £25,985.60.

The cost of sales figure was £155,215.35

Other expenses were:

Wages	£ 65,500.00
Advertising	£ 12,576.00
Heat and light	£ 10,040.50
Administration	£ 12,875.70
Vehicle costs	£ 4,950.75

TOTAL = £ 105,942.95

Calculate:

a) The total sales income = £284,942.10

b) Gross profit = £129,726.75

c) Net profit = £23,783.80

4 Multiplication and division

4.1 Multiplying in accounting

Many calculations that you perform in an accounting office will require you to multiply or divide.

 Definition

Multiplying means adding the same amount a number of times. If you need to find the cost of more than one item you multiply the cost of the item by the number of items needed.

Multiplying a number by another will **increase** the original amount.

Case study

A customer of How Two Ltd has bought the following goods and has asked you to calculate the total sales price.

- 5 AG 355 15" laptop computer @ £299.00
- 3 Tamsing 10" Tablet PC @ £199.00
- 8 Shogun USB External Hard Drive @ £50.00
- 1 Tiger Antivirus Pro (10 licenses) @ £29.99

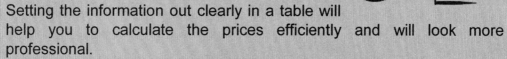

Setting the information out clearly in a table will help you to calculate the prices efficiently and will look more professional.

Item	Quantity	Unit Price (£)	Total Price (£)	*Calculation*
AG 355 15" laptop computer	5	299.00	**1,495.00**	*5 x 299*
Tamsing 10" Tablet PC	3	199.00	**597.00**	*3 x 199*
Shogun USB External Hard Drive	8	50.00	**400.00**	*8 x 50*
Tiger Antivirus Pro (10 licenses)	1	29.99	**29.99**	*1 x 29.99*
Total Sales Price			**2,521.99**	*1495.00+ 597.00+ 400.00 +29.99*

4.2   Division in accounting

 Definition

Dividing a number means splitting it into parts. If you know the cost of a number of items and want to find the cost of just one of them you will use division.

Dividing a number by another will **decrease** the original amount.

Case study

The How Two customer has seen some mouse mats for sale at £12.50 for a pack of 5. The customer would like to know the cost for each mouse mat.

To calculate the cost per unit, divide the total cost by the number of units

Total cost per pack of mouse mats is	£12.50
Divided by the number of units	5

Calculation:

12.5 ÷ 5 =
2.5

Each individual mouse mat costs **£2.50**

The same principles as those above for calculating prices could also be used for a variety of key daily routines of an accounting department. Let us consider the payroll function to test how multiplication and division are useful.

[handwritten notes in left margin:]
payroll = folha de pagamento
payslip = contra-cheque; holerite

 Test your understanding 3

You have been asked to calculate the weekly gross pay for the following employees.

Gross pay is the total amount of money paid to an employee before taxes or other deductions are made.

- Kamal worked for 35 hours and is paid £7.20 per hour. *= £252.00*
- Pamela worked for 35 hours and is paid £8.50 per hour. *£297.50*
- Jason worked for 16 hours and is paid £8.50 per hour. *= £136.00*
- Sana worked for 8 hours and is paid £7.20 per hour. *= £57.60*

£743.10

Required:

Set the information out in a table and calculate

a) The gross pay for each employee
b) The total gross pay for all employees. *£743,10*

Test your understanding 4

You have been given the following information from the previous payroll.

Kamal is paid £7.20 per hour. Last week Kamal earned £216.00.

Calculate how many hours Kamal worked last week.

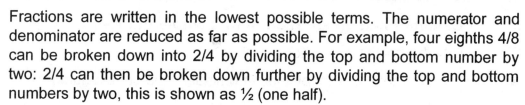

£216.00 ÷ £7.20 = 30 hours last week worked by Kamal.

5 Fractions and ratios

5.1 Using fractions

 Definition

Fractions are another way of representing parts of whole numbers.

If something is shared out equally between two people, each receives a half of the total, and that is written as $\frac{1}{2}$

The top half of a fraction is the **numerator.** The bottom half of a fraction is the **denominator.**

The numerator is divided by the denominator to show the decimal form of the fraction.

$$\frac{1}{2} = 1 \div 2 = 0.5$$

Fractions are written in the lowest possible terms. The numerator and denominator are reduced as far as possible. For example, four eighths 4/8 can be broken down into 2/4 by dividing the top and bottom number by two: 2/4 can then be broken down further by dividing the top and bottom numbers by two, this is shown as ½ (one half).

Remember! Whatever you do to the top number, you must do the same to the bottom number when trying to break a fraction down into its lowest form.

Large fractions can be reduced by dividing both the denominator and the numerator by the largest number that goes into both exactly.

For example, each number in the fraction 18/54 can be divided by 18 so, the fraction is reduced to:

$$\frac{18 \div 18 = 1}{54 \div 18 = 3} \quad \text{or one third}$$

📖 Case study

As part of her assessment, Jessica must be able to demonstrate that she can calculate simple fractions and then convert them into decimals:

Breaking the fractions down into their lowest form:

a) 50/100 (divide both numbers by 10) = 5/10 (divide both numbers by 5) = ½

b) 4/16 (divide both numbers by 2) = 2/8 (divide both numbers by 2) = ¼

c) 30/150 (divide both numbers by 5) = 6/30 (divide both numbers by 6) = 1/5

d) 20/200 (divide both numbers by 10) = 2/20 (divide both numbers by 2) = 1/10

Note: It doesn't matter what number you divide by so long as it goes into both the top and bottom number equally.

Jessica must then be able to convert fractions into decimals:

Converting the above fractions into decimals:

a) ½ = 1 ÷ 2 = 0.5

b) ¼ = 1 ÷ 4 = 0.25

c) 1/5 = 1 ÷ 5 = 0.2

d) 1/10 = 1 ÷ 10 = 0.1

5.2 Calculating a given fraction of a whole number

To calculate the fraction of a whole number:

- divide the whole number by the denominator (the bottom number)

- multiply the answer by the numerator (the top number).

KAPLAN PUBLISHING

Example

Bennett & Sons produce and sell home appliances, including electrical equipment for domestic use. The company has four branches in the UK: South Park, North Park, East Park and West Park.

The total sales income for all branches was £2,700,000.

North Park made $\frac{2}{3}$ of the sales.

How much sales income did North Park make?

1. Divide the total sales income by the denominator (the bottom number).

$$\frac{£2,700,000}{3} = £900,000$$

2. Multiply the £900,000 by the numerator (the top number).

$$2 \times £900,000 = £1,800,000$$

The calculation can be written as:

$$\frac{£2,700,000}{3} \times 2$$

North Park made £1,800,000 worth of sales.

Tip:

To use your calculator efficiently leave the zeros out of your calculation:

$$\frac{27}{3} \times 2 = 18$$

Just remember to add back the zeros you didn't calculate: 1800000 and to include the currency sign and thousand separators. £1,800,000.

 Test your understanding 5

How Two Ltd manufactures mouse mats in three different colours: blue, black and red. The production manager has estimated that 540,000 mouse mats will be produced next month and $\frac{3}{5}$ will be black.

How many black mouse mats will be produced?

540 ÷ 5 × 3 =
108 × 3 = 324

324,000

Test your understanding 6

How Two Ltd has 45,000 customers at one of their branches. $\frac{2}{3}$ of these customers pay on credit. $\frac{3}{3} - \frac{2}{3} = \frac{1}{3}$ $45 \div 3 \times 1 = 15 \times 1 = 15$

How many of the customers are cash customers?   *15,000 customers*

 Test your understanding 7

The Director of How Two Ltd has organised a meal in a restaurant for three of the managers and their families as a reward for their hard work over the last month.   *£210.56 ÷ 11 = £19,14 per person*

The Morris family consists of two adults and three children.   *5 = £95,71*

The Kazee family consists of two adults and two children.   *4 = £76,57*

The Thomas family consist of one adult and one child.   *2 = £38.28*

The restaurant bill totals £210.56. How can the bill be split so that each family pays a fair proportion of the £210.56?   *Bill can be split per head.*

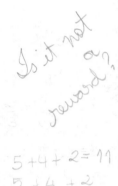

Is it not a reward?

5 + 4 + 2 = 11

$\frac{5}{11} + \frac{4}{11} + \frac{2}{11}$

5.3   Expressing a number as a fraction of another number

When expressing a number as a fraction of another number you simply use the smaller number as the numerator (the top number) and the bigger number as the denominator (the bottom number).

You then break the fraction down into its lowest form.

 Example

Bennett & Sons made the following sales of kitchen appliances in one week at their North Park branch:

Day	Number of kitchen appliances sold
Monday	20
Tuesday	40
Wednesday	50
Thursday	10
Friday	60
Total	**180**

To express the number of kettles sold each day as a fraction of the total number sold during the week:

Monday   20/180 = 2/18 = 1/9

Tuesday   40/180 = 4/18 = 2/9

Wednesday   50/180 = 5/18

Thursday   10/180 = 1/18

Friday   60/180 = 6/18 = 1/3

Note: You can check your answer by doing the following:

Monday   180 ÷ 9 x 1 = 20

Tuesday   180 ÷ 9 x 2 = 40

Wednesday   180 ÷ 18 x 5 = 50

Thursday   180 ÷ 18 x 1 = 10

Friday   180 ÷ 3 x 1 = 60

5.4   Ratios

Ratios give exactly the same information as fractions but they are written in a different way so that comparisons can be made between two numbers.

They are a way of comparing amounts of something. For example, if there were 15 men and 12 women in the Sales department, this would be expressed as 15:12 *'fifteen to twelve'*.

This could be broken down into its lowest form the same way as a fraction could (by dividing both numbers by the same number):

15 ÷ 3 = 5

12 ÷ 3 = 4

This would be written as 5:4; *pronounced 'five to four'*.

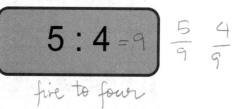

The two numbers given in a ratio are the fraction numerators.

The denominator is not shown - it can be calculated by adding together the two numerators

In this ratio, 3 and 1 are the fraction numerators.

The denominator is 4.

This ratio is pronounced 'three to one'.

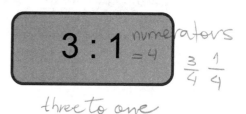

Case study

How Two Ltd are reviewing two of their retail outlets with total sales of £56,000.

The pattern of sales for Store A and Store B has been given as ratio of 3:1 respectively. This means that Store A has 3 *times* more sales than Store B.

To calculate the ratio the two numerators are added together to find the denominator: 3 + 1 = 4.

We can then apportion the total sales of £56,000 between to the two retail outlets as follows:

Store A $\dfrac{56,000}{4}$ x 3 = £42,000

Store B $\dfrac{56,000}{4}$ x 1 = 14 = £14,000

You may be asked to calculate the ratio or proportion of two given numbers. Let's use the numbers from the two stores above.

 Case study

Store A has sales of £42,000 and Store B has sales of £14,000. This time you have been asked to find out the ratio of Store A's sales to Store B's.

First, divide   Store A's sales $\dfrac{£42,000}{£14,000} = 3$

By   Store B's sales

We are comparing Store A to Store B, so the ratio answer is written as 3:1.

 Test your understanding 8

How Two Ltd has two departments who use the canteen at their headquarters. There are 125 employees in the production department and 25 employees in the administration department.

What is the ratio of production department employees to administration staff? 5:1

$\dfrac{125}{25} \dfrac{P}{A} = 5$

KAPLAN PUBLISHING

Test your understanding 9

Bennett & Son's West Park branch has cost of sales of £75,000 and sales of £225,000.

What is the ratio of cost of sales to sales? 1 : 3

$\frac{225}{75} = 3$

6 Percentages

6.1 The use of percentages

Percentages are another method used to compare figures. 'Per cent' means 'out of a 100' so the denominator of the percentage is 100.

Percentages can be shown as fractions or decimals:

$$25\% = \frac{25}{100} = 0.25$$

$$10\% = \frac{10}{100} = 0.10$$

Tip: It is more efficient to calculate percentages on a calculator by using the decimal equivalent.

 Test your understanding 10

Use your calculator to fill in the missing figures from the table below.

Percentage	Fraction	Decimal
25%	$\frac{25}{100}$	0.25
2%	$\frac{2}{100}$	0.02
10%	$\frac{10}{100}$	0.10
1%	$\frac{1}{100}$	0.01
50%	$\frac{50}{100}$	0.50
5%	$\frac{5}{100}$	0.05

6.2 Finding a percentage of a whole number

 Case study

Jessica will need to be able to find a percentage of a whole number, for example when calculating how much discount to deduct from a sales invoice, or when adding VAT on to an invoice.

 Definition

VAT (Value Added Tax) is a government tax on some consumer goods. Organisations that are registered for VAT must collect this tax from customers on behalf of the government. In 2017 the VAT rate was 20%.

To calculate percentages efficiently on a calculator, you must first convert the percentage to a decimal; you can then use this figure in your calculation.

We will now look at two examples to illustrate this method – the first shows how to find a percentage from a total value (in this case, of sales) and the second relates the same method to VAT.

Example

Bennett & Sons has four branches in the UK: South Park, North Park, East Park and West Park.

North Park had Month 1 sales of £24,560.

The total sales to date for all branches was £122,800.

To express North Park's Month 1 sales as a percentage of the total sales:

24,560 ÷ 122,800 = 0.2
x 100 = 20%

North Park's Month 1 sales as a percentage of total sales = 20%

Note: You can check your answer by doing:
122,800 ÷ 100 x 20 = 24,560

Example

A customer (Pipers Plumbers) has bought a monitor worth £150.00 from How Two Ltd and has been offered 10% discount.

VAT of 20% is to be added to the invoice amount.

You are to calculate the total amount the customer owes.

Discount

- Convert 10% to a decimal: $10\% = \dfrac{10}{100} = 0.10$

- Multiply £150.00 by 0.10 = £15.00 discount
- **Subtract** £15.00 from £150.00 to find the net amount = £135.00

VAT

- Convert 20% to a decimal: $20\% = \dfrac{20}{100} = 0.20$

- Multiply the net amount of £135.00 by 0.20 = £27.00 VAT
- **Add** £27.00 to £135.00 to find the total amount = £162.00

These calculations are shown on the following invoice:

How Two Ltd	
VAT NO. 456 7656 909	
Pipers Plumbers	Invoice no: i459009
Bolton Close	Tax point: 24 May 2017
Rochdale	
FG1 3SQ	
Monitor	£150.00
Less Discount 10%	-£15.00
Total after discount	£135.00
VAT at 20%	£27.00
Total	£162.00
Payment terms: 15 days net	

Test your understanding 11

Complete the following invoices.

How Two Ltd
VAT NO. 456 7656 909

Grange Theatre
Blackburn Avenue
Diggle
LF2 689

Invoice no: 5678
Tax point: 23 September 2017

HDMI Cable	£75.00
Less Discount 5%	£ 3.75
Total after discount	£ 71.25
VAT at 20%	£ 14.25
Total	£ 85.50

Payment terms: 7 days net

How Two Ltd
VAT NO. 456 7656 909

H Kazee
Bristol Street
Gloucester
AL9 867

Invoice no: 35281
Tax point: 26 September 2017

5 x HB78 @ £15.00	£ 75.00
10 x AN5787 @ £2.30	£ 23.00
Sub total	£ 98.00
Less 15% discount	£ 14.70
Total after discount	£ 83.30
VAT at 20%	16.66
Total	£ 99.96

Payment terms: 7 days net

6.3 Calculating the percentage of one number in relation to another

 Example

The East Park branch of Bennett & Sons has sales of £890,000 and gross profit of £267,000. We need to calculate gross profit as a percentage of sales.

Divide gross profit
Into sales

$$\frac{£267,000}{£890,000} = 0.30 \text{ then multiply by } 100 = 30\%$$

Gross profit is 30% of sales.

Check your answer by multiplying sales of £890,000 by 0.30 = £267,000.

 Test your understanding 12

The human resources department has analysed the number of employees at one of How Two's regional offices.

	No of employees	Percentage of the total number of employees
Production department	8	47.1%
Marketing department	3	17.6%
Accounts department	2	11.8%
Sales department	4	23.5%
Total number of employees	17	100%

Calculate the number of employees in each department as a percentage of the total number of employees. Round your answers to one decimal place.

7 Calculating averages

7.1 Calculating the range

 Case study

As part of the job role at How Two Ltd., Jessica must be able to calculate the range of a set of figures.

The range is the difference between the highest and lowest figure in a set of data.

 Case study

How Two Ltd have collated information on the number of hours worked by the admin staff in their main office over a week.

Adam – 35 hours

Steph – 38 hours

John – 42 hours

Maisie – 45 hours

Jim – 30 hours

Step One: Put them in order to make it easier to see the highest and the lowest.

30, 35, 38, 42, 45

The highest number is 45 and the lowest number is 30.

Step Two: Find the difference by subtracting the lower number from the highest number.

45 – 30 = 15

The range is 15.

7.2 Identifying the mode

 Case study

As part of the job role at How Two Ltd., Jessica must be able to identify the most frequently occurring number in a set of numbers (**the mode**).

To find the mode, or modal value, first put the numbers in order, then count how many of each number there are. The number that appears the most often is the mode.

Note: It doesn't matter whether you list the numbers in ascending order (smallest to biggest) or in descending order (biggest to smallest), it's simply the number that appears the most.

 Case study

How Two Ltd have collated some information in relation to some of the stationery purchases for the first six months of the year.

Month	Number of boxes of paper	Number of packs of document wallets
January	15	33
February	21	29
March	17	28
April	20	33
May	19	27
June	17	31

To work out the mode of the number of boxes of paper purchased in ascending order:

15, 17, 17, 19, 20, 21

The mode is 17 as this is the number that appears the most.

To work out the mode of the number of packs of document wallets purchased in descending order:

33, 33, 31, 29, 28, 27

The mode is 33 as this is the number that appears the most.

7.3 Calculating the mean

The mean is the most common measure of average. If you ask someone to find the average, this is the method they are most likely to use.

To calculate the mean (average) of a set of figures, you add up all of the numbers in the set of data given and then divide by how many numbers there are.

 Example

Bennett & Sons are looking at the profit that has been made by their branches in the UK for the first quarter of the year.

Branch	Profit
North Park	£15,987.56
South Park	£21,877.64
East Park	£12,563.22
West Park	£18,245.58

To work out the mean (average) profit:

Step One: Add up the total profit from each of the branches:

15,987.56 + 21,877.64 + 12,563.22 + 18,245.58 = 68,674.00

Step Two: Then divide the total by the number of branches:

68,674 ÷ 4 = 17,168.50

The mean (average) profit made by the branches is £17,168.50.

Note: You can check your answer by doing the following:

17,168.50 x 4 = 68,674

68,674 − 15,987.56 − 21,877.64 - 12,563.22 − 18,245.58 = 0

This means that your answer is correct.

But what happens if someone make a loss? This would mean that negative figures would come into the calculation. Adding a negative number is the same as subtracting the number (without the negative). For example 3 + (−2) = 3−2 = 1.

Example

Bennett & Sons are looking at the profit or loss made by North Park over the last year.

Rather than looking month on month, they have requested that the information be viewed in quarters.

North Park	Profit or Loss
January – March	-£3,485.75
April – June	£31,895.24
July – September	-£5,635.22
October - December	£54,251.79

To work out the mean (average) profit or loss per quarter:

Step One: Add up the total profit or loss over the year:

-£3,485.75 + £31,895.24 - £5,635.22 + £54,251.79 = 77,026.06

Step Two: Then divide the total by the number of quarters:

77,026.06 ÷ 4 = 19,256.515

The mean (average) profit made by North Park per quarter is £19,256.52 to 2 decimal places.

 Test your understanding 13

The Payroll Clerk has been asked to work out the averages of the hours worked by an employee in the production department in a week:

Day	Hours worked
Monday	8
Tuesday	7
Wednesday	8
Thursday	9
Friday	10

Calculate the following:

a) The range of hours works ~~7 8 8 9 10 => 10 – 7 = 3~~

b) The mode of hours worked ~~7 8 8 9 10 => 8~~

c) The mean (average) number of hours worked (rounded to the nearest hour) ~~8 + 7 + 8 + 9 + 10 = 42 ÷ 5 = 8.4 = 8~~

8 Identifying differences and checking results of calculations

8.1 Identifying differences between figures over time

 Case study

When looking at a set of figures Jessica may be asked to identify differences over a period of time. This would involve looking at the increases or decreases over the period.

 Example

Bennett & Sons are looking at the sales that have been made by South Park over the last year.

South Park	Profit
January	£15,872.51
February	£15,475.34
March	£17,233.32
April	£18,565.28
May	£15,227.84
June	£19,288.45
July	£18,799.73
August	£14,276.11
September	£16,993.21
October	£17,665.32
November	£18,325.45
December	£19,445.44

To work out the increase or decrease, you work out the difference between one month and the next. To do so, take the latest figure and subtract the previous figure from it e.g. February - January.

If the figure you are left with is a negative number it suggests a decrease, however if it is a positive number it suggests an increase.

South Park	Increase/Decrease	Amount
January – February	Decrease	£397.17
February – March	Increase	£1,757.98
March – April	Increase	£1,331.96
April – May	Decrease	£3,337.44
May – June	Increase	£4,060.61
June – July	Decrease	£488.72
July – August	Decrease	£4,523.62
August – September	Increase	£2,717.10
September – October	Increase	£672.11
October – November	Increase	£660.13
November – December	Increase	£1,119.99

8.2 Using estimation/rounding

Before working out a calculation, it is a good idea to estimate what you think that the answer will be. This will help to ensure that the answer you arrive at is accurate.

To do this you need to round the numbers. What you round the number to depends on the size of the figures you are working with; it could be to the nearest 10, 100 or 1,000.

 Example

Bennett & Sons are looking at the wages for a member of the sales staff at West Park over a month. The person is paid £8.90 an hour.

	Hours worked	Rounded question	Estimated answer	Accurate answer
Week 1	42	40 x 9	£360	£373.80
Week 2	41	40 x 9	£360	£364.90
Week 3	34	30 x 9	£270	£302.60
Week 4	35	40 x 9	£360	£311.50
Total	152		£1,350	£1,352.80

The difference between the estimated answer and the accurate answer is **£2.80.**

Test your understanding 14

How Two Ltd are looking at the wages for the machine operatives in the factory of one of their depots over a week.

depositos

The machine operatives are paid £7.80 an hour.

	Hours worked	Rounded question	Estimated answer	Accurate answer
Monday	633	600 × 8	£9,800	£4,937.40
Tuesday	742	700 × 8	£5,600	£5,787.60
Wednesday	649	600 × 8	£4,800	£5,062.20
Thursday	682	700 × 8	£5,600	£5,319.60
Friday	724	700 × 8	£5,600	£5,647.20
Total			£26,400	£26,754.00

(handwritten margin note: didn't mention nearest rounded. Can I choose? nearest 10, 100 ....)

The difference between the estimated answer and the accurate answer is £...354.00.....

(handwritten: RESUMO E ENTREVISTA AVALIAÇÃO)

(handwritten margin note: Resumo e Avaliação da Entrevista)

9 Summary and Interview Assessment

In this chapter we have looked at the common maths functions used in accounting and how numbers can be calculated and presented for business purposes.

You will need to practice the techniques learnt in the chapter to make sure you are able to perform the calculations quickly and confidently on a calculator. And, where needed, use the checking and estimating tools suggested to ensure your answer looks correct.

Returning to our case study, the first part of Jessica's interview assessment for the role at How Two Ltd now follows – see how well you can apply the numbers in business by completing it.

Case study activity 3 – Interview Assessment

Jessica has been set the following tasks to complete as part of her interview:

Task 1

Work out the mean, mode and range of the following estimated sales for the next 6 months:

January	February	March	April	May	June
10,000	9,500	14,000	13,500	14,000	15,500

Mean: 10,000 + 9,500 + 14,000 + 13,500 + 14,000 + 15,500 = 76,500 ÷ 6 £12,750

Mode: £14,000

Range: 15,500 − 9,500 = £6,000

Task 2

Below is a breakdown of the profit of one of our shops over the last 6 months:

January	February	March	April	May	June
4,500	5,000	6,750	6,900	6,300	5,400

Identify the increase/decrease in profit month on month:

Jan – Feb = increase by £500

Feb – Mar = increase by £1,750

Mar – Apr = increase by £150

Apr – May = decrease by £600

May – Jun = decrease by £900

Task 3

Below are the hours worked for three members of staff at one of the shops. Calculate their total pay for the week.

Rate of pay £9.50 per hour					
	Mon	**Tue**	**Wed**	**Thu**	**Fri**
Jim	7 hours	5.5 hours	6 hours	7 hours	6 hours
Dave	8 hours	7.5 hours	4 hours	7.5 hours	5 hours
Ahmed	6 hours	7.5 hours	8 hours	8 hours	6.5 hours

Jim: 31.5 hours x £9.50 = £299.25

Dave: 32 hours x £9.50 = £304.00

Ahmed: 36 hours x £9.50 = £342.00

Task 4

Calculate the VAT and gross amounts of the following invoices and then write the gross figures as a fraction of the total for each invoice:

	Net	VAT	Total
Invoice 101	100.00	£ 20.00	£120.00
Invoice 102	150.00	£ 30.00	£ 180.00
Invoice 103	200.00	£ 40.00	£ 240.00
Invoice 104	233.34	£ 46.668	£ 280.01
Invoice 105	150.00	£ 30.00	£ 180.00
Totals	833.34	£ 166.668	£1,000.01

Fractions:

Invoice 101 = $\frac{12}{100} \sim \frac{6}{50} \sim \frac{3}{25}$

Invoice 102 = $\frac{18}{100} \sim \frac{9}{50}$

Invoice 103 = $\frac{24}{100} \sim \frac{12}{50} \sim \frac{6}{25}$

Invoice 104 = $\frac{28}{100} \sim \frac{14}{50} \sim \frac{7}{25}$

Invoice 105 = $\frac{18}{100} \sim \frac{9}{50}$

Task 5

a) Round the following quarterly sales and cost of sales figures to the nearest £'000.

b) State the ratio of the sales figures to cost of sales

c) Break the ratios down into their lowest form

	Jan - Mar	Apr - Jun	Jul - Sep	Oct - Dec
Sales	11,754	15,789	29,659	49,200
Cost of sales	3,256	7,770	6,250	6,825

Rounded

	Jan - Mar	Apr - Jun	Jul - Sep	Oct - Dec
Sales	12,000	16,000	30,000	49,000
Cost of sales	3,000	8,000	6,000	7,000

Ratios:

Jan – Mar = 12:3 = 4:1

Apr – Jun = 16:8 = 2:1

Jul – Sep = 30:6 = 5:1

Oct – Dec = 49:7 = 7:1

Answers to chapter activities

 Test your understanding 1

a)   The weekly credit sales are £108,219.70

> 22399 + 23210.5 + 22225.2 + 24375 + 16010 =
>
> ## 108219.7

b)   The weekly cash sales are £12,646.69

> 2499.99 + 3325.5 + 2769 + 2005 + 2047.2 =
>
> ## 12646.69

c)   The total weekly sales are £120,866.39

> 108219.70 + 12646.69 =
>
> ## 120866.39

 Test your understanding 2

a)   The total sales income is £284,942.10

> 258956.5 + 25985.6 =
>
> ## 284942.1

b)   The gross profit is £129,726.75

> 284942.1 - 155215.35 =
>
> ## 129726.75

c)   The net profit is £23,783.80

> 129726.75 - 65500 - 12576 - 10040.5 - 12875.7 - 4950.75 =
>
> ## 23783.8

Test your understanding 3

a)

	Hours worked	Pay per hour	Gross pay	*calculation*
Kamal	35	£7.20	£252.00	*35 x 7.2*
Pamela	35	£8.50	£297.50	*35 x 8.5*
Jason	16	£8.50	£136.00	*16 x 8.5*
Sana	8	£7.20	£57.60	*8 x 7.2*
	Total weekly gross pay		£743.10	*252. +* *297.5 +* *136.+ 57.6*

b) The total weekly gross pay is £743.10.

 Test your understanding 4

The total cost of Kamal's weekly wage was   £216.00

Divided by the cost per hour   £7.20

216. ÷ 7.2 =

30

Last week Kamal worked for **30 hours.**

 Test your understanding 5

$\dfrac{540,000}{5}$ x 3 = **324,000 black mouse mats.**

Test your understanding 6

How Two Ltd. has 45,000 customers

$\frac{2}{3}$ of customers pay on credit - 45,000 ÷ 3 x 2 = 30,000 credit customers.

The remainder must be cash customers – 45,000 – 30,000 = **15,000**

You can also work this out by calculating the fraction for cash customers. If credit customers account for $\frac{2}{3}$, cash customers must account for $\frac{1}{3}$ so 45,000 ÷ 3 x 1 = **15,000.**

 Test your understanding 7

Firstly, you need to determine how many people there are in total:

The Morris family has 5 members, the Kazee family has 4 members and the Thomas family has 2 members, so there are 11 people in total. This is the denominator.

The fraction of the total bill that the Morris family should pay is $\frac{5}{11}$, for the Kazee family it is $\frac{4}{11}$, and for the Thomas's it is $\frac{2}{11}$

The bill should be split as follows:

Morris family $\frac{210.56}{11}$ x 5 = 95.70909, a monetary value of £95.71

Kazee family $\frac{210.56}{11}$ x 4 = 76.56727, a monetary value of £76.57

Thomas family $\frac{210.56}{11}$ x 2 = 38.28363, a monetary value of £38.28

Check that the total bill will be paid correctly: 95.71 + 76.57 + 38.28 = 210.56

Test your understanding 8

Divide 125 by 25 to give an answer of 5.

We are comparing production *to* administration, so the ratio is written as **5:1.**

There are 5 times more employees who work in production than in administration.

 Test your understanding 9

Divide 225,000 by 75,000 = 3

We are comparing cost of sales *to* sales, so the ratio is expressed as **1:3**. For every £1 of cost of sales there are £3 of sales.

Test your understanding 10

Percentage	Fraction	Decimal
25%	$\frac{25}{100}$	**0.25**
2%	$\frac{2}{100}$	0.02
10%	$\frac{10}{100}$	0.10
1%	$\frac{1}{100}$	**0.01**
50%	$\frac{50}{100}$	0.50
5%	$\frac{5}{100}$	0.05

KAPLAN PUBLISHING

Test your understanding 11

How Two Ltd
VAT NO. 456 7656 909

Grange Theatre
Blackburn Avenue
Diggle
LF2 689

Invoice no: 5678
Tax point: 23 September 2017

HDMI	£75.00
Less Discount 5%	**£3.75**
Total after discount	**£71.25**
VAT at 20%	**£14.25**
Total	**£85.50**

Payment terms: 7 days net

How Two Ltd
VAT NO. 456 7656 909

H Kazee
Bristol Street
Gloucester
AL9 867

Invoice no: 35281
Tax point: 26 September 2017

5	HB78 @ £15.00	£75.00
10	AN5787 @ £2.30	£23.00
Sub total		**£98.00**
Less Discount 15%		**£14.70**
Total after discount		**£83.30**
VAT at 20%		**£16.66**
	Total	**£99.96**

Payment terms: 7 days net

Note: VAT should always be rounded DOWN to the nearest penny.

Test your understanding 12

	No of employees	Percentage of the total number of employees	Calculation
Production department	8	**47.1%**	$\frac{8}{17}$ x 100 = 47.05 (rounded to 47.1)
Marketing department	3	**17.6%**	$\frac{3}{17}$ x 100 = 17.64 (rounded to 17.6)
Accounts department	2	**11.8%**	$\frac{2}{17}$ x 100 = 11.76 (rounded to 11.8)
Sales department	4	**23.5%**	$\frac{4}{17}$ x 100 = 23.52 (rounded to 23.5)
Total number of employees	17	**100%**	$\frac{17}{17}$ x 100 = 100

The total of all the individual percentages should always equal 100%.

 Test your understanding 13

a)   The range of hours worked = 10 – 7 = 3

b)   The mode is 8

c)   The mean number of hours worked is:

8 + 7 + 8 + 9 + 10 = 42

42 ÷ 5 = 8.4

The mean is 8 hours (rounded to the nearest hour)

Test your understanding 14

Day	Hours worked	Rounded question	Estimated answer	Accurate answer
Monday	633	630 x 8	£5,040	£4,937.40
Tuesday	742	740 x 8	£5,920	£5,787.60
Wednesday	649	650 x 8	£5,200	£5,062.20
Thursday	682	680 x 8	£5,440	£5,319.60
Friday	724	720 x 8	£5,760	£5,647.20
Total			£27,360	£26,754

The difference between the estimated answer and the accurate answer is **£606.**

Case study activity 3 – Interview Assessment

Task 1

Mean: 10,000 + 9,500 + 14,000 + 13,500 + 14,000 + 15,500 = 76,500

76,500 / 6 = **12,750**

Mode: 14,000

Range: 15,500 – 9,500 = **6,000**

Task 2

Jan – Feb = Increased by £500

Feb – Mar = Increased by £1,750

Mar – Apr = Increased by £150

Apr – May = Decreased by £600

May – Jun = Decreased by £900

Task 3

Jim = 31.5 hours x 9.50 = £299.25

Dave = 32 hours x 9.50 = £304.00

Ahmed = 36 hours x 9.50 = £342.00

Task 4

	Net	VAT	Total
Invoice 101	100.00	20.00	120.00
Invoice 102	150.00	30.00	180.00
Invoice 103	200.00	40.00	240.00
Invoice 104	233.34	46.66	280.00
Invoice 105	150.00	30.00	180.00
Totals	833.34	166.66	1000.00

Fractions:

Invoice 101 = 120/1000 = 12/100 = 6/50 = 3/25

Invoice 102 = 180/1000 = 18/100 = 18/100 = 9/50

Invoice 103 = 240/1000 = 24/100 = 12/50 = 6/25

Invoice 104 = 280/1000 = 28/100 = 14/50 = 7/25

Invoice 105 = 180/1000 = 18/100 = 18/100 = 9/50

Task 5

Rounded

	Jan - Mar	Apr - Jun	Jul - Sep	Oct - Dec
Sales	12,000	16,000	30,000	49,000
Cost of sales	3,000	8,000	6,000	7,000

Jan – Mar = 12,000:3,000 = 12:3 = **4:1**

Apr – Jun = 16,000:8,000 = 16:8 = **2:1**

Jul – Sep = 30,000:6,000 = 30:6 = **5:1**

Oct – Dec = 49,000:7,000 = 49:7 = **7:1**

Tools and techniques to present numerical data

Introduction

Having established some of the key calculations used in business and the main mathematical functions required, we will now focus on how numerical data can be presented and used in spreadsheets.

In the workplace, although you may use a calculator to perform some calculations, it is likely that many will be performed using formulas electronically. In this chapter, we will look at how to use spreadsheet formulas when completing the calculations covered previously, and how formatting can help to present this data more effectively.

KNOWLEDGE	CONTENTS
Using numbers in business	1 Using spreadsheets to present numerical data
1 Perform simple business calculations	2 Formatting numerical data
1.4 Complete calculations	3 Formulas
2 Calculate decimals, fractions, percentages, proportions and ratios	4 Summary and further questions
2.1 Calculate decimals, fractions and percentages of numbers	
3 Use tools and techniques to present numerical data	
3.1 Formulas	
3.2 Formatting	

spreadsheet = planilha.

1 Using spreadsheets to present numerical data

1.1 Case study: an introduction

📖 Case study

Jessica is confident with her understanding of the calculations needed for her interview assessment. She now looks to revise for the other part of the interview – the basic functionality of spreadsheets.

Jessica understands that in the workplace spreadsheets are often used to calculate and present financial data and therefore that revising formatting tools and formulas will also be useful for her future roles.

Previously, she has studied spreadsheets as part of her ICT GCSE and has seen her parents using them to organise the family finances. Show now looks to get a better understanding of their many uses for those in an accounting role.

1.2 The benefits of using tools and techniques to present numerical data

When working in finance, it is important to present numerical information in a logical format which is easily understood by the user. Spreadsheets are often used as they are versatile, can automate many processes and create efficiency when preparing accurate financial information.

They allow calculations to be performed automatically, which reduces the risk of error (which can be often present with manual calculations). Spreadsheets can be formatted to present data in a variety of formats including tables, charts and graphs, presenting information in a visually-appealing way which is seen to be more accessible for those outside the accounting department. This is particularly useful for business owners when they want to see information quickly and be able to make business decisions promptly from the summary of findings.

Spreadsheets are used in accounting for a variety of tasks such as quotations and invoicing, managing inventory, producing and monitoring budgets and producing year end financial statements. These are just a few examples, but the list is endless. There are also many templates available within the software which helps as a starting point as it saves time creating worksheets from scratch.

There are many advantages of using spreadsheets within finance. For most businesses, the use of spreadsheets is free; Microsoft Excel is part of the Microsoft Office package, which is widely used within business, alternatively Google Workspace's Google Sheets is another popular option. What makes these attractive to businesses is that they are available immediately via an internet connection and can be used by multiple users at one time if used within the cloud as opposed to via the desktop.

To be able to enter data into a spreadsheet requires minimal training. This is advantageous when new members of staff join a team, and the business requires them to be completing tasks quite quickly.

There are many functions available within spreadsheets and training can be delivered up to an expert level. This keeps employees interested as they can learn new functions and features at the pace required for their role and ability. There are many free training resources available which makes it a cheaper option in comparison to other software.

1.3 Spreadsheet basics

The following examples and screen shots are generated using Microsoft Excel. There are many other spreadsheet options available and whilst they may look slightly different, the principles and features remain very much the same.

There are numerous ways to open the application and the way that you do it will depend on the version of Excel that you are using and personal preference.

- Click the Windows button in the bottom left of the screen (or the Start Menu)
- Scroll through the list of programs
- Select 'Excel'
- Alternatively, you can access it via the app

Microsoft Excel can be located from the program list or via the app tile. Once clicked, Excel will open.

features = características

pace = ritmo (cadência)

whilst = enquanto

scroll = rolagem is it not drag.

workbook = pasta de trabalho) spreadsheet = planilha.
default = padrão

1.4   Workbooks and worksheets

worksheet = planilha.

> ### 🔍 Definition
>
> A **worksheet** is a single page or sheet in the spreadsheet. A new spreadsheet will have 3 of these by default (called 'Sheet1', 'Sheet2', 'Sheet3'), but this can be changed, and worksheets can be added or deleted or renamed. The term worksheet is often abbreviated to **Sheet**.
>
> A **workbook** is the spreadsheet file, made up of one or more worksheets. The default blank workbook is made up of 1 worksheet. The workbook name is the filename of the spreadsheet.

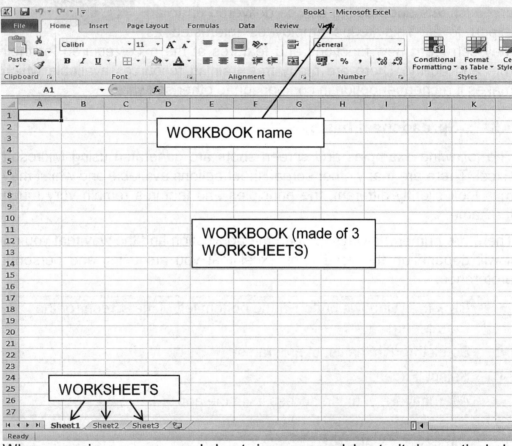

When opening a new worksheet in a spreadsheet, it is particularly important to become familiar with the toolbar. This is the row of tabs and icons at the top of the screen which allows you to quickly use and understand certain commands used to perform a task.

1.5   The Ribbon

The 'Ribbon' is Excel's menu system. It is made up of various tabs and buttons, allowing you access to all of Excel's features. There are many, many options within the Ribbon – the good news is that most people only use a few of them. We will concentrate on the key features only.

RIBBON

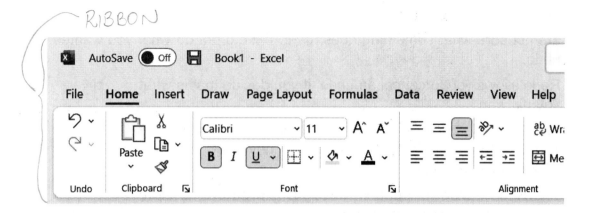

Tabs

There are usually 10 **tabs** across the top of the Ribbon – File, Home, Insert, Draw, Page Layout, Formulas, Data, Review, View, and Help. Clicking on these offers different options. Sometimes more tabs appear depending on context – for example if you are editing a graph, the Chart Tools tabs appear.

Click on the name of the tab to change it and see the different options.

Buttons

The buttons on each tab perform a series of tasks – formatting, spreadsheet appearance, analysis etc. Some of them open a new menu.

Although it seems like a lot to take in, the more you use these menu options, the more familiar with them you will become. Also, due to the way they are grouped with similar commands, you can often find what you need by looking in these menus.

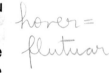
hover = flutuar

Note that if you are not sure what a particular option does, hover the mouse pointer over it for a second or two and more information will be shown.

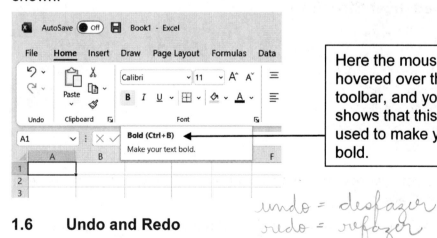

Here the mouse has hovered over the **B** on the toolbar, and you can see it shows that this button is used to make your text bold.

undo = desfazer
redo = refazer

1.6   Undo and Redo

Probably the most frequently used command within Excel. Undo, as the name suggests, cancels the last thing you did. The most useful thing about this is that it means you should not be afraid to experiment – if you

whichever = qualquer que seja

greyed out
acinzentado

are not sure what something does, try it. If it did not do what you wanted, undo.

Redo allows you to cancel an undo, if you decide that is what you did want!

The Undo button (the top arrow) is located in the top-left corner of the file. It is always visible, whichever tab you have clicked on in the ribbon.

The Redo button (the bottom arrow) is greyed out as there are currently no commands to redo.

Clicking on the top arrow will undo the last command. Clicking on the small triangle will allow you to undo more than one recent command.

To test this, enter 10 into cell A1 and then click the 'undo' arrow. After clicking Undo, the 10 which had been typed in has gone – this has been 'undone'. Note that the redo button has now appeared and is no longer greyed out – if we click on that, the command (typing 10 into cell A1) will be 'redone'.

Remember, formatting, data entry and formula entry can all be 'undone', so if things start to look wrong, undo what you have done. If you realise you were right, simply redo!

Shortcut

- **Ctrl-z** (hold Ctrl, then press z) will undo the last command
- **Ctrl-y** will redo the last undone command

1.7 Spreadsheet Structure

rows
columns
cells

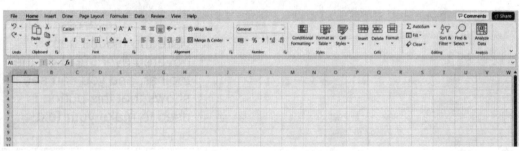

The spreadsheet (worksheet) shown above is made up of 'Rows', 'Columns' and 'Cells:

- The 'Rows' are numbered down the left hand-side from 1 onwards.
- The 'Columns' are lettered along the top from A onwards.
- The 'Cells' are the junction of columns and rows [example cell A1 is the junction of Column A and Row 1].

active cell = aonde o cursor esta.

- The 'Active' cell is where you are be able to enter data and is highlighted with a bold border [See A1 above]. Both the column letter and the row number are also highlighted.

Shortcut

Ctrl-Home takes you to cell A1.

Ctrl-End takes you to the cell furthest into the worksheet that has been active (even if the content has been removed).

1.8 Entering data into your worksheet

Selecting cells

To select a cell, left-click on the cell you wish to select. This is now the Active Cell. The value or formula in the Active Cell will be shown in the Formula Bar, and the Cell Reference will be shown in the Name Box.

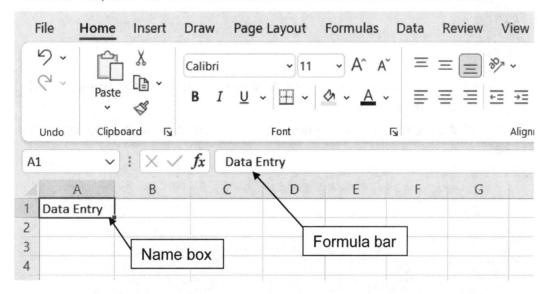

You can also change the selection by using the arrow keys to move the Active Cell Box around the screen until you reach the cell you require, or by typing the cell you require into the Name Box and pressing 'Enter'.

shortcut = atalho.
left click = go to the cell you wish to select. = active cell.

Selecting multiple cells

Selecting several cells at once is easiest using the mouse.

> - Using the mouse, **Left-Click** on a cell to select it, but **HOLD DOWN** the mouse button
> - **DRAG** the mouse pointer to select neighbouring cells.

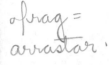

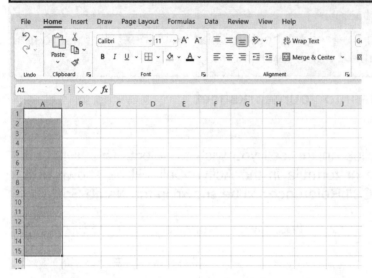

If you wish to select non-contiguous (not neighbouring) cells, press the Ctrl key while selecting individual cells.

To select **ALL** cells in a worksheet, click on the box in the top-left of the sheet.

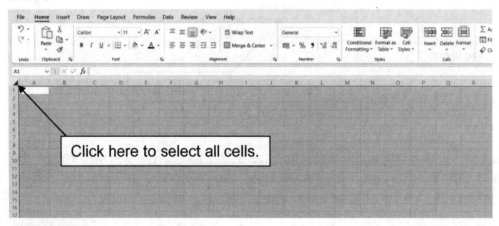

Click here to select all cells.

Cell ranges

As we have seen, each cell in Excel has a name (A1, B7 etc). If you select multiple cells, this is a **RANGE** of cells. If you select 2 separate cells, for example C2 and E5, the cells would be separated by a comma, so this would be displayed as **(C2, E5)**. If, as is more common, a **BLOCK** of cells is selected, these are displayed as: **(Top left cell:Bottom right cell)**

Example

To refer to the cells selected here, we would enter **(A3:C8)**.

This notation becomes important when we deal with functions later.

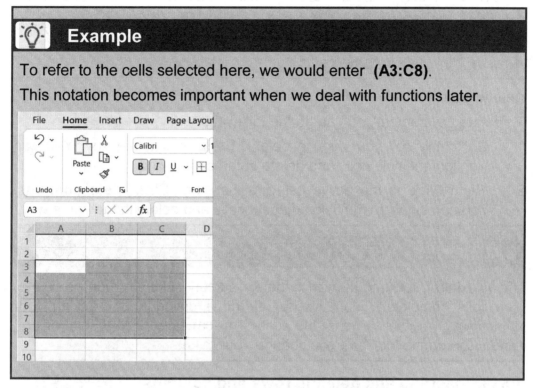

Entering data

To enter data into the active cell, simply type the data required into the cell – either numeric or text. This will overwrite any existing data.

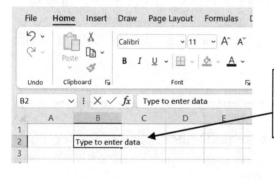

As you type, the data will be displayed on the spreadsheet itself and within the Formula Bar.

1.9 Editing and deleting cell content

Editing existing data

If a cell already contains data and you wish to edit it without overwriting, there are two ways to do this, via the Formula Bar or directly in the cell:

- **Double Click** on a cell to edit it

Or

- With the cell selected, **Left-click** in the **Formula Bar** to edit its contents.

Shortcut

Press **F2** to edit the Active cell.

Deleting data

To **delete** cell content you can do the following

1   Go to the cell you wish to delete. Press the delete key. You can highlight multiple cells and delete in the same way.

2   'Right-Click' in the active cell and then 'Left-Click' **clear contents.** You can highlight multiple adjacent cells and delete in the same way.

CAUTION!!!

If you 'Right-Click' and then click 'delete' Excel thinks you want to delete the cells completely. You will be offered a dialogue box asking you which way you want to shift the cells. You can click 'Edit, Undo' or the undo icon on the toolbar if you change your mind.

10.10   Inserting and deleting rows and columns

You can insert both rows and columns into your 'Worksheet'. Doing so will not increase or decrease the number of rows and columns in your worksheet. Excel will merely insert a blank row(s) or column(s) and shift the other rows or columns down/right. Excel cannot insert if the last row or column are in use. You would need to delete a row or column from elsewhere first.

To add a row to your worksheet

- Select the **'Home'** tab
- Click on the arrow under **'Insert'** in the **Cells** section of the toolbar
- Select **'Insert Sheet Rows'**

A row will be inserted, and the row with the Active Cell in it will be shifted **DOWN**.

To add a column to your worksheet

- Select the **'Home'** tab
- Click on the arrow under **'Insert'** in the 'cells section of the toolbar
- Select **'Insert Sheet Columns'**

A column will be inserted, and the column with the Active Cell in it will be shifted **RIGHT**.

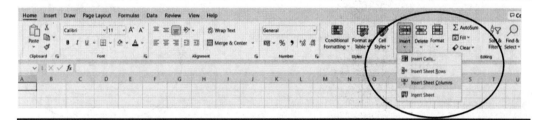

Shortcut

'Right-Click' the row number or column letter where you wish to insert, then click **'Insert'**.

Example

Right clicking on the **'5'** brings up this menu – select **Insert** to add a new row here.

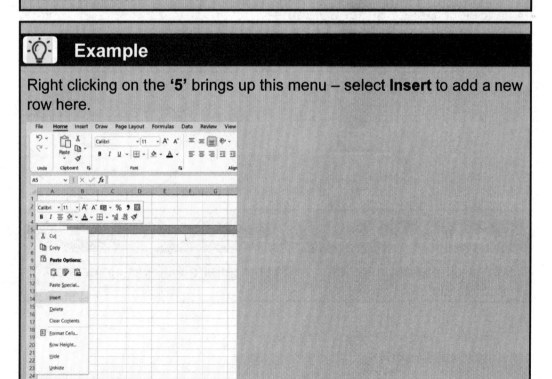

To delete a row from your worksheet

- Select the **'Home'** tab
- Click on the arrow under **'Delete'** in the **Cells** section of the toolbar
- Select **'Delete Sheet Rows'**

The data in the row will be deleted, and the rows underneath shifted **UP**

To delete a column from your worksheet

- Select the **'Home'** tab
- Select **'Delete'**
- Select **'Delete Sheet Columns'**

The data in the column will be deleted, and the columns underneath shifted **UP**

Shortcut

'Right-Click' the row number(s) or column letter(s) you wish to delete, then click **'Delete'**

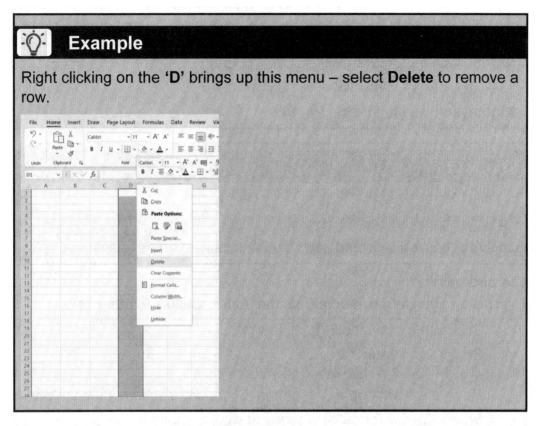

1.11 Copy, Cut, Paste and AutoFill

Copy and paste

Excel allows you to copy data from the 'Active Cell(s)' to other cells.

- Click in the active cell(s)
- Select the **'Home'** tab
- Press the **'Copy'** button in the 'Clipboard' section of the toolbar
- Select the cell (or cells) where you wish to copy to
- Press the **'Paste'** button

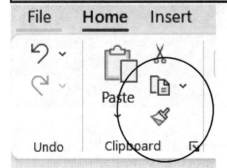

It is FORMAT Painter, not paste.

Shortcut

'**Right-Click**' the 'Active Cell(s)'. Click '**Copy**'.

Select the cell(s) where you wish to copy to.

'**Right-Click**' and then click '**Paste**'.

Shortcut

Highlight the active cells.

Ctrl-c will copy the selected cell(s)

Ctrl-v will paste the copied cell(s) to the location you have selected

Cut and paste

Excel allows you to move data from the 'Active Cell(s)' to other cells.

- Click in the active cell(s)
- Select the '**Home**' tab

- Press the '**Cut**' button ✂ in the 'Clipboard' section of the toolbar
- Select the cell (or cells) where you wish to move to

- Press the '**Paste**' button 🖌

Shortcut

'**Right-Click**' the 'Active Cell(s)'. Click '**Cut**'.

Select the cell(s) where you wish to copy to.

'**Right-Click**' and then click '**Paste**'.

Shortcut

Highlight the active cells.

Ctrl-x will copy the selected cell(s)

Ctrl-v will paste the copied cell(s) to the location you have selected

AutoFill

The AutoFill tool is an incredibly useful feature within Excel. In the main it is used to quickly copy data into neighbouring cells, but it has several other uses that can save time and effort.

To copy a cell's contents into adjacent cells, hover the mouse pointer over the **bottom right** of the cell. The mouse pointer should change from a fat cross (⊞) to a normal thinner cross.

arrastar

Once the pointer has changed, **left click** and **drag** the mouse in the direction you wish to copy the information.

Release the mouse button to complete the fill.

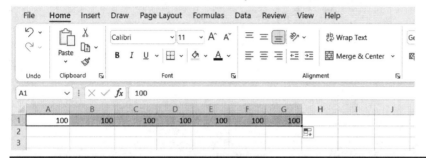

Example

Autofill becomes especially useful when copying formulas (see later), and can also be used to save time when typing out common lists, such as days of the week, or repetitive sequences.

Here, 'January' has been typed into cell A1. Autofill has been used to 'drag' the cell down for 12 rows. You can see a pop up over B13 there's a box saying 'December'. – this is telling us that the Autofill is going to put 'December' in cell A12 – the last cell in the fill.

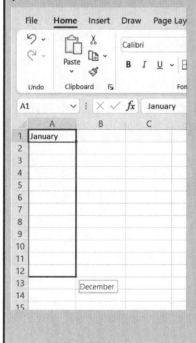

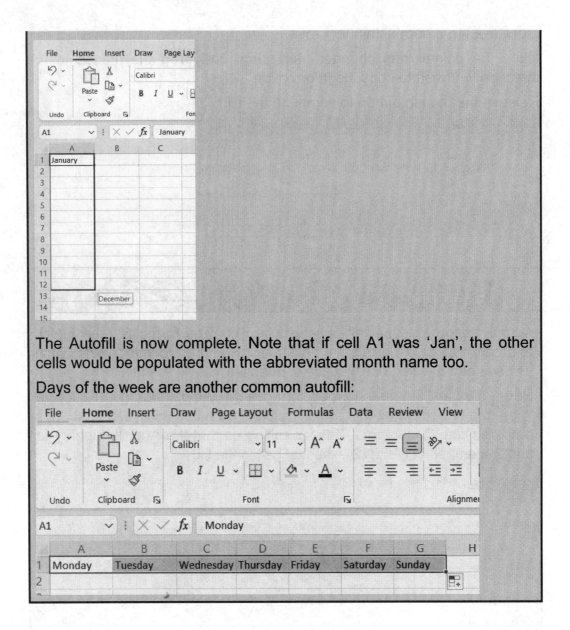

The Autofill is now complete. Note that if cell A1 was 'Jan', the other cells would be populated with the abbreviated month name too.

Days of the week are another common autofill:

You can also autofill sequences of numbers.

To do this you need to have at least the first 2 numbers of the sequence. Highlight both cells and then 'drag' the cells down.

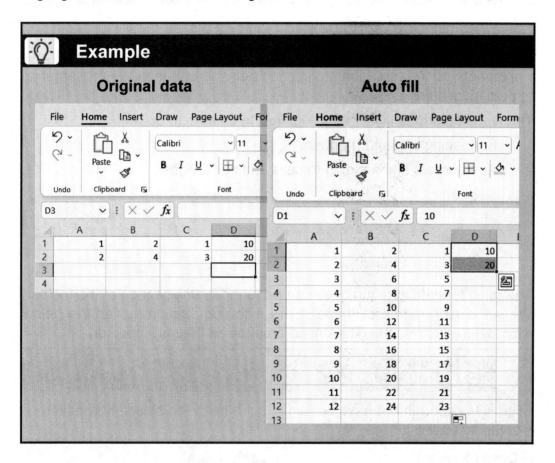

2 Formatting numerical data

2.1 Formatting techniques

Formatting is a process whereby you change the visual aspects of your worksheet. Using formatting techniques helps to enhance the presentation of numerical data.

The types of formatting you are required to be able to do are:

1 Formatting text and numbers

2 Add borders and shading to cells and cell ranges.

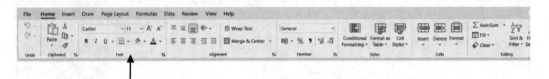

The main formatting techniques can be found in this section of the toolbar. We will explore some of these in the following sections using the below example to illustrate the different commands as they are covered.

Example

The sales department have been given the following sales information for the last week:

Credit Sales	Cash Sales
Monday - 15678.98	Monday – 3210.66
Tuesday - 21386.54	Tuesday – 3548.21
Wednesday - 24733.12	Wednesday – 4890.34
Thursday - 18450.55	Thursday – 2997.65
Friday – 20433.74	Friday – 5623.92

You have been asked to:

a) Give the spreadsheet a suitable title

b) Enter the above information into a spreadsheet

c) Format the data to enhance the presentation

d) Use a formula to add up the total credit sales for the week

e) Use the AutoSum function to add up the total cash sales for the week

2.2 Formatting titles

The starting point for this task is to open a new worksheet and enter the details. The first part of the task is to a add a suitable title. For this we will use 'Total Sales for the Week'. When adding a title into a spreadsheet, it is common to enter this into cell A1.

The next part of the task is to enter the given data into the worksheet. When using spreadsheets, it is important to select a row for headings.

Using a header row helps the reader see the category of the data within each column. For this exercise 'row 3' will be used for the headings. In the example given, there are days of the week, credit sales and cash sales. These categories will form the headings on row 3 as shown below:

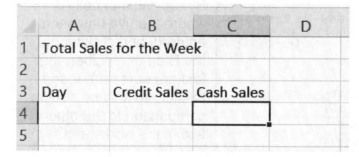

hover = flutuar

Note: If you cannot see all text within a certain cell, you can hover your mouse over the line between the relevant columns on the grey bar (the mouse pointer will change to ⬌) double click and it will automatically resize so that the text is clearly visible.

The data can now be added to the spreadsheet as shown below. Remember to use the AutoFill command when adding the days of the week into the worksheet.

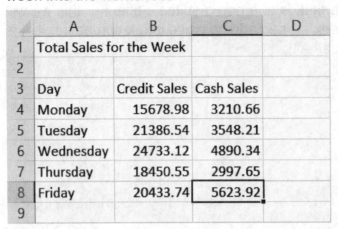

	A	B	C	D
1	Total Sales for the Week			
2				
3	Day	Credit Sales	Cash Sales	
4	Monday	15678.98	3210.66	
5	Tuesday	21386.54	3548.21	
6	Wednesday	24733.12	4890.34	
7	Thursday	18450.55	2997.65	
8	Friday	20433.74	5623.92	
9				

The advantage of using a spreadsheet as opposed to manually working with this data is that it can be formatted to make certain information stand out.

For example, the title should stand out to the reader to it catches their attention and they know what information they are looking at. In this example the title will be made 'bold', slightly bigger and underlined.

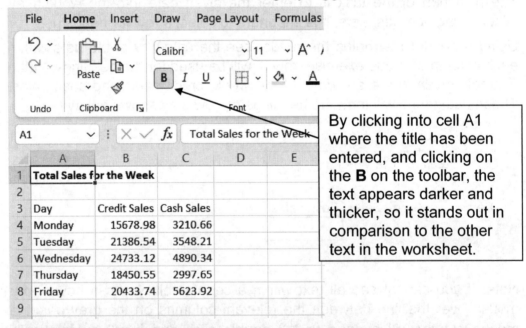

By clicking into cell A1 where the title has been entered, and clicking on the B on the toolbar, the text appears darker and thicker, so it stands out in comparison to the other text in the worksheet.

Shortcut

Ctrl-B - Clicking into cell A1, holding down the CTRL key and pressing B on the keyboard will also make the text bold.

The title can also be underlined (using U) to make it obvious to the reader that it is a title.

Shortcut

Ctrl-u - Clicking into cell A1, holding down the CTRL key and pressing U on the keyboard will also underline the text within the cell(s).

The column titles will be made bold and in italic text to make them clear. You do not need to perform these tasks one cell at a time, you can perform actions on multiple cells at one time. This is another benefit of using spreadsheets as it saves lots of time and creates efficiency when preparing and manipulating data.

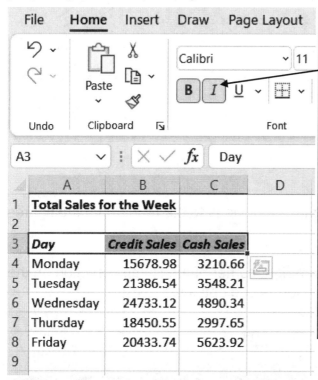

By the three cells containing headings, and clicking on the *I* on the toolbar, the text will be formatted in italics. In this example, the headings have been made bold too, using the same method as above.

Data in a cell can also be made italic by using a shortcut. Clicking into cell A1, holding down the CTRL key and pressing I on the keyboard will also make the text italic.

Shortcut

Ctrl-i - Clicking into cell A1, holding down the CTRL key and pressing i on the keyboard will also make the text italic within the cell(s).

2.3   Formatting numbers

The sales figures provided in the example are in pounds. However, at present they simply look like a set of numbers.

To format numbers, you can use a variety of methods which will be covered throughout this chapter. Firstly, we will use a thousand separator which will insert a comma to separate the thousands from the hundreds, tens and units.

throughout = por toda

Remember, actions can be performed on multiple cells at one time by highlighting the relevant data.

Highlight all of the cells relevant to the action you want to perform. In this case it is all of the numbers.

To insert the thousand separator, click on the **'** in the 'Number' section of the toolbar. You will see this will insert a thousand separator (comma) in all of your figures.

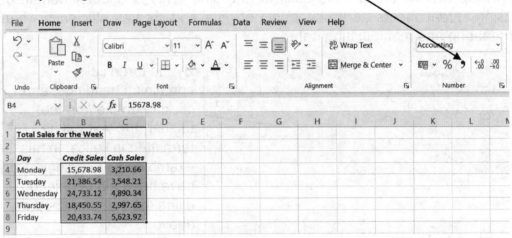

We will now enter a £ sign to make it obvious to the reader that the figures shown are in GBP.

Clicking on the � in the bottom right corner of the Number section on the toolbar will bring up the number formatting options.

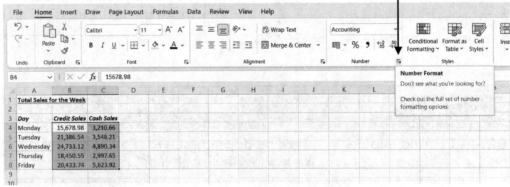

Highlight all the cells relevant to the action you want to perform. In this case it is all the numbers.

Click on the 〔↘〕 in the bottom right corner 'Number' section of the toolbar. The above screen appears. The figures need to be presented in £'s so we select 'Currency' from the options on the left hand side. The figures need to be displayed to 2 decimal places with a £ sign. When the correct options have been selected, click [OK]

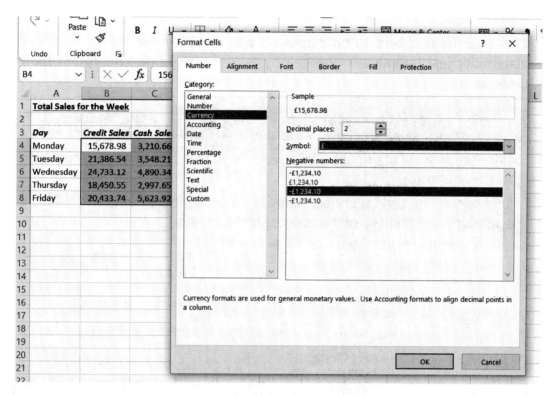

The figures in the spreadsheet are now presented in £'s with a thousand separator and to two decimal places, as per the options selected:

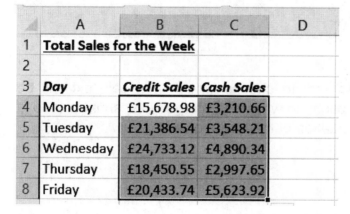

Note: Although the name 'Number' implies that this menu affects numbers, this option will change the way information within all selected cells will be displayed. Its primary use is to display numeric information in a user-friendly fashion. However, as you can see from the options above, this command can also be used to format dates, time, percentages etc. The negative number option can be used to display negative numbers as red, with or without a minus sign.

Accounting

This is very similar to **Currency**, but decimal points and currency symbols will be lined up in a column, potentially making it easier to interpret data.

It's a matter of personal choice as to which you prefer.

Percentage

This enables numbers to be displayed with a '%' symbol at the end, and also multiplies the value in the cell by 100 – this will be covered in more detail later.

Shortcuts

There are several shortcuts available to change the Number Format on the **Home menu**.

Number formats can be chosen directly, or percentage symbols, 1000 separators and number of decimal points changed:

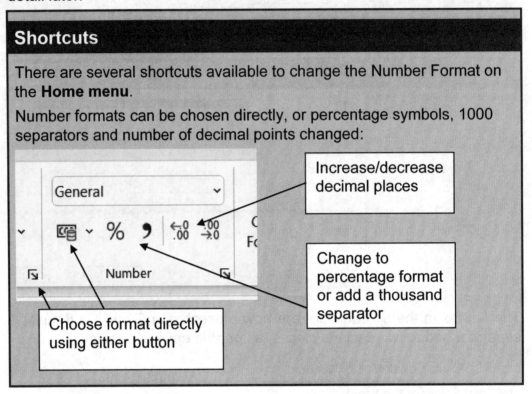

Alignment

The **Alignment** tab allows you to choose where in a cell text will be displayed, as well as the options to wrap text, merge cells, shrink text to fit in cells and also adjust orientation of the text in a cell.

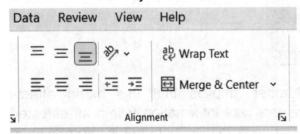

KAPLAN PUBLISHING

Using the example we have been working through to illustrate the commands within Excel, use the 'Merge and Centre' command to centralise the title over all three columns.

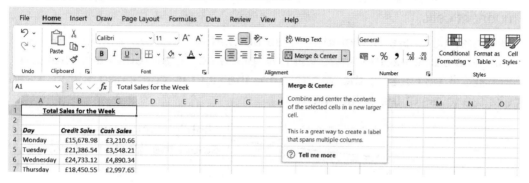

2.4 Formatting text

Font

This is used to change the font type, size, and colour and to add effects to the text.

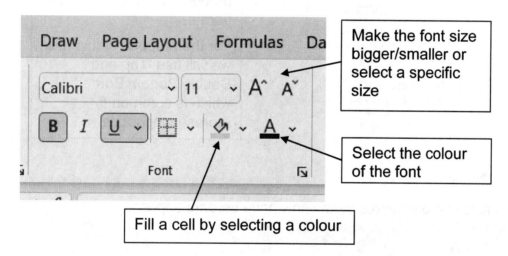

Make the font size bigger/smaller or select a specific size

Select the colour of the font

Fill a cell by selecting a colour

2.5   Formatting borders

As the name suggests, the Border button allows you to place a border around a cell or cells, to improve the look of the spreadsheet, or highlight important cells.

If several cells are selected, the same borders will be applied to each. Using the same example, we will now place borders around the total cells, to make it obvious to the reader that the figures contained within these cells are totals of the columns.

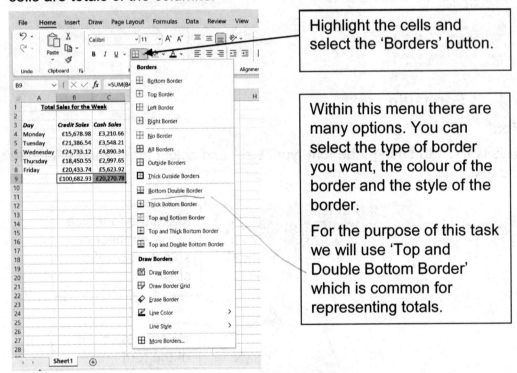

Highlight the cells and select the 'Borders' button.

Within this menu there are many options. You can select the type of border you want, the colour of the border and the style of the border.

For the purpose of this task we will use 'Top and Double Bottom Border' which is common for representing totals.

The totals in the example below now have borders applied:

	A	B	C
1	**Total Sales for the Week**		
2			
3	*Day*	*Credit Sales*	*Cash Sales*
4	Monday	£15,678.98	£3,210.66
5	Tuesday	£21,386.54	£3,548.21
6	Wednesday	£24,733.12	£4,890.34
7	Thursday	£18,450.55	£2,997.65
8	Friday	£20,433.74	£5,623.92
9		£100,682.93	£20,270.78
10			

Test your understanding 1

Formatting can enhance the presentation of numerical information.

Match the icons given with the relevant description.

Icon	Description
←0 .00	Changes font colour.
B	Makes text bold.
A ˅	Centralises the text in the cell.
🖼 ˅	Changes to percentage format.
%	Switches to accounting format.
,	Increases the number of decimal places.
≡	Add a thousands separator.

3 Formulas

3.1 Using formulas when performing calculations

One of the main advantages of using spreadsheets in finance is because it replaces the need for a calculator. Human error can easily occur when manually working with large amounts of data. Using formulas in a spreadsheet eradicates this and ensures the accuracy of calculations. You can enter formulas to add, subtract, multiply or divide figures quickly and easily. Saving time and increasing accuracy within financial records is of great benefit to all businesses.

We have already seen how to enter numeric and text information into cells. However, Excel's primary purpose is to manipulate the raw data through calculations and formulas. One of the main things you will use Excel for is simple calculations. The most basic (and most common) calculations are the mathematical functions addition +, subtraction -, multiplication * and divide /.

To use these, you need to tell Excel that you are using a **FUNCTION**. To do this, enter an equals sign, '=' in the formula box, before the calculation you require.

For simple formulas you can simply enter = followed by the numerical values and mathematical operations you wish to perform. To add numbers together you use the plus sign (+), to subtract figures you use the minus sign (-), to multiply figures you use the asterisk (*) and to divide figures you use the forward slash (/). For example, if you want to do 256 divided by 8, this would be as follows:

SUM		⌄	⋮	✕ ✓ *fx*	=256/8

	A	B	C	D
1	=256/8			
2				

When you press enter, the answer will be automatically generated, and the calculation remains in the formula box as shown below:

A1		⌄	⋮	✕ ✓ *fx*	=256/8

	A	B	C	D
1	32			
2				

The example we have been working through requires you to add up the total credit sales for the week.

As there is more than one number within the calculation, this can be done as illustrated below:

Firstly, click in the cell that you want the answer to be shown. In this case this will be B9.

Enter = in the formula box and then click on each figure you would like to include in the calculation. You can see in this example that by doing this, you are generating the formula required.

When you press enter, the answer will be displayed in cell B9.

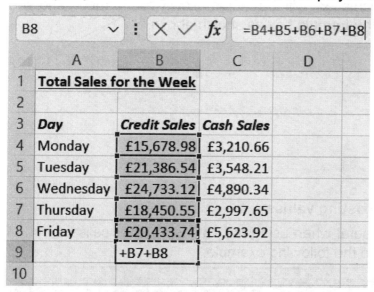

The answer is displayed in cell B9:

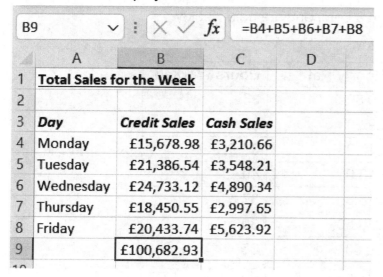

The example we have been working through also requires you to add up the total cash sales for the week. The other way of doing this is to use the AutoSum function.

This is a quicker way of adding up more than one figure and can be done as follows:

Highlight all the figures you wish to add up, and the cell in which you want the answer to be displayed. In this example we are adding up the 'total cash sales' and we want the answer to be displayed in cell C9.

Click on the Σ AutoSum button which is in the Editing tab on the toolbar and press enter. The calculation will be automatically performed, and the formula generated in the formula box as shown above.

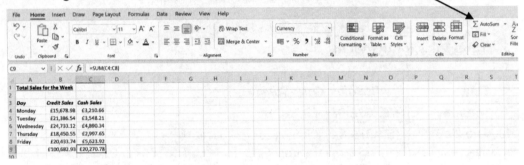

Calculations using existing values

Excel is particularly useful when using the values in other cells as part of your calculations. Take the following example:

Example

Ten employees within a company are paid weekly.

The details are as follows:

Name	Hourly Rate	Hours Worked
Fletcher	£9.80	35
Wilson	£9.20	37
Parker	£15.25	37.5
Eastwood	£18.00	40
Ahmed	£18.00	37.5
Divilli	£10.50	30
Davies	£9.80	35
Flanagan	£12.00	30
Brown	£21.00	37.5
Mitchell	£17.50	40

You have been asked to calculate the total wages for each employee for the week using a spreadsheet:

a)   Open a new workbook and insert a suitable title; use bold, underline and merge and center

b)   Insert appropriate headings including a column for 'Total Pay'. Headings should be formatted in bold italics

c)   Enter the above information into the worksheet in the font style 'Arial' size 12 (make sure the text is readable by adjusting the column width if necessary)

d)   Format the 'hourly rate', 'hours worked' and 'total pay' columns by making the information contained within each cell central, the hourly rate in the 'Accounting' format and the hours worked formatted by number to 1 decimal place

e)   Use a formula to calculate the total pay for each employee

f)   Use the AutoSum function to add up the total wages for the week

You should now be able to perform parts a – d of the above example by putting into practice the skills learnt so far in this chapter. When you have done this, your spreadsheet should look as follows:

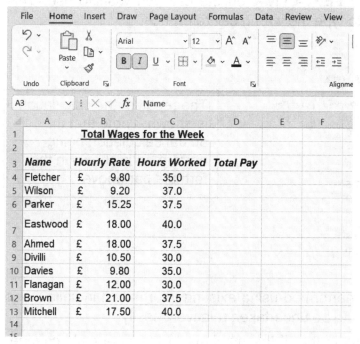

Name	Hourly Rate	Hours Worked	Total Pay
Fletcher	£ 9.80	35.0	
Wilson	£ 9.20	37.0	
Parker	£ 15.25	37.5	
Eastwood	£ 18.00	40.0	
Ahmed	£ 18.00	37.5	
Divilli	£ 10.50	30.0	
Davies	£ 9.80	35.0	
Flanagan	£ 12.00	30.0	
Brown	£ 21.00	37.5	
Mitchell	£ 17.50	40.0	

To calculate the total pay we need to multiply the hourly rate by the number of hours worked. You could simply type each one of these in, for example '=9.80*35' for Fletcher. However, this would be time consuming and not much better than using a pen and paper.

We can instead tell Excel to 'take the value in cell B4 and multiply by the value in cell C4'.

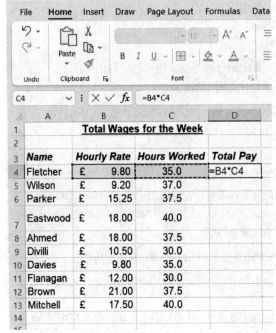

Each cell is referred to by its column and row reference. To perform the calculation, start with the '**=**' sign to show that you want to perform a calculation. Then type the cell reference of the cell you wish to use. A box will appear around the cell.

Finish off the calculation as required – the cell references are just saying "use whatever number is in this cell".

Note: When entering cell references into a formula, rather than typing the reference '**B2**', you can **LEFT-CLICK** on the cell you wish to use. This way you are less likely to type the wrong cell reference.

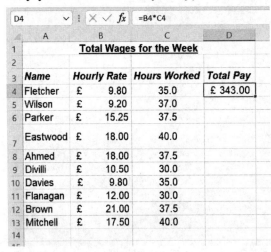

The result of the calculation is shown – note that the actual calculation being performed is shown in the formula bar above.

Any calculation can be performed using existing information in cells – this allows complex analysis to be undertaken relatively easily.

One huge benefit of this is that if the numbers in the data cells change, then the calculation will be updated to reflect this.

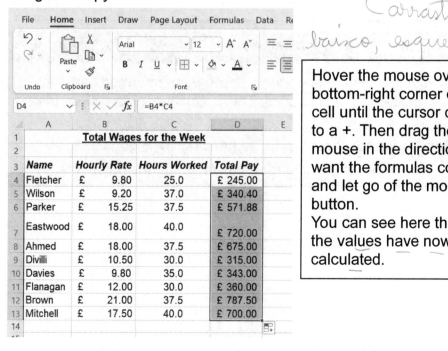

D4		fx	=B4*C4	
	A	B	C	D
1		**Total Wages for the Week**		
2				
3	**Name**	**Hourly Rate**	**Hours Worked**	**Total Pay**
4	Fletcher	£ 9.80	25.0	£ 245.00
5	Wilson	£ 9.20	37.0	
6	Parker	£ 15.25	37.5	
7	Eastwood	£ 18.00	40.0	
8	Ahmed	£ 18.00	37.5	
9	Divilli	£ 10.50	30.0	
10	Davies	£ 9.80	35.0	
11	Flanagan	£ 12.00	30.0	
12	Brown	£ 21.00	37.5	
13	Mitchell	£ 17.50	40.0	
14				

> Changing the hours worked to 25 will automatically give an updated value in the total pay column.

3.2 Copying formulas

In the previous example, a formula has been entered into cell D4. We need to perform the same calculation for the other 9 members of staff. It would be incredibly time consuming to have to manually enter the calculation into each cell – sometimes spreadsheets can have several thousand rows!

Fortunately, Excel deals with this problem very easily. Using the same copy and paste feature seen earlier in the chapter, you can duplicate formulas used to speed up calculations.

Another quick way to copy formulas is to use the Autofill function explained earlier in the chapter. Formulas can be "dragged" up, down, left, or right to copy them:

arrastar para amg baixo, esquerda ou direita

File	Home	Insert	Draw	Page Layout	Formulas	Data	Re

D4		fx	=B4*C4	
	A	B	C	D	E
1		**Total Wages for the Week**		
2				
3	**Name**	**Hourly Rate**	**Hours Worked**	**Total Pay**
4	Fletcher	£ 9.80	25.0	£ 245.00
5	Wilson	£ 9.20	37.0	£ 340.40
6	Parker	£ 15.25	37.5	£ 571.88
7	Eastwood	£ 18.00	40.0	£ 720.00
8	Ahmed	£ 18.00	37.5	£ 675.00
9	Divilli	£ 10.50	30.0	£ 315.00
10	Davies	£ 9.80	35.0	£ 343.00
11	Flanagan	£ 12.00	30.0	£ 360.00
12	Brown	£ 21.00	37.5	£ 787.50
13	Mitchell	£ 17.50	40.0	£ 700.00
14				

> Hover the mouse over the bottom-right corner of the cell until the cursor changes to a +. Then drag the mouse in the direction you want the formulas copied and let go of the mouse button.
> You can see here that all of the values have now been calculated.

The total wages for the week can now be calculated using the AutoSum function.

| F20 | | fx | | |

	A	B	C	D	E
1		**Total Wages for the Week**			
2					
3	**Name**	**Hourly Rate**	**Hours Worked**	**Total Pay**	
4	Fletcher	£ 9.80	25.0	£ 245.00	
5	Wilson	£ 9.20	37.0	£ 340.40	
6	Parker	£ 15.25	37.5	£ 571.88	
7	Eastwood	£ 18.00	40.0	£ 720.00	
8	Ahmed	£ 18.00	37.5	£ 675.00	
9	Divilli	£ 10.50	30.0	£ 315.00	
10	Davies	£ 9.80	35.0	£ 343.00	
11	Flanagan	£ 12.00	30.0	£ 360.00	
12	Brown	£ 21.00	37.5	£ 787.50	
13	Mitchell	£ 17.50	40.0	£ 700.00	
14					
15			Total wages for the week	£5,057.78	
16					
17					

Shortcut

Instead of dragging the Autofill box down, **DOUBLE CLICK** to automatically copy formulas down to the bottom of a block of cells.

Example

Continuing with the same example, you have been informed that each employee is entitled to a 10% bonus. This is calculated as 10% of their total pay.

a) Insert an additional column with the heading '10% bonus'

b) Enter an appropriate formula to calculate the bonus payments

When calculating a percentage of one figure within a spreadsheet, you can enter a simple formula such as, '=D4*10%'

AutoFill can then be used to generate the bonuses for the 9 remaining employees and AutoSum can be used to quickly add up the total of the 'bonus' column:

E4		⌄ : ✕ ✓ *fx*	=D4*10%	

	A	B	C	D	E
1			**Total Wages for the Week**		
2					
3	**Name**	**Hourly Rate**	**Hours Worked**	**Total Pay**	**10% Bonus**
4	Fletcher	£ 9.80	25.0	£ 245.00	£ 24.50
5	Wilson	£ 9.20	37.0	£ 340.40	£ 34.04
6	Parker	£ 15.25	37.5	£ 571.88	£ 57.19
7	Eastwood	£ 18.00	40.0	£ 720.00	£ 72.00
8	Ahmed	£ 18.00	37.5	£ 675.00	£ 67.50
9	Divilli	£ 10.50	30.0	£ 315.00	£ 31.50
10	Davies	£ 9.80	35.0	£ 343.00	£ 34.30
11	Flanagan	£ 12.00	30.0	£ 360.00	£ 36.00
12	Brown	£ 21.00	37.5	£ 787.50	£ 78.75
13	Mitchell	£ 17.50	40.0	£ 700.00	£ 70.00
14					
15			Total wages for the week	£5,057.78	£ 505.78
16					

3.3 Completing calculations and the order of precedence

You are going to use simple mathematical functions to analyse your data but in order that you can do this you need to understand the order of priority given to each function. Excel follows the same mathematical rules. Below is a list of the order of precedence (priority).

This is not the full list, but it is what you need to know in order to perform basic calculations:

Operator	Symbol	Order of Precedence
Brackets	()	1
Multiplication	*	2
Division	/	2
Addition	+	3
Subtraction	-	3

The order of precedence determines which operators Excel will use first in its calculations. It can be seen above that Excel will calculate a formula that contains multiplication or division before it calculates an addition or subtraction. By inserting brackets around part of a formula, it forces Excel to calculate the content of the brackets first, followed by the remainder of the formula.

Important

You may have come across the phrase BODMAS during a maths class. This stands for Brackets Off, Divide, Multiply, Add, Subtract – the order of precedence.

Continuing with the same example, we can demonstrate the order of precedence. We need to calculate the tax each person will pay, as 20% of their total pay.

To calculate this using one formula, we need to add up two cells, and then multiply the total by 20%. However, due to the order of operations, care must be taken.

If we simply instructed Excel to add up the two cells then multiply by 20, Excel reads this as: Multiply E4 by 20%, and then add on D2.

So, the answer comes out as £249.90, which is incorrect:

E4			f_x =D4+E4*20%			
	A	B	C	D	E	F
1			**Total Wages for the Week**			
2						
3	**Name**	**Hourly Rate**	**Hours Worked**	**Total Pay**	**10% Bonus**	**Tax @ 20%**
4	Fletcher	£ 9.80	25.0	£ 245.00	£ 24.50	=D4+E4*20%
5	Wilson	£ 9.20	37.0	£ 340.40	£ 34.04	
6	Parker	£ 15.25	37.5	£ 571.88	£ 57.19	
7	Eastwood	£ 18.00	40.0	£ 720.00	£ 72.00	
8	Ahmed	£ 18.00	37.5	£ 675.00	£ 67.50	
9	Divilli	£ 10.50	30.0	£ 315.00	£ 31.50	
10	Davies	£ 9.80	35.0	£ 343.00	£ 34.30	
11	Flanagan	£ 12.00	30.0	£ 360.00	£ 36.00	
12	Brown	£ 21.00	37.5	£ 787.50	£ 78.75	
13	Mitchell	£ 17.50	40.0	£ 700.00	£ 70.00	
14						
15			Total wages for the week	£5,057.78	£ 505.78	
16						

To get round this problem, you must use brackets – put the calculation you want to happen first in brackets, to force the order required as follows:

F4			f_x =(D4+E4)*20%			
	A	B	C	D	E	F
1			**Total Wages for the Week**			
2						
3	**Name**	**Hourly Rate**	**Hours Worked**	**Total Pay**	**10% Bonus**	**Tax @ 20%**
4	Fletcher	£ 9.80	25.0	£ 245.00	£ 24.50	£ 53.90
5	Wilson	£ 9.20	37.0	£ 340.40	£ 34.04	
6	Parker	£ 15.25	37.5	£ 571.88	£ 57.19	
7	Eastwood	£ 18.00	40.0	£ 720.00	£ 72.00	
8	Ahmed	£ 18.00	37.5	£ 675.00	£ 67.50	
9	Divilli	£ 10.50	30.0	£ 315.00	£ 31.50	
10	Davies	£ 9.80	35.0	£ 343.00	£ 34.30	
11	Flanagan	£ 12.00	30.0	£ 360.00	£ 36.00	

(handwritten) =(D4 + E4) * 20%

You can see here that by adding brackets into the 'addition' part of the formula, Excel knows to add up the values of these cells first, and then multiply the answer by 20%

 It's often worth sense checking the result of a calculation – a simple typo can give unpredictable results!

Again, using the AutoFill function is a quick and easy way of calculating the tax for all of the remaining employees. The AutoSum function can also be used to update the spreadsheet with the total tax payable by the employees.

	A	B	C	D	E	F	G
	F18		fx				
1			Total Wages for the Week				
2							
3	Name	Hourly Rate	Hours Worked	Total Pay	10% Bonus	Tax @ 20%	
4	Fletcher	£ 9.80	25.0	£ 245.00	£ 24.50	£ 53.90	
5	Wilson	£ 9.20	37.0	£ 340.40	£ 34.04	£ 74.89	
6	Parker	£ 15.25	37.5	£ 571.88	£ 57.19	£ 125.81	
7	Eastwood	£ 18.00	40.0	£ 720.00	£ 72.00	£ 158.40	
8	Ahmed	£ 18.00	37.5	£ 675.00	£ 67.50	£ 148.50	
9	Divilli	£ 10.50	30.0	£ 315.00	£ 31.50	£ 69.30	
10	Davies	£ 9.80	35.0	£ 343.00	£ 34.30	£ 75.46	
11	Flanagan	£ 12.00	30.0	£ 360.00	£ 36.00	£ 79.20	
12	Brown	£ 21.00	37.5	£ 787.50	£ 78.75	£ 173.25	
13	Mitchell	£ 17.50	40.0	£ 700.00	£ 70.00	£ 154.00	
14							
15			Total wages for the week	£5,057.78	£ 505.78	£ 1,112.71	
16							

Example

Continuing with the same example, you have been asked to calculate the net pay. This can be calculated by adding together the total pay and bonus and then subtracting the tax.

Note: *National insurance is not applicable for the purpose of this exercise.*

a)   Insert an additional column with the heading 'Net Pay

b)   Enter an appropriate formula to calculate the net pay for each employee

NET PAY = (D4 + E4) - F4

Using the order of precedence, you must use brackets – put the calculation you want to happen first in brackets, to force the order required as follows:

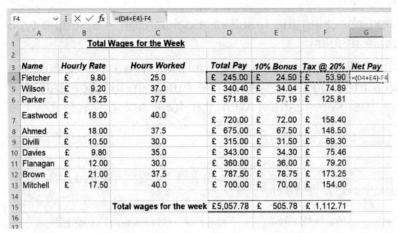

You can see above that by adding brackets into the 'addition' part of the formula again, and then subtracting the figure in the 'tax' column using the correct cell reference, the formula is generated in the formula bar.

When pressing enter, the figure is automatically updated.

Using the necessary formatting techniques, your spreadsheet should look as follows:

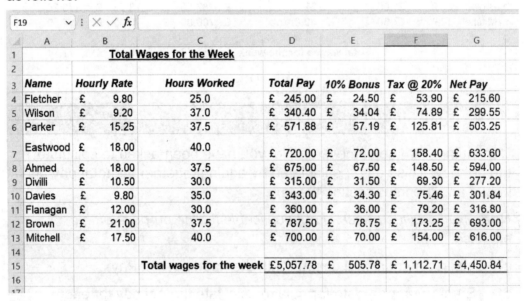

Tasks

a)   Enter the title 'Sales Invoices 11/07/XX' into cell A1.

b)   Enter headings on row 3 as follows; Customer Name, Discount, Net, VAT, Total – format them so they are central within the columns.

c)   Format all text to Arial Size 12.

d)   Merge and Center the title in Bold and Underlined.

e)   Format the headings in Bold Italics.

f)   Input the Customer Names and Net Amounts appropriately – *Note: Your whole spreadsheet needs to be formatted in Arial Size 12.*

g)   In cell A10, enter Total.

h)   In the discount column, enter an appropriate formula to calculate any discounts applicable to the customers. Where a discount is not applicable, enter 0.

i)   In the VAT column, calculate the VAT applicable on each invoice. VAT is charged at 20%.

   Note: Remember that the formula will need to subtract any discount applicable before the VAT can be calculated.

j)   In the Total column, calculate the Total of each invoice by adding together the Net and VAT figure.

k)   Total each column using AutoSum and format with a Top and Double bottom border around the totals.

l)   Format the figures within the spreadsheet to 'Accounting', centralising all figures within each cell

Answers to chapter activities

Test your understanding 1

Icon	Description
⬅.00 0	Increases the number of decimal places.
B	Makes text bold.
A ⌄	Changes font colour.
🏛 ⌄	Switches to accounting format.
%	Changes to percentage format.
,	Adds a thousands separator.
≡	Centralises the text in the cell.

Test your understanding 2

Formula	Type of calculation completed
=B8*C2	Multiplication
=C2/A6	Division
=B8-A8	Subtraction
=SUM(B2:B7)	Total of data
=B7+C7	Addition

KAPLAN PUBLISHING

Case study activity 4 – Interview Assessment

Spreadsheet Format and Figures

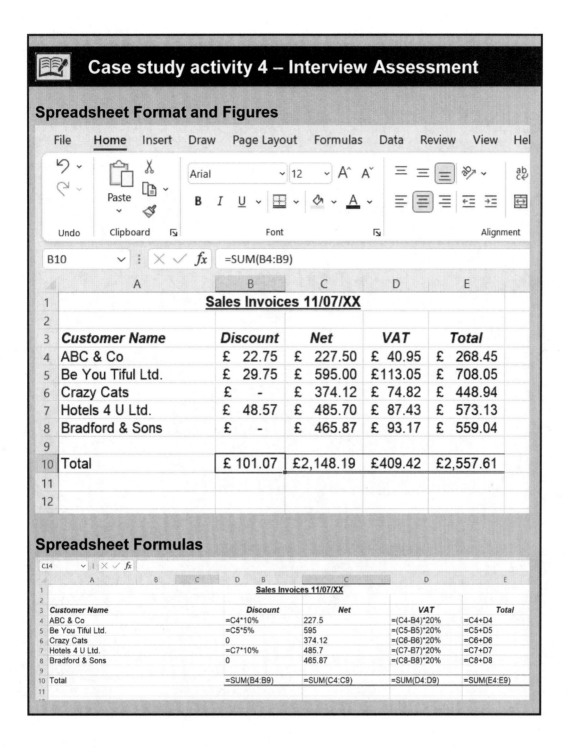

Cell B10: =SUM(B4:B9)

Sales Invoices 11/07/XX

Customer Name	Discount	Net	VAT	Total
ABC & Co	£ 22.75	£ 227.50	£ 40.95	£ 268.45
Be You Tiful Ltd.	£ 29.75	£ 595.00	£113.05	£ 708.05
Crazy Cats	£ -	£ 374.12	£ 74.82	£ 448.94
Hotels 4 U Ltd.	£ 48.57	£ 485.70	£ 87.43	£ 573.13
Bradford & Sons	£ -	£ 465.87	£ 93.17	£ 559.04
Total	£ 101.07	£2,148.19	£409.42	£2,557.61

Spreadsheet Formulas

Sales Invoices 11/07/XX

Customer Name	Discount	Net	VAT	Total
ABC & Co	=C4*10%	227.5	=(C4-B4)*20%	=C4+D4
Be You Tiful Ltd.	=C5*5%	595	=(C5-B5)*20%	=C5+D5
Crazy Cats	0	374.12	=(C6-B6)*20%	=C6+D6
Hotels 4 U Ltd.	=C7*10%	485.7	=(C7-B7)*20%	=C7+D7
Bradford & Sons	0	465.87	=(C8-B8)*20%	=C8+D8
Total	=SUM(B4:B9)	=SUM(C4:C9)	=SUM(D4:D9)	=SUM(E4:E9)

Developing skills for the workplace

4

Introduction

When starting a new role within an organisation, it will be vital to understand and develop the skills needed within the workplace. This includes the importance of team working, communication, effective time management and the need for professional behaviour.

This chapter will introduce you to the business environment and explore the skills required to be successful within the workplace.

KNOWLEDGE	CONTENTS
Working in the business environment	1 Workplace policies and procedures
1 Develop skills for the workplace	2 Working with others
1.1 The responsibilities of the employee and employer	3 Keeping data and information secure
1.2 Working and communicating with others	4 Summary and further questions
1.3 Time management	
1.4 Professional behaviour	
1.5 The importance of keeping data and information secure	

1 Workplace policies and procedures

1.1 Case study: an introduction

 Case study

Jessica passed her interview assessment with flying colours and impressed in her interview, Jessica was successful at securing the job at How Two Ltd.

She is now starting her new role with the company and is really looking forward to starting her first full time finance role.

Jessica's first full week will mainly be an induction into the organisation and introduction to the team she will be working with.

Jessica is keen to understand more about the organisation, including key policies and procedures to be followed and the rules and regulations and policies that she needs to adhere to.

 Definition

An induction is a short programme which introduces new employees to the working environment.

The induction programme will introduce you to the organisation, you will learn about the company objectives and values and the employee code of conduct. The induction process also provides information around the key regulations and policies which all employees must follow.

1.2 The responsibilities of the employer

When an organisation employs someone new, they must provide an induction that includes communication of the organisation's policies and procedures.

The purpose of the induction process is to introduce the new member of staff to the culture and policies of the organisation. An effective induction process will ensure the new staff member feels valued but will also give a clear understanding of what is expected of them within the organisation and their role.

The induction process will also introduce health and safety requirements, to ensure a safe working environment.

An effective induction process will take place over the first few days of employment and will:

- Support the integration of new staff, helping them to perform effectively
- Ensure staff understand the organisation's values, business strategy and vision
- Provide the necessary information in relation to policies and procedures to ensure effective working
- Help to define performance expectations and harness good working relationships
- Identify the training and development needs of new staff
- Identify any additional support required to meet their individual needs

Many employers will have a staff handbook which will be provided to new staff at induction; this will set out the policies, procedures, and rules to be followed. Employers must make sure that all staff have access to the staff handbook at all times.

The information included in the staff handbook will vary from organisation to organisation but there will be common topics such as:

- An introduction to the company
- Health and safety
- Equal opportunities
- Disciplinary and grievance policies and procedures
- Data protection
- Time off and absence
- Flexible working and homeworking
- Email, internet and social media policies.

 Examples

Dress Code: If your employer has a dress code, ensure that you respect it and dress accordingly, especially if meeting customers.

Social Media: Most companies state that computers in the workplace should not be used to access social media or for personal online use. This is not just due to the risk of reduced productivity but is also to avoid the danger of a security breach or accidentally acquiring a computer virus that could disable the whole organisation's systems. Likewise, many limit the use of mobile phones during working hours and therefore it is usually best to keep them on silent or switch them off.

1.3   Health and safety in the workplace

Employers also have a responsibility to provide a safe working environment for all staff. Providing a safe work environment will help to prevent accidents and ill-health caused by the working conditions or working practices.

Employers must consider working conditions in relation to space, temperature, lighting, ventilation, humidity and welfare facilities such as access to toilets and drinking water.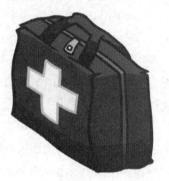

Any employer with five or more employees must have a written health and safety policy, which is updated regularly and accessible to all staff.

Health and safety policies within an office environment will cover the following:

- risk assessments
- computer equipment and IT set up
- lone working
- personal protective equipment
- reporting accident procedures
- location of first aiders
- fire drill and evacuation procedures
- location of fire extinguishers
- security alerts.

As part of the induction process, employers must make new staff aware of health and safety policies and procedures. This will not only help to protect new staff but also existing staff and site visitors. If an employer is found to be responsible for an injury sustained whilst on their premises, they may held liable and legal action may be taken against the organisation.

Because Health and Safety at work is so important all businesses must provide appropriate training and written rules that all employees and visitors must follow to reduce risks to individuals.

It is the employee's responsibility report to their manager if they see anything that could be considered unsafe, or anything that could cause an accident. Failure to report hazards would be a breach of the organisation's Health and Safety policy and could result in disciplinary action.

One way that you can help to maintain health and safety in the workplace is to keep your own work area clean and tidy. You should make sure that walkways are not blocked by boxes of papers, or trailing wires that could cause someone to trip.

Many workers find themselves overwhelmed by the amount of clutter on their desks, so by taking a few minutes each day to tidy up your work area you can make your office surroundings more professional, healthier and less stressful.

Keeping your work area tidy will also help you to prevent any confidential information to be left lying around – the need to do this will be covered later in this chapter.

1.4 The responsibilities of the employee

It is the responsibility of all employees within an organisation to follow policies and procedures. They will impact almost every aspect of everyday working, from behaviour in the workplace to departmental tasks undertaken.

A policy sets out how an organisation wants and expects activities to be undertaken, providing a clear guide of how actions should be taken, and decisions made. A procedure provides a step by step process of how to undertake an activity, for example, a procedure could be provided on the banking process.

All new staff have a responsibility to ensure that they are aware of and understand the policies and procedures relevant to their job role and organisation. Taking responsibility for this during the induction process and going forward:

- contributes to compliance
- improves efficiency
- protects all staff and visitors
- protects the organisation (including information and assets).

All employees must understand and follow all health and safety policies and report any concerns to the relevant person. Many organisations may have a designated Health and Safety Officer or Fire Marshall. For example, this could be as simple as reporting a tripping hazard in the office such a trailing wires across the office floor.

Employees need to take responsibility for a range of health and safety issues including:

- how to use equipment and any relevant safety measures

- fire drill and evacuation practices
- non-smoking policies
- reporting health and safety risks/hazards
- reporting accidents.

Test your understanding 1

Today is Marvin's first day in his new job. He has been told that he will have an induction day.

Which of the following should Marvin expect during the induction day (tick all that apply)?

Options	✓
A job interview	
Information about the company's policies	✓
An introduction to key staff in the company	✓
An overview of the company's values	✓
Lots of fun games and activities with other new starters	
To finish work early	
A promotion	

Test your understanding 2

Marvin has been with his new employer for a week. He has been warned by a colleague about using his mobile phone during work hours. He is unsure of the company's policy regarding this.

Where should he look to find out? Tick the most appropriate answer.

Options	✓
The job specification	
The company handbook	✓
The company website	
A government employment website	

KAPLAN PUBLISHING

Test your understanding 3

Marvin overhears three statements from his colleagues in his first week with the company.

For each one, decide if they are true or false and tick the correct box.

Statement	True	False
"As we work at a desk in the office and not in the warehouse, health and safety is not relevant to us."		✓
"Don't worry about that loose cable next to your desk – it is not your responsibility to report it."		✓
"Everyone here has a duty of care to keep things safe for both our colleagues and visitors".	✓	

Test your understanding 4

Health and safety in the workplace is the responsibility of:

Options	✓
The government	
The managers	
The employees	✓
The managers and the employees	

Test your understanding 5

Marvin has been given a laptop to work from but the only plug socket available is across the other side of the office. The only way he can plug it in is to use an extension lead and trail the wire across the office.

Should Marvin do this?

Options	✓
Yes, it is his first week with the company, so he does not feel comfortable saying no	
Yes, it will be fine so long as the wire is visible, so his colleagues know to step over it	
No, this is a trip hazard, he should speak to his manager and explain the situation	✓

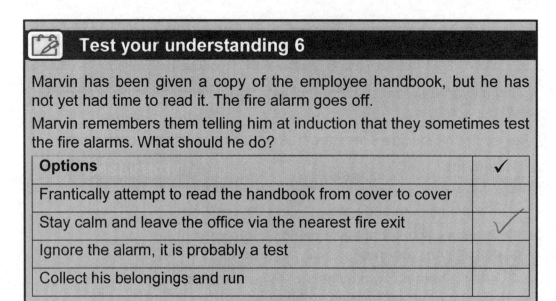

Test your understanding 6

Marvin has been given a copy of the employee handbook, but he has not yet had time to read it. The fire alarm goes off.

Marvin remembers them telling him at induction that they sometimes test the fire alarms. What should he do?

Options	✓
Frantically attempt to read the handbook from cover to cover	
Stay calm and leave the office via the nearest fire exit	✓
Ignore the alarm, it is probably a test	
Collect his belongings and run	

1.5 Sustainability

Sustainability is an important topic for most organisations.

 Definition

Sustainability means meeting the needs of the present generation without compromising the ability of future generations to meet their own needs.

Organisations have a duty to protect society and future generations and there are three areas to consider:

- Economic
- Social
- Environmental.

Economic sustainability looks to ensure organisations are profitable in order to support growth and future development. Businesses should reinvest in local communities and projects and ensure they pay the correct taxes; this ensures they remain economically sustainable.

Social sustainability looks to support people, which can include consulting staff and the local community in relation to key business decisions. Businesses should provide a safe and healthy work environment for their employees and provide training and work development opportunities to remain socially sustainable.

 Example

Many organisations now have a wellness programme for their staff and provide employee benefits such as physical and mental health support.

Environmental sustainability looks to reduce the impact of business activities on the environment, which can include using less energy and creating less pollution. Examples include recycling to reduce as much waste as much as possible and reducing energy where possible to help save the environment.

All businesses and finance professionals have a responsibility towards supporting sustainability.

On a day to day basis, finance professionals should:

- champion sustainability
- promote a sustainable culture
- take into account economic, social and environment factors when making decisions
- raise awareness of sustainable responsibility
- promote diversity and provide equal opportunities for all.

 Test your understanding 7

Refer to the following examples and state which category of sustainability they fall under:

- Economical
- Social
- Environmental

Example	Category
Paperless systems/think before you print – reduce printing in turn reducing paper usage	*Environmental*
Offering employees a healthcare plan as part of their benefits package	*social*
Saving energy by installing motion sensor lights – reduces energy bills and increases profits	*Economical*

1.6   Professional behaviour

Any successful organisation will rely heavily on its staff and their effectiveness to build good working relationships with both internal and external stakeholders.

Staff will need to demonstrate professional behaviour and have sound personal qualities and skills in order to harness these relationships. It is important to portray a keen attitude to work at all times by being punctual. Arriving at work on time, keeping to break times and not leaving early shows commitment to the role and that you are adhering to the employee code of conduct.

> **Definition**
>
> **Punctuality:** Being punctual means being on time, both in terms of arriving at your place of work on time and completing a required task at an agreed time. Adhere to break times and do not leave work early.

There are many skills and attributes a finance professional will need to possess including:

- respect
- trust
- responsibility
- reliability
- co-operation
- initiative
- problem solving

These skills will be used to interact with others as well as being able to work independently.

1.7   Polite communication with colleagues and customers

It is important to portray yourself in a polite and professional manner at all times in the workplace. Communication in the most important attribute in business as it helps the effective and efficient operation of a successful organisation.

For example, when in meetings it is important to engage fully with what is being communicated. If you don't listen properly, you could miss a vital piece of information that is relevant to you successfully completing a task. It projects an image to the employer of someone who is disinterested in their role and who doesn't take it seriously.

An excellent communicator will become an integral part of the team who others can rely on. This is important if you want to progress within your career.

The following principles of polite communication should be followed:

Use correct names

In the workplace it may be acceptable to address your colleagues by their first name unless they direct otherwise. When speaking to customers remain respectful, address them as Sir/ Madam/ Mr/ Mrs/ Miss.

Listen to the other person

Show an interest in what the other person is saying. Maintain eye contact when speaking face to face. Never interrupt someone when they are on the telephone or face to face.

Appropriate language

Avoid the use of slang terms, swearing and offensive humour

Remember your manners

It is important to be courteous both in terms of words and actions. For example, use 'please' and 'thank you' wherever necessary/appropriate and hold the door open for those behind you. Likewise, shaking hands when you first meet a customer is considered sound business etiquette.

Avoid using slang when communicating. The use of slang can be confusing, and people may not understand the message you are trying to get across. Swearing in the workplace in not professional and can lead to complaints/disciplinary action.

Humour in the workplace

The use of humour in the workplace can lighten the mood and reduce stress. However, it is important not to use too much humour or offensive humour as it can sometimes cause offense. The workplace is made up of a diverse range of personalities therefore it is important to be self-aware and avoid causing offense unnecessarily.

1.8   Personal qualities required for the workplace

Honesty

Honesty is about doing the right thing, even in difficult situations. For example, if a colleague asked you to complete a task for them but you did not know how to do it, by accepting the task to help them out would not be the honest thing to do. Ultimately the task would not be completed correctly which would have an impact on others within the team. By being honest with your colleague and explaining you do not feel comfortable doing it, they will have more respect for you than if you were to attempt it incorrectly.

Another example of being honest is owning up to your own mistakes. Hiding mistakes in fear of getting into trouble could cause issues to the wider business.

Honesty is the foundation for trust; it is vital to build trusting relationships at work so that people know they can rely on you to keep your promises and commitments.

Adaptability

Willing to learn

Adaptability is important in the workplace to ensure success. Adaptability is about being able to being able to embrace change and contribute to innovative ways of working to ensure maximum efficiency in business. Employees who are considered adaptable, often like a challenge and become successful when it comes to taking on new projects, or contributing new ideas, as they can often encourage others to adapt to change too.

Trustworthiness

A trustworthy employee is one who is honest, reliable and dependable. It is important for any employer to be able to give a task to an employee and to be able to trust that it will be completed on time and to the required standard. Trust is particularly important when working in a team because if your colleagues trust you and you trust them, you are more likely to be open and honest with each other as it provides a sense of safety.

Commitment

A committed employee will add value to the organisation as they are invested in its culture and values. Commitment is particularly important when working in a team as everyone is relying on each other to achieve their objectives. If someone within a team is not committed, it is not good for team morale or productivity which ultimately breeds an unhealthy workplace.

conformidade.
Compliance = the action or fact of complying with a wish or command.

Demonstrating commitment at work helps the business achieve success which ultimately helps promote your own success, often leading to career development opportunities.

 Test your understanding 8

A key client, Tony Foster, the Managing Director of Bolsover Breweries has called to raise a complaint with an invoice. Having spoken to one of Marvin's colleagues, the call has been put through to Marvin for him to advise the customer.

Which is the best way for Marvin to start the conversation? Tick the most suitable answer.

Options	✓
Good morning Mr Foster. This is Marvin. How can I help?	✓
Good morning Tony. How's things there?	
This is Marvin speaking. How can I help?	
Hi Sir. How's things there?	
Hello Mr Bolsover. How can I help?	

 Test your understanding 9

Which of the following suggest that Marvin is listening to others when they are in a department meeting?

Tick the TWO most appropriate answers.

Options	✓
He is constantly checking his watch to ensure that he can get back to focus on his e-mails	
He asks further questions based on the comments made by this manager	✓
He becomes easily distracted by a chart of sales figures on the wall of the room	
He often completes one of his colleague's sentences to save time, assuming he knows what he is going to say	
He makes notes as other people speak and occasionally nods when a key point is made	✓

Test your understanding 10

Which of the following would NOT be appropriate if you were meeting an important customer for the first time (tick ALL that apply)?

Options	✓
Shaking hands with the customer and introducing yourself to him	
Calling the customer by his first name despite having not met him previously	✓
Crossing your arms and shaking your head when you do not agree with what the customer is saying	✓
Smiling and making eye contact as the customer tells you about their company's history	
Showing the customer something that made you laugh on social media, which is not work-related	✓
Swearing about one of the customer's competitors who do not use your company as a supplier	✓
Appearing comfortable by slouching in the chair, with your legs crossed in a relaxed manner	✓

2 Working with others

2.1 The characteristics of effective team working

Each department within an organisation is subdivided into teams so that all the work can be shared out to ensure it is completed on time. Team working means that the work will be completed more efficiently and effectively rather than each individual working independently.

 Definition

A team is more than a group of individuals. A team can be described as any group of people who must significantly relate with each other in order to accomplish shared, specified aims.

Therefore a team usually:

- shares a common goal
- is committed to achieving that goal
- enjoys working together to achieve it.

To be able to work effectively in a team you will need to develop good team working skills. These skills include mutual support for each other; respect for others opinions, and the sharing of information. Where working effectively, the members of a team show collective loyalty and possess a strong sense of **team spirit.**

The team leader will allocate the tasks that the team needs to complete to individual members of the team. Each member of the team will then have certain tasks to do by a specific deadline. It is therefore important to identify what your specific role and responsibility is within the team. In some instances, other members of your team will need information from you before they can complete their work; this puts you in a position of trust. To ensure that the organisation as a whole can operate successfully, co-operation amongst you and your colleagues is key.

There are usually realistic deadlines to work towards. It is therefore important that you share good communication skills with the team, so that everybody is aware if a task may not be completed on time.

If something happens which means that the team cannot complete a task on time, the team leader will have a **contingency plan.** For example, the team leader may build in some spare time in each team member's weekly schedule to allow them to step in to help other individuals if something has happened which means that they cannot keep to the planned schedule

Timekeeping is particularly important when working in a team. Knowing how long a particular task will take helps with planning. Managers can delegate tasks to individual team members, each working towards a common goal. It is important to work efficiently and to keep to the expected timescales as other people within the team may be relying on the completion of your work before they can complete theirs.

If you are struggling to meet a deadline, it is important to highlight this straight away to your manager so that arrangements can be made for other members of the team to help you complete the work, or deadlines can be amended to prevent issues further down the line.

It is also important to agree time off with your manager as far in advance as possible. When team members take time off work for holidays, their workload will need to be shared amongst the rest of the team. It is not possible to have multiple people absent from work at the same time as it could have major impacts on deadlines and the wider business. For this reason, it is always important to agree your leave dates with your manager before booking them following the organisation's procedure.

The benefit of team working is that a lot more can be achieved than if the work was being completed by one individual. The key to a successful team is reliability. Each member of the team is depending on the other to complete their part of the task and they are being trusted to complete work without supervision. If one person cannot be trusted to complete their work on time and with accuracy, this can have a major impact on the wider team and the wider business.

Professionalism is a key characteristic to possess when working as part of a team. Professionalism promotes a positive culture and increases productivity, thus projecting a positive image of yourself and the organisation. Presenting yourself well in terms of your behaviour, appearance and attitude shows professionalism in the workplace.

2.2   The benefits of team working

> ### 🔍 Definitions
>
> **Leadership** is an influence directed toward the achievement of a goal or goals. Leadership is therefore is concerned with setting goals and then inspiring people to achieve them.
>
> Collaboration is when two or more persons work together to complete a task, share ideas or contribute to a change in process.

Effective leadership and staff co-operating collaboratively promotes a positive working environment. Everyone has different strengths and weaknesses, and these can be used to achieve the best possible outcome.

Rather than individuals feeling like they are in competition with each other, working together allows them to get to know each other, share their ideas and build positive working relationships. Individual skills and expertise can be used to improve weaknesses in others which helps with individual development but also helps to improve the overall skillset of the team.

People join teams at different times, therefore there will always be a range of expertise to call upon to help if there is a lack of understanding. Sharing learning experiences in this way helps to build confidence and competence within a team which ultimately results in promotion. This can assist in keeping team morale high, which in turn can increase productivity. The team can achieve common goals and promote success within an organisation.

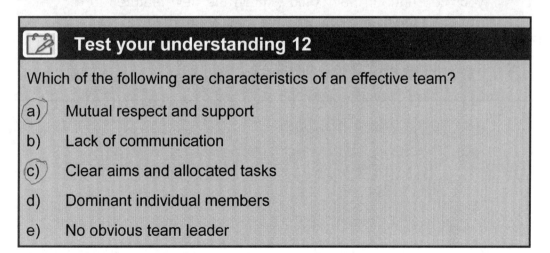

Test your understanding 11

It is lunchtime and you have completed all of your work for the day. Your colleague is struggling to meet their deadline of the end of the day.

What do you do?

Options	✔
Keep quiet and look busy	
Book a half day holiday	
Offer to help them complete their work to ensure the deadline is met	✓

Test your understanding 12

Which of the following are characteristics of an effective team?

a) Mutual respect and support

b) Lack of communication

c) Clear aims and allocated tasks

d) Dominant individual members

e) No obvious team leader

Test your understanding 13

Which FOUR of the following are benefits of good team working?

Options	✔
Increased motivation of staff	✓
Higher staff morale	✓
Better staff pay	
Better use of a mixture of skills	✓
Tighter control over staff	
More staff doing other people's work for them	
Increased productivity and success for the organisation	✓

Test your understanding 14

Your accounting software has done an automatic update and there are some new features that you are unsure of. Your colleague is an expert with the use of the software and attended an update training day.

What should you do?

Options	✔
Play around with the system to try and figure out what benefit the new features might have when completing your tasks	
Ask your colleague if they could explain the new features to you and ask if they can show you how to operate them	✓
Move onto a new task and hope instructions on how to use the new features are sent via email	

3 Keeping data and information secure

3.1 Confidentiality

Information that is being processed by a bookkeeper will be both sensitive and/or private. Whether the information is held on paper or held electronically on a computer, a bookkeeper must make sure that confidential information is kept in a safe and secure way. This will help to prevent loss and the unauthorised sharing of information.

The potential impact of not keeping this information confidential should be serious for both the individual and the organisation. It could be considered a breach of the individual's employment contract (most users will need to complete some form of IT security/ 'Acceptable use of IT' training when joining a company), a breach of the AAT Code of Professional Ethics, or a data protection violation or breach (see section 3.3), which could result in a fine for the business.

breach = brecha
breach = quebrar a lei.

3.2 Commercial information

Information held by the accounts department or being processed by a bookkeeper may be commercially sensitive. For example, the price paid for a particular product, or discounts given to customers. If a competitor of the business knew this information they might be able to use it as a competitive advantage. It is therefore imperative to protect customer information and to only share information with authorised personnel, otherwise this could be damaging to the business.

3.3 Personal information

Personal information held about individuals such as employees, customers, supplier etc. is protected by law. The Data Protection Act 2018 is the UK's implementation of the General Data Protection Regulation (GDPR). This sets out rules about how personal data can be used.

The act sets out the following principles that must be followed when processing and using personal data.

The information must be:

1.   collected and used fairly, transparently, and lawfully

2.   used for limited, specifically stated purposes

3. used in a way that is adequate, relevant, and limited to what is necessary in relation to the purposes for it is intended

4. accurate and kept up to date

5. kept for no longer than is absolutely necessary

6. kept safe and secure - the principle of integrity and confidentiality requires businesses to handle personal data in a manner that will protect against accidental loss or damage

7. handled responsibly in compliance with the other principles – organisations should have written policies and processes to ensure all staff are accountable for the way in which data is handled.

Any organisations who process personal data must register with the Information Commissioner's Office in order to be permitted to process data. The information Commissioner's Office (ICO) is the UK's independent body set up to uphold information rights. You can find out how personal information is protected by visiting their website: https://ico.org.uk/

Whether personal and sensitive information is held on a computer or in paper based format, it is vitally important that it is kept safe and secure. This means necessary steps must be taken to reduce the risk of unauthorised access or sharing of information.

When sending information to others, it is important to make sure they are authorised to receive the details and if sending this information via email, the sender should double check they have the correct recipient to prevent information getting into the wrong hands.

Without the correct safety precautions in place, information could be lost or corrupted due to computer failure or viruses. Information should only be shared with people who are authorised to view it. It is a legal requirement of all businesses to keep sensitive information such as customer details confidential, any breach could result in penalties being imposed on the individual who has caused the issue, the company or both.

Not only would this be a breach of the individual's contract of employment and GDPR regulations, but it would also be a breach of the AAT Code of Professional Ethics. This could have a detrimental impact on the individual's reputation, the reputation of the organisation and ultimately could result in loss of business.

3.4 The security of confidential information

Advances in technology have enabled organisations to process more and more personal data, and to share information more easily. This has obvious benefits, but it also gives rise to equally obvious security risks.

If a bookkeeper is given sensitive information to work with, it is their responsibility to keep it safe and secure. There are some basic steps that can be taken such as:

- not sharing laptops/computers
- not working in public spaces where others may be able to see what you are doing
- conducting meetings in private
- the agenda for meetings not covering anything that is confidential and cannot be shared with all attendees
- discussing confidential matters with others in a place where unauthorised personnel are unable to hear what is being discussed
- using a secure network or VPN (Virtual Private Network) for remote or hybrid working
- restricting staff access to systems to the level required for their role. For example, an employee responsible for inputting invoices on the accounting system, does not necessarily need access to the bank account.

Although it is important to not keep unnecessary information, organisations do need to consider legal requirements. Financial information must be kept for 6 years from the end of the last company financial year they relate to. It is best practice to archive old records whether that be physically archiving and storing paperwork or archiving electronic files so they are hidden and only retrieved if and when required.

Below are some examples of how to keep confidential information secure in an accounting office.

retrieved - past of retrieve = find or extracted information stored in a computer. get or bring (something) back from somewhere.

Example

Situation	Paper based filing system	Information held on a computer
Confidential information you are currently working with.	Any confidential information you are responsible for should be kept close by you at all times so that you are aware if anyone tries to read it. To avoid the information being seen by anyone passing by your desk, all confidential paperwork should be kept face down or in a folder until you need to work with it.	You may need to change the position of your computer screen to make sure that unauthorised people cannot see information on your computer screen as you are working. If this is not possible, you may need to move desks or offices to ensure that you can carry out the work. Sensitive information held on computers should be protected by multi-level passwords so that employees only see what is relevant to them. Never share your password with unauthorised people.
If you have to leave your workstation	If you have to leave your desk always put any confidential papers in a locked drawer or filing cabinet.	You should use the screen lock on your computer so that confidential information cannot be read by people passing your desk when you are away.
Storage of confidential information	Sensitive information should be kept in a locked filing cabinet, until it is needed.	Regular back-ups of computer data should be taken and stored in fireproof cabinets.
Out of date information	When confidential information is no longer needed it should be shredded before being recycled.	Data should be removed or deleted from computers by authorised staff from the Information Technology (IT) department.

Definition

Authorised person – Someone who has been given permission to do something on somebody else's behalf. For example, an employee who has been authorised to input confidential information onto a computer.

Test your understanding 15

Tick the appropriate box for the statements provided:

Commercial information is information that can be sold to anyone, so it does not have to be kept confidential.

True ☐ or False ☑

You have finished working on a document, you have made notes on paper that you do not need anymore. Are you going to:

Discard the paper in the bin ☐   Shred the paper ☑

You have sent an e-mail containing personal information to the wrong client. Is this:

A breach of data protection regulations (GDPR) ☑

Nothing to worry about, as the data is not commercial ☐

3.5   Cybersecurity

Definition

Cybersecurity is how individuals and organisations protect hardware, software and data cyberattacks.

Businesses need to consider the best way of protecting themselves such as using a secure network, installing firewalls or asking for authentication before allowing access to cloud-based information.

Remote working/hybrid working is becoming more common, but it does increase the risk to the security of confidential information. Many companies use Microsoft Office for their day to day operations and this now operates in the cloud via Office 365. It is best practice to enable two factor authentication so that if a person is logging onto their Office Sharepoint, a code will be sent to another device such as their mobile phone to verify it is them before access is granted.

Firewalls provide protection against outside cyber attackers by shielding your computer or network from malicious or unnecessary network traffic. Firewalls can also prevent malicious software from accessing your computer or network via the internet.

blindagem protect from a dangers risk

3.6 Passwords

As a bookkeeper, you will have many passwords for different systems and processes. For example, you will have a password to be able to gain access to the computer system itself, you will then need another password to gain access to the accounting software and the chances are that other documents will be password protected for you to be able to view them.

It is important that you keep your password safe and secure and change it regularly in line with the company procedures or immediately if you suspect that someone has found out what your password is. You should avoid the use of names or dates that are personal to you as quite often these can be easy to guess. Ideally you should create a password that contains both upper and lower case letters, numbers and symbols. The harder it is for someone to guess your password, the harder it is for them to access sensitive information.

Test your understanding 16

You have recently set up online banking for your current account.

You need to set a password for access to the online banking facilities. Which of the following would make a good password? Tick the TWO best answers from the options given.

Options	✔
Something you cannot remember	
Something other people are not likely to know	✓
Something obvious	
The word 'password'	
Your name and year of birth	
A combination of letters, numbers and symbols	✓
Something you saved on your PC in a file called Passwords	

KAPLAN PUBLISHING

| ![pencil icon] Test your understanding 17 |

Below is a list of statements. State which are true and which are false.

Statement	True/False
Passwords can be shared with colleagues who are doing the same type work.	FALSE
All cabinet drawers with personal or commercial information in should be kept locked.	TRUE
If leaving your work station, you must ensure that the screen is blank and computer access blocked.	TRUE

3.7 Viruses

The best way to understand the concept of a computer virus is to think about a human being having the flu virus; let's call them the 'host.' When they come into contact with another human they infect them with the virus.

The virus can just keep on replicating itself and spreading from human to human until there is an epidemic. In the same way a computer virus needs a 'host' cell such as a program, file or document. When that is sent to another computer that too becomes infected.

'involuntariamente' *(without being aware,)*

These viruses are cleverly hidden and can be unwittingly sent from user to user. People often do not realise that they have an infected computer until *unintentionally.* they experience problems with their programs. The more severe viruses have been known to spread to millions of users and have damaged their systems, or in some cases have destroyed them completely.

Unfortunately, viruses are created by people who write bad codes intended to change the way in which a computer operates. There have been instances where people experimenting have accidently sent out bad codes, however it is usually an intentional action by someone who is commonly known as a **cybercriminal**. They send the bad code out and it will attach itself to a program or file on the recipient user's computer. The virus may not do any damage immediately, it will only become active when you run the file that it has attached itself to (until then it is effectively sleeping). Once you run that program the bad code becomes active, you now have an infected computer that can infect other computers on the same network.

A virus attack can completely destroy accounting data/files resulting in the loss of client and business information. A severe attack can destroy an

---

accounting system completely making it unusable. An attack can also create openings for unauthorised users known as hackers to view and steal sensitive information and data. The nature of accounting often means sending customers information electronically and therefore if you have a virus on your computer, it could be inadvertently sent to the client.

3.8   Backups

The first line of defence against a virus is to backup data and save it in a safe place such as a locked fire proof cabinet. It is good practice to have a further backed up copy stored in outside premises in case something happens to the file that is kept in the office. If storing data in the cloud, backups should be regularly updated to capture new data, the computer is set to automatically do a backup and as the information stored is real-time information, the most up to date data is always available to access.

3.9   Anti-virus software

Anti-virus software is another key way in which an organisation can keep confidential information safe and secure. This is a piece of software that is installed onto the computer system which will then scan information such as emails for viruses and will block any content that appears suspect. Viruses can be extremely dangerous as they can shut down a whole system in a very short space of time. If data becomes corrupt, you will not be able to see or use it therefore it is very important that an organisation protects itself with anti-virus software.

Test your understanding 18

You have been working on a confidential document on your computer and have to leave the office for ten minutes to deal with a customer. How can you keep the information on your screen confidential?

Options	✓
Switch the computer off	
Use the screen lock facility to lock the computer screen	✓
Stay at your desk	
Put some papers over the screen to hide the information	

Test your understanding 19

Complete the following sentences:

a) I need to go to the bathroom, I should use my computer ___screen___ lock.

b) I have finished with this confidential paper so I am going to ___shred___ it.

c) I don't want anyone to read this paperwork so I am going to put it ___face down___ on my desk.

d) ___Anti – virus___ software is another way of keeping information safe and secure.

e) Backed up computer data should be stored in ___fire proof___ cabinets.

3.10 Hacking   — _assaltante_

Just like a burglar enters premises without permission, hackers gain access to people's computers without permission. Once they have done so, the hackers can do anything from stealing information to having control of the computer. Sophisticated hackers can see everything that the user is doing.

Hackers can gain access to computers in several ways such as through viruses, insecure wireless connections, e-mails, fake internet sites and social media. Hackers are constantly looking for weaknesses in computer programs and, just like a burglar will take advantage of an open window and sneak in, a hacker will do the same with a vulnerable computer. _esqueivar- se_

If a hacker manages to access accounting data they can cause irreparable damage to the business. They can access all the clients' information and use it to commit identity theft, steal passwords and change or delete data.

These kind of attacks can cause huge financial losses to an organisation. The firm would have to inform all its clients that this had happened, resulting in damage to the reputation of the company and potentially the loss of clients.

To protect accounting data from hackers, effective use of passwords by employees is key. It is important to keep passwords safe and secure and change them regularly in line with the company procedures or immediately suspecting that someone has found out what the password is.

An organisation with a number of employees will usually have a system that prompts the user to change their password when it is time to do so. In addition, you should not use the same password for different programs, this way if a hacker guesses one password they do not have access to everything.

Encrypting data is effective against hackers. This is where your information is scrambled up so that it looks like nonsense. Only people who have access to the key stored on your hardware can unscramble it. So, a hacker may still manage to break in to the computer but they would not be able to understand the information.

Another way of protecting an organisation from hackers is to only keep the data that is of use. Client/customer information such as credit card numbers, dates of birth or other personal or sensitive data may be of no use, but is tempting for hackers. Therefore employees must be vigilant and remove the information yourself or get your client to remove it. Again, ensuring that you have a good security software package and keeping it updated is another way in which data can be kept secure. Individuals should NEVER share your password with anyone and should always close your computer screen when you leave your workstation and lock the screen to avoid unauthorised people from viewing information or using your computer.

3.11 Phishing

Phishing is an attempt to trick people into revealing sensitive information such as passwords, bank details or any other kind of sensitive financial information. The ultimate goal is financial theft. There are also phishing attacks where they not only try to steal information but also attach a virus to your system.

Phishing usually occurs in the form of an e-mail that looks like it came from a genuine organisation, for example a bank. A common trick is to tell the recipient that there has been some unusual activity on their account. They must sign into the account using the link provided (fake web address that looks like the banks) and verify their details in order to be able to continue using their account. It will say that an immediate response is required or your account will be suspended or closed.

Anyone clicking the link and providing the information has just given a thief all they need to steal from their bank account. People often receive these kinds of e-mails from organisations that they don't even have an account with. Companies may receive an e-mail that appears to be from one of their genuine clients. They are designed to trick the user into giving out financial information about the company or may activate a virus once opened.

Example

A recent phishing scheme e-mail reported in the USA targeted accounting firm employees. It looked like it was from a genuine client and asked the employee to open an attachment.

When opened, key-logging malware was launched that could see every keystroke the employee made.

It even got past encrypted data because the keystrokes were recorded by the malware before they were encrypted.

Phishing can cause a major threat to accounting data because sensitive data about clients and their customers can be used to gain access to their bank accounts or be used for other fraudulent financial transactions. Information about a company can be divulged to competitors or in some cases sold for the purpose of causing financial ruin.

If users wish to protect your data from phishing, they need to remember that no reputable organisation will EVER contact them and ask for a password. If the sender of an e-mail is not known, e-mails should not be opened and a virus scan should be performed.

If you are unsure of an e-mail because you know the sender, contact them to ask if they have sent you the e-mail. Hover over any strange looking links with your cursor to see if it is spelled correctly or is an unusual address. You should delete any obvious suspicious e-mail unopened and if you are unsure, you should report any strange activity to the I.T department.

3.12 System crashes

If a system crashes, it means that the system stops working properly and shuts itself down. This happens because data or other files can suddenly develop errors that the system cannot handle or recognise. These corrupt files are commonly known as computer bugs.

Power failures and problems with other programs or networks can also cause a system to crash. If this happens, there is a chance that all data files could be lost and therefore it is essential to protect data by taking regular backups. If a system has to be restored using a backup from before the crash happened, any transactions completed since would need to be re-entered. However, if data is stored in the cloud, it is automatically backed up on a regular basis. This means that when the system is backup and running, the number of transactions that need to be re-entered is minimal.

3.13 Employee fraud in accounting

Employee fraud is where an employee steals money from a business by altering or creating accounting records, in order to make missing money that they have stolen, look like legitimate transactions.

There are many ways in which this can happen, as shown here:

 Example

Accounts payable fraud – an employee sets up a fake supplier and charges the company for goods or services that have not actually been provided.

Personal purchases – an employee uses company funds to pay for personal purchases and records the payments as legitimate business expenses in the accounting system.

Payroll fraud – an employee processing payroll transactions sets up ghost employees on the system and pays them, intercepting the money for themselves.

Not only do these instances of fraud cause financial losses for the business, but often the employee is altering data either by deleting, adding or changing figures. This affects the integrity of the accounting data which is used to produce the year-end financial statements and to calculate their taxes. Incorrect information can lead to penalties and fines. There is also a risk of the system crashing or the employee causing a bad code to be generated and introduce a virus.

To protect accounting data from employee fraud, the company should introduce segregation of duties across the department/accounting process. Segregation of duties is where more than one employee is responsible for every stage of an accounting process. By having work checked more than once, this reduces the risk of employee fraud occurring and the temptation to attempt it.

 Examples

The cashier taking cash to the bank on behalf of a business should not be the same person who writes out the paying in slip to the bank. This reduces the danger of cash disappearing into the cashier's pocket.

There should also be a supervisor/line manager overseeing accounting activities on a regular basis. This involves checking things such as data entries onto computers, payments etc. with specified limits on payments over a certain amount e.g. payments over £2,500 need to be authorised by a senior member of staff.

Employees should also be encouraged to report suspicious activity.

3.14 Corrupt files

Corrupt files are files that suddenly stop working. There are several reasons for this happening.

A common reason is that the file has developed a bad sector - this is something that can happen randomly and unfortunately little can prevent it. Sometimes there is a fault or bug that may cause a file not to work properly, but it starts working again. The problem may never recur but the system needs checking by the IT department to ensure nothing more serious is happening behind the scenes.

The more serious way of files becoming corrupt is if a bug occurs due to the system having a virus. This poses a threat to accounting data as it can result in the loss of some or all accounting data. To protect against this, regular backups of data should be taken. Storing data in a cloud will ensure that the most up to date information is always available. Frequent virus checks will also help protect files from becoming corrupt.

3.15 Natural disasters and accidental deletion

Unexpected events occur in all over the world and are classed as natural disasters. These include fires, floods and earthquakes. Data is always vulnerable in the case of one of these events.

Accidental deletion is when someone removes a file or other data that should not have been removed from the system. This is usually by mistake or because of human error. Accidental deletion can happen by clicking on the wrong key or sequence of keys on the computer or by trying to correct an entry by deleting it incorrectly. Sometimes people try to speed up some of their working practices by copying and pasting information but sometimes this can lead to accidental data loss.

Accidental deletion or natural disasters could result in the loss of all accounting data files which causes major setbacks for a business. If client information is lost, this could lead to financial loss as well as having a negative effect on their reputation.

In order to protect accounting data, backup data should be stored in a fireproof cabinet high off the floor. Backups should be taken on a regular basis, and at least once a day in most businesses. In addition, individual files should regularly be backed up whilst working on them. There is little more frustrating than spending an hour producing a document or a spreadsheet only to lose it and not to have a backup.

Copies of backups should be kept securely to prevent unauthorised access or accidental damage. It is good practice to keep a backup at a secure location off the premises. This way, if there is a fire or a burglary the backup data will not be destroyed or stolen. Storing data in cloud is also another secure method as it is always accessible from anywhere with an internet connection.

Test your understanding 20

Viruses can.....

Tick all of the options below that complete the sentence correctly.

Options	✔
Cause loss of information	✓
Can be easily fixed	
Cause the system to crash	✓
Infect all computers on the same network	✓
Only be harmful for s short period of time	
Cause a loss in productivity	✓

Test your understanding 21

You receive an email from a client asking you to click on a link. It is unusual for them to contact you via email, what do you do?

There are TWO correct answers. Put a tick in the relevant boxes.

Options	✔
Ignore the email	
Hover over the address and if it looks genuine, click on the link	✓
Forward it to your supervisor	
Click on the link	
Contact the client to ask if they have sent the email	✓

KAPLAN PUBLISHING

Case study activity 6

Jessica is aware that certain personal qualities are required to be a valuable team member and employee.

Use the pick list below to show which of these qualities are best being demonstrated by Jessica and her colleagues in each example. Use each option only once.

It is only Jessica's second week with the company and she has been asked to check a batch of old invoices which seem to have not been paid. Although the task is bigger than expected, Jessica gets into the office an hour early every day for a week to ensure the work is completed.	*Commitment*
As part of the task, Jessica spends a couple of hours making telephone calls to customers who have unpaid invoices. Although she is getting through to voicemails and has been shouted at by some angry clients, she remains courteous, professional and respectful on the calls and offers to make her team colleagues a hot drink when she has finished.	*Polite communication with others.*
Lucy works in the customer service team, in the same office as Jessica. When it is busy, or to ensure the process runs smoothly, she sometimes helps the credit control team to chase debts and the despatch team to pack orders.	*Adaptability.*
Jessica is helping to input business documentation and having checked her work, she realises that she has entered a purchase order number incorrectly on a sales invoice. This will mean that the customer might not pay. Jessica realises her error and immediately tells her manager and asks how best to correct it.	*Honesty*

Pick list

Honesty

Adaptability

Commitment

Polite communication with others

Case study activity 7

Jessica is in a training session at work as part of her induction. The trainer asks her a question that she does not understand. What should Jessica do? Tick the most appropriate option.

Options	✓
Make a joke and laugh about it	
Explain that she is not sure and politely ask them to explain the answer	✓
Tell the trainer she does not know and suggest they ask someone else	
Tell the trainer that they are not explaining themselves very well and suggest improvements to the session	
Politely make her excuses and leave the room for a while	

Case study activity 8

As part of Jessica's induction week, she has been asked to offer some ideas on ways How Two Ltd can consider environmental sustainability within the everyday activities of the business.

Make a list of environmental issues which could be considered.

- Recycle bin area; (Hub)
- Avoid printing on paper. Paperless system,
- Energy usage.
- Cycling schemes/car share.

10

 Case study activity 9

Jessica has been given a temporary desk in the corner of the office, until an existing Finance Assistant leaves the company next week.

The desk is surrounded by archive boxes and confidential files.

What should Jessica do?

Options	✓
Sit at the desk and get on with the work she has been given	
Report the hazards to her manager and see if they can relocate her	✓
Read through some of the files to familiarise herself with the company	
Immediately shred all of the documentation to avoid the risk of data protection breach.	

 Case study activity 10

Jessica has been asked to create her own unique password for the accounting system.

Which of the following passwords should she use?

a)   Password123

b)   JHoward011200

c)   JessHowTw0

d)   4yXkj2fR!*

Case study activity 11

During a conversation in the staff canteen, several members of staff were discussing their rates of pay and the company bonus.

One of them, Neelam is upset that other people are being paid more than her. She asks Jessica to find out for her if one of her colleagues, Jason, is indeed being paid more than her.

What reply should Jessica give?

Statement	Correct?
Jessica confirms the amount that Jason does indeed receive more money than Neelam.	
Jessica tells Neelam that she will speak to her manager to see if she can tell her the information.	
Jessica explains to Neelam that this information is confidential and cannot be disclosed.	✓
Jessica ensures that all pay rates are accessible to all employees to avoid any future debate.	

 Case study activity 12

Jessica has a colleague who is also a good friend. They have forgotten their password to the system and need to quickly amend some figures before their meeting.

They have asked to use your password temporarily, what do you do?

Put a tick in the correct box.

Options	✓
Give them her password but tell them not to tell anyone else what it is	
Give them her password for now and then change it when they have gone into their meeting	
Refuse to give them her password	✓
Log in for them so they don't know what her password is	

KAPLAN PUBLISHING

Answers to chapter activities

⬛ Test your understanding 1

Options	✓
A job interview	
Information about the company's policies	✓
An introduction to key staff in the company	✓
An overview of the company's values	✓
Lots of fun games and activities with other new starters	
To finish work early	
A promotion	

⬛ Test your understanding 2

Options	✓
The job specification	
The company handbook	✓
The company website	
A government employment website	

Test your understanding 3

Statement	True	False
"As we work at a desk in the office and not in the warehouse, health and safety is not relevant to us."		✓
"Don't worry about that loose cable next to your desk – it is not your responsibility to report it."		✓
"Everyone here has a duty of care to keep things safe for both our colleagues and visitors".	✓	

Test your understanding 4

Options	✓
The government	
The managers	
The employees	
The managers and the employees	✓

Test your understanding 5

Options	✓
Yes, it is his first week with the company, so he does not feel comfortable saying no	
Yes, it will be fine so long as the wire is visible, so his colleagues know to step over it	
No, this is a trip hazard, he should speak to his manager and explain the situation	✓

Test your understanding 6

Options	✓
Frantically attempt to read the handbook from cover to cover	
Stay calm and leave the office via the nearest fire exit	✓
Ignore the alarm, it is probably a test	
Collect his belongings and run	

Test your understanding 7

Example	Category
Paperless systems/think before you print – reduce printing in turn reducing paper usage	**Environmental**
Offering employees a healthcare plan as part of their benefits package	**Social**
Saving energy by installing motion sensor lights – reduces energy bills and increases profits	**Economical**

Test your understanding 8

Options	✓
Good morning Mr Foster. This is Marvin. How can I help?	✓
Good morning Tony. How's things there?	
This is Marvin speaking. How can I help?	
Hi Sir. How's things there?	
Hello Mr Bolsover. How can I help?	

Test your understanding 9

Options	✓
He is constantly checking his watch to ensure that he can get back to focus on his e-mails	
He asks further questions based on the comments made by this manager	✓
He becomes easily distracted by a chart of sales figures on the wall of the room	
He often completes one of his colleague's sentences to save time, assuming he knows what he is going to say	
He makes notes as other people speak and occasionally nods when a key point is made	✓

Test your understanding 10

Options	✓
Shaking hands with the customer and introducing yourself to him	
Calling the customer by his first name despite having not met him previously	✓
Crossing your arms and shaking your head when you do not agree with what the customer is saying	✓
Smiling and making eye contact as the customer tells you about their company's history	
Showing the customer something that made you laugh on social media, which is not work-related	✓
Swearing about one of the customer's competitors who do not use your company as a supplier	✓
Appearing comfortable by slouching in the chair, with your legs crossed in a relaxed manner	✓

Test your understanding 11

Options	✓
Keep quiet and look busy	
Book a half day holiday	
Offer to help them complete their work to ensure the deadline is met	✓

Test your understanding 12

The following are characteristics of an effective team:

Mutual respect and support (a)

Clear aims and allocated tasks (c)

Test your understanding 13

Options	✓
Increased motivation of staff	✓
Higher staff morale	✓
Better staff pay	
Better use of a mixture of skills	✓
Tighter control over staff	
More staff doing other people's work for them	
Increased productivity and success for the organisation	✓

Test your understanding 14

Options	✓
Play around with the system to try and figure out what benefit the new features might have when completing your tasks	
Ask your colleague if they could explain the new features to you and ask if they can show you how to operate them	✓
Move onto a new task and hope instructions on how to use the new features are sent via email	

Test your understanding 15

Commercial information is information that can be sold to anyone, so it does not have to be kept confidential.

False ✓

You have finished working on a document, you have made notes on paper that you do not need anymore.

Shred the paper ✓

You have sent an e-mail containing personal information to the wrong client. Is this:

A breach of data protection regulations (GDPR) ✓

Test your understanding 16

Options	✓
Something you cannot remember	
Something other people are not likely to know	✓
Something obvious	
The word 'password'	
Your name and year of birth	
A combination of letters, numbers and symbols	✓
Something you saved on your PC in a file called Passwords	

Test your understanding 17

Statement	True/False
Passwords can be shared with colleagues who are doing the same type work.	False
All cabinet drawers with personal or commercial information in should be kept locked.	True
If leaving your work station, you must ensure that the screen is blank and computer access blocked.	True

Test your understanding 18

Options	✓
Switch the computer off	
Use the screen lock facility to lock the computer screen	✓
Stay at your desk	
Put some papers over the screen to hide the information	

Test your understanding 19

a) I need to go to the bathroom, I should use my computer **screen lock**.

b) I have finished with this confidential paper so I am going to **shred** it.

c) I don't want anyone to read this paperwork so I am going to put it **face down** on my desk.

d) **Anti-virus** software is another way of keeping information safe and secure.

e) Backed up computer data should be stored in **fireproof** cabinets.

Test your understanding 20

Options	✔
Cause loss of information	✔
Can be easily fixed	
Cause the system to crash	✔
Infect all computers on the same network	✔
Only be harmful for s short period of time	
Cause a loss in productivity	✔

Test your understanding 21

Options	✔
Ignore the email	
Hover over the address and if it looks genuine, click on the link	✔
Forward it to your supervisor	
Click on the link	
Contact the client to ask if they have sent the email	✔

Test your understanding 22

Statement	Threat
Enters your computer from infected files or programs	Viruses
Enters your computer through emails	Phishing
Can trace every stroke of a key you make on your computer	Hacking

Case study activity 5

Statement	Policy	✓ / X
I knew you would be here! I knew you wouldn't let me down	c	✓
No, you cannot see if anyone has shared or commented on your post in work time	e	X
I am so glad you're always on time or early, we will get to see the start	a	✓
No, I can't come to work in my jeans and t-shirt, the boss wouldn't like it	b	✓
Gosh you're keen, I've only just given you that work and you've done it already	d	✓
You had better switch that off, I can hear it vibrating in your pocket even though it's on silent	f	X

Case study activity 6

It is only Jessica's second week with the company and she has been asked to check a batch of old invoices which seem to have not been paid. Although the task is bigger than expected, Jessica gets into the office an hour early every day for a week to ensure the work is completed.	**Commitment**
As part of the task, Jessica spends a couple of hours making telephone calls to customers who have unpaid invoices. Although she is getting through to voicemails and has been shouted at by some angry clients, she remains courteous, professional and respectful on the calls and offers to make her team colleagues a hot drink when she has finished.	**Polite communication with others**

Lucy works in the customer service team, in the same office as Jessica. When it is busy, or to ensure the process runs smoothly, she sometimes helps the credit control team to chase debts and the despatch team to pack orders.	**Adaptability**
Jessica is helping to input business documentation and having checked her work, she realises that she has entered a purchase order number incorrectly on a sales invoice. This will mean that the customer might not pay. Jessica realises her error and immediately tells her manager and asks how best to correct it.	**Honesty**

Case study activity 7

Options	✓
Make a joke and laugh about it	
Explain that she is not sure and politely ask them to explain the answer	✓
Tell the trainer she does not know and suggest they ask someone else	
Tell the trainer that they are not explaining themselves very well and suggest improvements to the session	
Politely make her excuses and leave the room for a while	

Case study activity 8

- Paperless systems/think before you print – reduce printing in turn reducing paper usage
- Removal of disposal plastic cups within the office – offer reusable cups for visitors/staff
- Recycling Hub – encourage all staff/visitors to recycle paper/plastic/glass
- Energy usage – encourage all staff to turn off computers/electrical items overnight / turn off lights in toilets or meeting rooms when not in use
- Cycling schemes/car share – encourage staff to cycle to work, or take public transport or car share

10

Case study activity 9

She should use:

d)   4yXkj2fR!*

9

Case study activity 10

Options	✓
Sit at the desk and get on with the work she has been given	
Report the hazards to her manager and see if they can relocate her	✓
Read through some of the files to familiarise herself with the company	
Immediately shred all of the documentation to avoid the risk of data protection breach.	

Case study activity 11

Statement	Correct?
Jessica confirms the amount that Jason does indeed receive more money than Neelam.	
Jessica tells Neelam that she will speak to her manager to see if she can tell her the information.	
Jessica explains to Neelam that this information is confidential and cannot be disclosed.	✓
Jessica ensures that all pay rates are accessible to all employees to avoid any future debate.	

Case study activity 12

Options	✓
Give them her password but tell them not to tell anyone else what it is	
Give them her password for now and then change it when they have gone into their meeting	
Refuse to give them her password	✓
Log in for them so they don't know what her password is	

KAPLAN PUBLISHING

Time management and communication skills

5

Introduction

Time management and communication skills are key traits to being successful in the workplace. This chapter will focus on these two key sets of skills, without which individuals cannot work effectively or efficiently.

In this chapter you will learn about the different tools and techniques to help you prioritise your workload. You will also learn about the different methods of communication within an office environment and how these should be presented in business.

KNOWLEDGE

Working in the business environment

Develop skills for the workplace

1.2 Working and communicating with others

1.3 Time management

1.4 Professional behaviour

CONTENTS

1 Time management
2 Planning aids
3 Communication skills
4 Written communication methods
5 Verbal communication methods
6 Spreadsheets and software for workplace communications
7 Summary and further questions

workload = carga de trabalho.
traits = caracteristicas

1 Time management

1.1 Case study: an introduction

 Case study

Jessica now feels that she has a good understanding of How Two Ltd as an organisation and the policies and procedures relevant to her.

She is now learning about some of the administrative tasks involved within her role and how to communicate information in different forms.

She is also aware of the importance of deadlines within a finance department and is keen to ensure that she applies the correct time management techniques to ensure that she completes her work on time.

1.2 The importance of time management

 Definition

Time management is the process of planning and controlling the amount of time that is spent on specific activities, usually with the aim of increasing your efficiency or productivity.

As we saw in the previous chapter, each employee within a team will be allocated tasks to complete.

It is then up to those individuals to organise their own workload so that they can make sure that these tasks are completed efficiently within the deadlines set by the team leader. In order to do this, they will need to use their time management skills.

1.3 Deadlines

It is important that you manage your time effectively as failure to meet a deadline can have a detrimental effect on the rest of the team. If you do not complete your allocated work on time, the next person in line will be delayed and the overall deadline for completion will not be met.

If you feel that you are going to struggle to meet a deadline it is really important to raise it with your manager as soon as possible. This will enable a plan to put in place for other members of the team to help with the task to ensure that the deadline can still be met.

Some deadlines may be classed as urgent, the work will be allocated appropriately and you will be informed of what should be classed as an 'urgent' task. You should plan allocated work based on the time available and prioritise your tasks in accordance with its urgency or importance. For example, if your manager has asked you to assist with month-end procedures and it is the end of the month, you will need to prioritise this as an important task and therefore complete it as soon as possible. This is because the month-end figures will be needed to generate the Management Accounts which will need to be presented to the Directors by a specific date.

2 Planning aids

2.1 Methods of planning

A work plan is simply a list of jobs to complete, organised into the order in which they will be tackled and the time when each will be completed. There are many different methods which can be used to plan your work and the ones you choose may depend on your own personal preference, or be recommended by your team leader.

Some common planning methods which can be used on their own or in combination are:

Some common planning methods which can be used in combination are:

To do Lists / Check Lists

A 'to do' list is a simple check list of all the activities that need to be carried out each day. The first five minutes of each day are set aside to write out the 'to do' list, and as each activity is completed it is crossed off the list. If anything is not completed that day, it can be added to the 'to do' list for the next day. However, if there is a task which cannot be completed within a certain time, then you will need to let your team leader know so that they can reschedule the task if necessary.

Digital to-do lists are an excellent way of planning your work to help manage your time effectively. You can often get an app for these too which helps as you can access your to-do list from anywhere at any time.

Another advantage of an online to do list is that it will not get lost and it can be easily amended.

You can share electronic to-do lists so that you can keep others up to date with your progress. It also helps when managing deadlines as other members of the team may be waiting for the completion of your work and they can plan their deadlines around the targets you have set yourself.

> ### Example
>
> ### THINGS TO DO TODAY
>
> Date......................
>
> 1 .... ☐
> 2 .... ☐
> 3 .... ☐
> 4 .... ☐
> 5 .... ☐
> 6 .... ☐
> 7 .... ☐

In Tray

You may have a set of letter trays on your workstation which can be used to organise the different types of documents you are working on.

For example, your job role may involve dealing with purchase orders, purchase delivery notes and purchase invoices. Each tray should be labelled accordingly for each different document so that you, and other members of the team, can find the documents quickly and easily.

A traditional method of using letter trays is to have three trays labelled 'In', 'Out' and 'Pending'. Any new documentation that you receive is put in the 'In' tray, any work that you cannot complete because you need information from someone else is placed in the 'Pending' tray, and any work that has completed and needs filing or passing on to another team member is placed in the 'Out' tray.

Each tray should be clearly labelled so that anyone leaving a document for you can put it into the correct tray without disturbing your work.

KAPLAN PUBLISHING

Online Collaboration Tools

An online collaboration tool is a piece of software which helps multiple people work on a project at the same time. Gone are the days of people having to physically sit in an office to share ideas or update others on their progress.

Online collaboration tools allow different parts of a project to be shared out amongst the team. Documents can be worked on by multiple people at the same time which speeds up time spent on the project and improves the overall efficiency.

Communication is also a great benefit of online collaboration. Rather than lots of separate emails being sent between different members of the team, everyone can communicate their ideas, thoughts, and opinions via the software.

There are many different types of collaboration software in the market, it is up to the organisation to choose one which works best for their needs.

 Test your understanding 1

Jodie is a member of the Purchase Ledger team at How Two Ltd. Jessica is shadowing her for the morning to learn about the administrative side of the job and pick up tips on time management.

Jodie has a series of necessary administrative tasks to complete in the morning before a large departmental meeting in the afternoon. Her manager Julie has informed her that the meeting is extremely important.

Tick the ONE most appropriate solution for Jodie from the list provided.

Options	✓
Jodie should do the straightforward jobs and leave the more difficult ones for her colleagues to complete after she has left for the meeting.	
Jodie should make a list of all that she needs to do in the morning and give each a timescale and priority.	✓
Jodie should realise that it will be difficult to perform all of the tasks so she should put them all off until the next day.	
Jodie should ignore the regional meeting and devote all her time to the tasks she needs to complete in the office.	

Test your understanding 2

Thomas has three tasks to complete, each of which will take two hours. His supervisor is expecting him to have completed them all by 10am tomorrow. Thomas was unable to perform any of the tasks this morning because his computer was not working. It is now 2pm. Thomas goes home at 5pm.

What should Thomas do in these circumstances?

A   Complete one of the tasks and start one of the others. He should be able to complete all of them by noon tomorrow.

B   Complete the most urgent task and take home the other two tasks. He is bound to be able to find time to finish them tonight.

C   Contact his supervisor immediately and explain the problem. He should suggest that he finishes what he considers to be the most urgent task first before starting one of the others.

D   Start all of the tasks and do parts of each of them. This way he has at least done something towards each of them before he goes home.

Test your understanding 3

Jodie has given Jessica a list of her tasks for the following week and has asked Jessica to have a go at putting these into a work schedule for her. She informed Jessica that she usually takes her lunch from 1pm until 2pm.

Jodie has told her not to worry - it is simply a training exercise - so she just wants to see how well Jessica is picking up the time management techniques.

Task list:

Check emails (must be done first thing every morning) – 1 hour

Checking supplier invoices – 2 hours each day

Supplier payment run – 2 hours on a Friday

Processing purchase orders – 2 hours each day except Fridays

Purchase Ledger Meeting – 2 hours at 10am Friday

Supplier account reconciliations – 3 hours anytime

Purchase Ledger reports – 1 hour

Filing documents – 4 hours

Enter the above tasks into the work schedule below, ensuring that all deadlines are met

	Monday	Tuesday	Wednesday	Thursday	Friday
9am - 10am	Check emails	Check emails	check emails	check emails	check emails
10am – 11am	Checking supplier invoices	Checking supplier invoices	Checking supplier invoices	checking supplier invoices	Purchase Ledger meeting
11am – 12pm	checking supplier invoices	checking supplier invoices	checking supplier invoices	checking supplier invoices	Purchase Ledger meeting
12pm – 1pm	Processing purchase order	Processing purchase ord.	Processing purchase or.	Processing purchase or.	supplier payment run
1pm – 2pm	Lunch	Lunch	Lunch	Lunch	Lunch
2pm – 3pm	Processing purchase or.	Processing purchase or.	processing purchase or.	Processing purchase or.	supplier payment runs
3pm – 4pm	supplier account reconciliation	supplier account reconciliation	supplier accounts reconciliations	Purchase Ledger report	checking supplier invoices
4pm – 5pm	Filling documents	Filling documents	Filling documents	Filling documents	checking supplier invoice

3 Communication skills

3.1 Case study: an introduction

 Case study

Having shadowed other members of staff at How Two Ltd, Jessica becomes aware of the importance of communication between both herself and her colleagues (internal) and between How Two Ltd employees and their suppliers and customers.

Jessica starts to consider the different types of communication and the software she can use in order to deliver business communications. She realises that different methods of communication will be better served to different types of task.

3.2 Formal and informal communication

 Definition

Communication is the two-way interchange of information, ideas, facts and emotions by one or more persons.

Typically business communication is either written or verbal (spoken), however communication can take place without any words at all, through body language (non-verbal communication).

There are various methods of communication. Accounting professionals will need to communicate regularly with internal and external customers and it is essential that you use an appropriate acceptable method for both of these groups. Poor communication can create an adverse impression of the organisation.

There are many different types of business documents that you will come upon in an accounting environment. The following should help you to identify the correct style to use:

Formal Language

Business English is the formal language used for business communications, especially when producing documents. Formal language is structured and professional and follows accepted grammatical rules and spelling conventions. You should not use slang or text language and words are written out in full and not abbreviated.

Informal Language

Informal language is a more casual means of communication and is less structured than formal language. It is most often used in speech, whether face-to-face or on the telephone. In some cases, it may be acceptable to use informal language in a business setting, for example when you are communicating with your peers. However, even when communicating with people you know well it is still possible for your message to be misunderstood if you use slang or text language. If you are in any doubt you should always use formal language.

Formal language is most commonly used with external customers. Informal language may be used when communicating with internal customers. However, even when using informal language you should make sure that the message is clear and easily understandable.

Test your understanding 4

Decide when you would use these examples of formal or informal language.

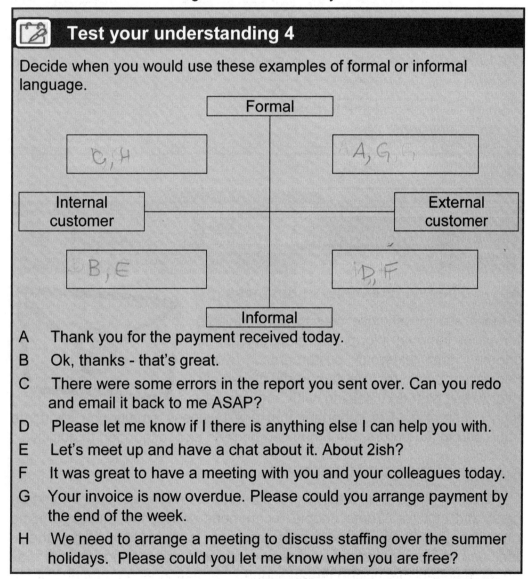

	Formal	
C, H		A, G, H
Internal customer		**External customer**
B, E		D, F
	Informal	

A   Thank you for the payment received today.

B   Ok, thanks - that's great.

C   There were some errors in the report you sent over. Can you redo and email it back to me ASAP?

D   Please let me know if I there is anything else I can help you with.

E   Let's meet up and have a chat about it. About 2ish?

F   It was great to have a meeting with you and your colleagues today.

G   Your invoice is now overdue. Please could you arrange payment by the end of the week.

H   We need to arrange a meeting to discuss staffing over the summer holidays. Please could you let me know when you are free?

Test your understanding 5

Classify the following communication activities as:

- formal or informal
- internal or external

	Formal / Informal	Internal / External
A letter to a member of the public responding to a complaint	*formal*	*external*
Asking a colleague whether or not an order has been fulfilled	*informal*	*internal*
A report for the directors analysing annual business performance	*formal*	*internal*
A Human Resources policy document for all staff	*formal*	*internal*
An e-mail to all customers regarding a new invoicing system	*formal*	*external*

4 Written communication methods

4.1 The use of e-mails in business

E-mails are an effective way to communicate formal or informal information electronically to internal and external customers. Many business people receive hundreds of e-mails every day and find dealing with emails very  time consuming. It is important that any business emails you send are short and to the point so that they can be read and responded to quickly.

4.2 Effective e-mail format

E-mails should have a clear subject line and the message itself should be clear and concise. Some people recommend writing the message in no more than five sentences so that the recipient is more likely to read the e-mail and respond quickly. If an e-mail contains detailed information, it may be more suitable to include the additional information as an attachment.

attachment, attachment, attachment, attachment

🔍 Definition

Attachment – An email attachment is a computer file, for example a document or spreadsheet, which is sent with an e-mail message.

Although e-mails are less formal that a printed business letter you should always write emails with the same care that you would use to write a formal letter. Remember that people are unlikely to be offended if you are too formal, but some may think you are being rude if you are too informal.

To: renbow@abc.net

Cc: accountsteam@newoft.co.uk

Subject: Returned faulty goods

Hello Jack

Further to our conversation today, I can confirm that the goods you returned to us have been received in our warehouse.

The warehouse team will check that the goods are faulty and, if so, we will send a credit note to you immediately.

Kind regards,

A. Wyatt

Accounts Administrator

📝 Test your understanding 6

Which of the following should always be present in business e-mail correspondence (tick all which apply):

Options	✓
A clear and purposeful subject heading	✓
Slang words	
Simple and well-structured content	✓
Jokes and personal comments	
Capital letters to stress the importance of your thoughts	
An appropriate sign off	✓

4.3 Business writing

Business documents follow a standard structure according to organisational guidelines.

In each case, they should be in the correct format, using clear and concise language, and they should be free from any grammatical or spelling mistakes.

4.4 Paragraphs and structure in business documents

All business documents should be structured by using paragraphs. Paragraphs help the reader to understand your message because:

- They break text down into manageable proportions

- Each sentence in a paragraph relates to the same topic

- Starting a new paragraph makes it clear to the reader that you are moving on to another topic.

In business documents there should be a short introductory paragraph; followed by one or two paragraphs with the main content. The final paragraph should be a short conclusion.

When writing business communications the pneumonic STRIPE is a useful structure to follow:

S	Salutation	A greeting, for example 'Dear ....'
T	Topic	The heading or subject
R	Reason	The main purpose of the communication
I	Information	Specific details or a request for information
P	Prompt to action	What you would like the reader to do.
E	End	A complimentary close and signature

4.5 The use of letters in business

Letters are used to communicate with **external** customers and should always be written using **formal** language.

All letters contain similar elements. However, you should also check your organisation's guidelines as it is important that all letters sent out by employees of the organisation are consistent with the organisation's house style.

Complimentary close (or closing salutation)

The choice of complimentary close depends on the opening salutation used.

When you know the name of the person you are addressing, e.g. 'Dear Mr or Mrs ...' the closing salutation should be 'Yours sincerely'

If you don't know the addressee's name, and you have used an opening salutation of 'Dear Sir or Madam' the closing salutation should be 'Yours faithfully'

Signature

The letter should be signed above the typed name and job title of the writer.

 Example

Friebe Motors
Top Lane
CHEETHAM
CH5 7TY

17 June 2022

Mr R Moore
Chippendale Lane
CHEETHAM
CH4 8PG

Dear Mr Moore

Re: Cheque Payment of £5,450

Thank you for your cheque payment of £5,450 received today.

Unfortunately, you did not send a remittance advice with the payment so we are not sure which invoices you are paying. Please could you send a remittance advice so that we can make sure that we allocate the payment to the correct invoices?

We look forward to receiving your remittance. In the meantime, if you need any more information please contact me at the above address.

Yours sincerely

D Francis

D Francis
Accounts Administrator

[handwritten note: remittance advice is a proof of payment letter sent by a customer to a supplier that verifies they have paid their invoice.]

Test your understanding 7

Jodie needs to write a letter to Steven Smart, the Managing Director of one of How Two Ltd's major customers, NB Solutions Ltd.

How should she start the letter? Tick the best option from those provided.

Options	✓
Hi Steven	
Hello	
Dear Mr Smart	✓
Dear NB Solutions	

Test your understanding 8

How would you sign off a business letter to someone whose name is not known to you?

Options	✓
Yours faithfully	✓
Yours sincerely	
Yours forever	
Kind regards	

Test your understanding 9

For which ONE of the following would a letter seem the most appropriate form of communication?

Options	✓
Informing staff of the company's performance and a pay rise	✓
Informing staff of the next training event	
Asking staff for feedback from the previous training event	

Test your understanding 10

Read through the letter shown below and identify TEN errors.

Morse Manufacturing

The Old Mill

Addison Drive

Newtown

NW24 8RP

Christopher Barrie

22 Loring Avenue

Little Hinton

Buckinghamshire

HP99 2AQ

no date

no relation with the content of the letter

Hello Barrie

Ref: 50% discount on all home furnishings

I am pleased to confirm that we have accepted your credit account application.

You're initial credit limit on the account will be £1,500 and you will be required to settle your account within 15 days of purchase.

after a trial period of three months, if payments have been received in a timely fashion, we will discuss your requirements further!

I hope that the above meets with your approval. If I could of been of any more assistance, please let me know. *could have*

Otherwise we look forward 2 hearing from you soon.

Yours faithfully,

Kevin Claydon *unappropriate signature, no job title.*
kevlovesit@hotmail.com *personal email*

4.7 The use of reports in business

Business reports are used to communicate information formally to internal and external customers.

Reports are used to present a lot of information all together in one document.

4.8   The structure of reports

The format of the report depends on the information being presented but could include:

headings

Title Page	The report will have a front cover or title page which will include: • The name of the person the report is for • The name of the person the report is from • The date of the report.
Summary	A short overview of what can be found in the full report.
Contents page	An index of page numbers where the information can be found.
Introduction	An outline of the report's structure.
Body	The main content of the report which may be sectioned into sub headings.
Conclusion	The main findings from the report.
Appendix	Graphs and charts which support the information in the main report.

 Test your understanding 11

Put the following sections of a report into the order in which you would expect to see them. Complete the boxes below using a), b), c) or d).

a)	Recommendations	First	c
b)	Conclusion	Second	a
c)	Introduction	Third	b
d)	Appendix	Fourth	d

4.9   Instant messaging

This is a useful way of communication within a company since most employees in accounts spend a lot of their working day using a computer. Instant messaging allows an employee to send a message from their computer to anyone within their department. It will immediately appear on the recipient's computer, this means that nobody has to leave their workstation.

5 Verbal communication methods

5.1 Telephone calls

Due to developments in both office and mobile telephone systems, perhaps the most common way for most colleagues to communicate is via telephone. And although much of this communication will be spoken, a text message to a colleague may get a more swift response.

Certain rules for telephone etiquette apply, as is the case for all of the written forms of communication addressed previously. It is vital to remain polite, positive and respectful when speaking on the phone and the appropriate use of language and tone are essential to avoid any misunderstandings.

There are many benefits of telephone conversations with colleagues and customers you know well. For example:

- They are a quick and easy method of instant two-way communication.

- Relating to this, telephone calls give a matter priority. They cannot typically be left for later as e-mails or letters can be due to work prioritisation by the receiver.

- Explanation is also often easier, especially if trying to address more complex issues. A telephone call more easily enables someone to check the other person understands and reword the subject matter if required.

It is important to remain professional when making a business telephone call. Speak clearly, avoid talking too fast. When talking to a customer show respect at all times, call them Sir/Madam/Mr/Mrs/Miss. On occasions they may instruct that you should call them by their first name, if this happens thank them and do as requested. However, if you have cause to contact them again in the future revert back to formality until again or if instructed differently. Avoid using any slang words or abbreviations regardless.

If you are making an internal call to one of your colleagues it may be acceptable to call them by their first name and to not be quite as formal. However, you must remain respectful at all times regardless of the person you may be conversing with, and therefore always use your manners and refrain from swearing.

5.2 Mobile telephones

Due to recent developments in mobile technology, it is now common for most key staff and those with jobs requiring a lot of time out of the office within a company to have business mobile telephones, or more recently, smartphones/tablets.

There are many advantages of increased use of business mobile telephones for a company:

- Staff are now available for more time and without delay
- Meetings can be held virtually and across large geographical areas
- Both customers and colleagues have greater access to the member of staff, allowing better team work and customer care
- The company can monitor phone usage
- Data can be more easily and quickly accessed by staff
- Mobile technology such as text reminders allows new methods of communication with customers.

Just as mobile telephones are more common in a business context, the majority of the population now have a personal device. Most companies will have in place a policy regarding personal calls and the use of mobiles during office hours. Therefore employees may need to sign an 'Acceptable Use' document for both IT and telephones when joining a company.

Using telephones for personal reasons during the working day is typically regarded as unacceptable, except in the case of an emergency or with a manager's permission. Personal calls or internet usage is therefore often restricted to break times. As discussed in the previous chapter, most companies will have a policy in place to specify when personal phone usage is permitted and how/when to utilise company equipment. Usually personal mobile telephones should be switched off in working hours, or at the least on silent mode to not distract the employee or their colleagues.

As well as causing a distraction and preventing productivity, there are also security risks which serve as a reason for these types of restrictions.

Test your understanding 12

The following two statements relate to telephones in business. Tick the boxes to show if they are true or false.

Statement	True	False
It is quicker and easier to communicate with colleagues using e-mail than to do so via telephone.		✓
Mobile telephones have no place in the workplace as they are only for personal use.		✓

5.3 Face to face communication and meetings

In addition to communicating with customers and colleagues who are not in the same location as you, there will also be numerous occasions where you will need to communicate face-to-face.

Most of these will be routine conversations in the office, and as such are considered informal communication. The need to be polite and communicate effectively with fellow team members was addressed in the previous chapter.

There will also be occasions when formal face-to-face communication is needed in the workplace. Most of these will be meetings, both with co-workers (for example, departmental staff meetings) and external participants (for example, customer and supplier meetings). Meetings can be both formal and informal and can take place in the office or off-site.

In terms of acceptable behaviour, the courtesy required on the telephone will also apply, however body language (so-called non-verbal communication) is more important.

 Definition

Non-verbal communication refers to the means of communicating in business without using words. Research suggests that up to 80% of communication is through our actions and the signals we show to others. This is commonly known as **body language**.

There are many tips on effective body language in the workplace, but on the whole it is important to appear enthusiastic and interested in what other people say. Using simple tools such as nodding and smiling when others speak and maintaining eye contact will achieve this. It is important not to interrupt others and if you feel the need to disagree or question them to do so in a polite and positive way.

Equally if the person you are talking to starts looking around the room, ensure you pick up on this and change your subject or approach to capture their attention.

5.4 Presentations

Presentations are perhaps the most obvious form of verbal communication. They are typically one person speaking to an audience, with limited interaction or discussion. As such, they provide a great opportunity to express and explain complex messages or brief staff or customers.

Presentations are not just important for managing directors seeking to inspire and inform their staff or salespeople looking to sell products or services to their clients. All parts of a company's business function may need to present their ideas and views to others in a way that their audience will respond to. For accountants, presentations can make an enormous spreadsheet or two hundred page report more digestible for others.

 Test your understanding 13

Rachel works in the accounts department at Hoops & Whoops Ltd, a company providing entertainment for children's parties.

An angry mother calls in to complain about one of the clowns the company use, who had ruined her child's party. She is asking for both an explanation and her money back.

What should Rachel say to the customer? Tick the correct answer.

Options	✓
With all due respect, that cannot be right. This clown is one of our finest entertainers and has been doing parties for over thirty years. Maybe you should check your facts and call us back?	
I am really sorry to hear that there were issues with the clown at the party, but there is nothing we can do about it now that the party is over. Maybe if you are not happy you should use another supplier next time?	
I am really sorry to hear that there were issues at the party; we take these matters very seriously. We could give you all of your money back if you promise not to ask us any more questions about this.	
I am really sorry to hear that there you were not happy with the clown at the party; we will look into the specific circumstances as we take quality very seriously. We can offer a 10% refund if we find that there was an issue.	✓

Test your understanding 14

How Two Ltd have been supplying NB Solutions Ltd's with computer and network equipment for a number of years and the account is now worth a substantial amount of money to How Two Ltd.

Otto, the Sales Manager at How Two, feels it would be good to set up a long-term contract with NB Solutions to confirm pricing, discounts and service levels for the future.

Which of the following would be the best way to discuss the future relationship between the two companies and negotiate terms? Tick the most appropriate answer.

Options	✓
A telephone call	
A face-to-face meeting	✓
A presentation by Otto	
An e-mail	

6 Spreadsheets and software for workplace communications

6.1 Spreadsheets

As we have already seen in Chapter 3, spreadsheets are common tools utilised for accounting functions. They provide a fast and efficient method of presenting and reporting data.

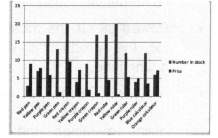

Performing calculations are straightforward as there is a formula function that allows the calculation to be done automatically. Spreadsheets can also process and manipulate data, with sorting and filtering among the most common tasks.

A spreadsheet allows figures to be presented easily in graphical form which is useful when analysing data such as month on month sales, for example.

When figures and information need to be communicated within the team they are easily transferred through the internal computer system to the relevant department or team member via a spreadsheet, in the format required by the business. Management find them useful to download and take to meetings so that they can refer to the information whenever figures need to be discussed.

6.2   Software for workplace communications

Many of the forms of communication we have detailed in this chapter are enabled by software programs. For example, it is rare for letters to be written by hand and visual aids in presentations tend to come in the form of PowerPoint slides rather than handwritten diagrams or notes.

If we consider the forms of communication described earlier, a corresponding Microsoft Office application will often exist to ensure their accurate and professional delivery. For example:

- Excel is the favoured program for devising spreadsheets. In addition to being able to perform mathematical functions, which are especially useful in accounting, Excel also can present the information in a variety of charts and graphs.

- Word is used for all forms of business writing. A word processing package, it can be used for writing e-mails, the written elements of a report and to type up the minutes of meetings. Spellings, grammar and punctuation can easily be checked and corrected in Word and fonts can be changed to match the most appropriate style.

- Outlook is the program utilised most often for sending e-mails – it also has a calendar feature to assist with time management. Within Outlook (or other email software), group emails can be set up to speed up the communication between groups of people. This is particularly useful when working as part of a team as the communication can be shared and contributions made by all.

- PowerPoint is the most widely used presentation software, allowing for the production of all aspects of presentations including animations.

- Microsoft Teams has become a popular method of communication within business. This is a piece of software that is often used for online meetings and shared communication. It has an instant messaging function, screen sharing ability, the ability to store and share resources and integrates with the Outlook calendar so reminders can be set for when meetings are due. In addition, online meetings can easily be accessed via your online calendar; having everything in one place promotes effective and efficient working regardless of the physical location of individuals.

Likewise, instant messenger apps may be connected to social media, but also may be connected to an e-mail system. For example, Google provide a chat feature and 'Hangouts' to operate alongside Gmail.

A lot of organisations have their own intranet. This is an internal website that is used exclusively by the employees of the organisation. An intranet is often used by employees to search for specific information, communicate with each other regardless of location and manage workflows and processes in a streamlined manner. It is a lot more secure than the internet and often they have an integrated social side to them where updates can be posted and people have the opportunity to comment, like and share posts.

7   Summary and further questions

In this chapter we have identified the different methods of communication in the workplace and the uses of both formal and informal language. You should now be able to identify the best method of communication and the most appropriate software required for any task.

You should be able to manage your time effectively. From the various suggestions in this chapter you may be able to identify which methods are likely to work best for you. You will have learnt how ineffective time manage can have a detrimental effect on other members of the team.

Let us return now to the case study to test your knowledge of these key skills for business.

Case study activity 13

During the course of a week Jessica is required to communicate using a number of methods of communication. Choose the most appropriate form of communication for Jessica to use for each situation below. Use the pick list provided.

Situation	Answer
Jessica needs to communicate a lot of information to internal and external customers	*Report*
Jessica has received a serious complaint in the post and needs to respond to it	*Letter*
Jessica has been asked to provide the latest figures from the system for the management to see	*Spreadsheet*
Jessica has been asked to contact a customer and speak to them urgently	*Telephone*
Jessica needs to see a colleague to tell them about some sensitive information	*Face-to-face*
Jessica has a query that anyone in the department may be able to help with – she needs to contact them all without leaving her desk	*Instant messaging*

Pick list

Letter	Spreadsheet
Instant messaging	Report
Face-to-face	Telephone

Case study activity 14

Jessica has been asked to write an e-mail to one of How Two Ltd's customers, NB Solutions Ltd, to detail some changes to their account.

It has been agreed that NB Solutions' credit limit will be increased to £30,000 and that weekly statements will be sent via e-mail. An early payment discount of 10% will apply when outstanding invoices are fully paid within 14 days of the goods being received. All deliveries to UK addresses will be free.

Jessica has been asked to contact Dawn-Marie, the Finance Manager at NB Solutions, with whom she has exchanged e-mails in the past.

Complete the e-mail below by selecting the best option from the three provided for each part:

1	Hey D-M	Hi Dawn-Marie	To whom it may concern
2	Further to your recent communications with Otto, I am pleased to confirm some of the new arrangements for your account with us.	Otto has told me to send you an e-mail because he is busy and he knows I have spoken to you before.	I have been asked to contact you as I understand you are not happy with the service How Two Ltd have been providing.
3	I am pleased to confirm that NB Solutions Ltd's credit limit will be increased to £30,000 and we will offer a 10% early payment discount if you pay within 14 days of the invoice dates.	I am pleased to confirm that NB Solutions Ltd's credit limit will be increased to £10,000 and we will offer a 30% early payment discount if you pay within 30 days of the invoice dates.	I am pleased to confirm that due to the fact NB Solutions Ltd is regarded as a very important customer, your credit limit will be increased and we will offer an early payment discount.
4	You will also receive a weekly statement via e-mail to save our postage costs,	You will also receive a weekly statement via e-mail to make sure you pay,	You will also receive a weekly statement via e-mail to keep you informed.
5	I am also pleased to confirm that you will receive a 10% discount on all UK deliveries.	Moving forward I am also pleased to confirm that you will not be charged for UK deliveries.	Due to your complaints, we have reluctantly agreed to not charge you for deliveries to the UK.
6	That should cover everything – sorry if it hasn't.	Please contact me with any queries regarding this.	If you have any queries, please look on our website.
7	Kind regards, Jessica	Yours faithfully, Jessica	Love, J xx

Case study activity 15

Jessica has been asked to select the most appropriate software for each of the following forms of workplace communication.

Use the pick list provided to find the most appropriate software for Jessica to use.

Jessica needs to send a newsletters, adding attachments such as data files and photographs	E-mail
Jessica is doing her reports and wants to work out formulas and other figures	spread-sheet
Jessica wants to write a letter and needs help with punctuation, grammar and spelling	Word Processing
Jessica needs to show what the company does and how it can benefit the customer, to a group of people.	Presentation

Pick list

Spreadsheet   E-mail

Word processing   Presentation

 Case study activity 16

Jessica has been asked to contact a customer to check which e-mail address an invoice should be sent to. She knows that the recipient of the e-mail is an accounts assistant called Ruth Maloney, but has never met her personally.

How should she end her e-mail?

Options	✓
See you later, Jessica	
Kind regards, Jessica	✓
Yours faithfully, Jessica	
Yours sincerely, Jessica	
Cheers, Jessica	

Answers to chapter activities

Test your understanding 1

Options	✓
Jodie should do the straightforward jobs and leave the more difficult ones for her colleagues to complete after she has left for the meeting.	
Jodie should make a list of all that she needs to do in the morning and give each a timescale and priority.	✓
Jodie should realise that it will be difficult to perform all of the tasks so she should put them all off until the next day.	
Jodie should ignore the regional meeting and devote all her time to the tasks she needs to complete in the office.	

Test your understanding 2

Thomas should:

C   Contact his supervisor immediately and explain the problem. He should suggest that he finishes what he considers to be the most urgent task first before starting one of the others.

Test your understanding 3

	Monday	Tuesday	Wednesday	Thursday	Friday
9am - 10am	Check emails	Check emails	Check emails	Check emails	Check emails
10am – 11am	Processing Purchase Orders	Processing Purchase Orders	Processing Purchase Orders	Processing Purchase Orders	Purchase ledger meeting
11am – 12pm	Processing Purchase Orders	Processing Purchase Orders	Processing Purchase Orders	Processing Purchase Orders	Purchase ledger meeting
12pm – 1pm	Checking supplier invoices	Checking supplier invoices	Checking supplier invoices	Checking supplier invoices	Checking supplier invoices
1pm – 2pm	Lunch	Lunch	Lunch	Lunch	Lunch
2pm – 3pm	Checking supplier invoices	Checking supplier invoices	Checking supplier invoices	Checking supplier invoices	Checking supplier invoices
3pm – 4pm	Supplier account reconciliations	Supplier account reconciliations	Supplier account reconciliations	Purchase Ledger reports	Supplier payment run
4pm – 5pm	Filing documents	Filing documents	Filing documents	Filing documents	Supplier payment run

Test your understanding 4

Decide when you would use these examples of formal or informal language.

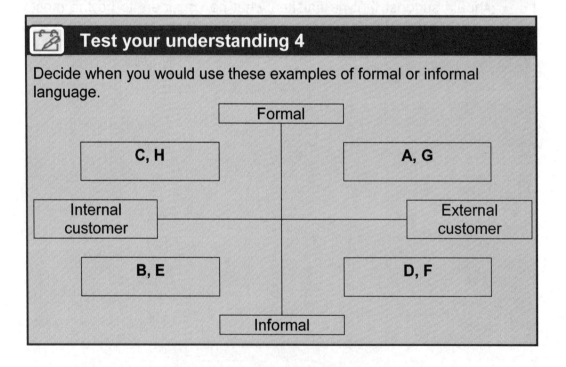

Formal

| C, H | | A, G |

Internal customer ———————————— External customer

| B, E | | D, F |

Informal

Test your understanding 5

	Formal / Informal	Internal / External
A letter to a member of the public responding to a complaint	Formal	External
Asking a colleague whether or not an order has been fulfilled	Informal	Internal
A report for the directors analysing annual business performance	Formal	Internal
A Human Resources policy document for all staff	Formal	Internal
An e-mail to all customers regarding a new invoicing system	Formal	External

Test your understanding 6

Options	✓
A clear and purposeful subject heading	✓
Slang words	
Simple and well-structured content	✓
Jokes and personal comments	
Capital letters to stress the importance of your thoughts	
An appropriate sign off	✓

Test your understanding 7

Options	✓
Hi Steven	
Hello	
Dear Mr Smart	✓
Dear NB Solutions	

Test your understanding 8

Options	✓
Yours faithfully	✓
Yours sincerely	
Yours forever	
Kind regards	

Test your understanding 9

Options	✓
Informing staff of the company's performance and a pay rise	✓
Informing staff of the next training event	
Asking staff for feedback from the previous training event	

Test your understanding 10

The following errors can be identified:

1. There is no date anywhere on the letter

2. The letter should start 'Dear Mr Barrie'. The salutation of Hello is not appropriate and 'Barrie' is the customer's surname, not first name.

3. The subject of the letter has nothing to do with the content (it is about the opening of a trade account, not discounted furnishings).

4. The third paragraph should start with a capital letter ('After').

5. 'You're' should be 'Your' before credit limit.

6. The second paragraph ends with an exclamation mark which is inappropriate in a business context.

7. In the third paragraph, 'could of' should be 'could have'.

8. In the final sentence the number 2 is used instead of the word 'to'. 'Text speak' is not acceptable in any business communications.

9. As the name of the recipient is known, the letter should end with 'Yours sincerely' rather than 'Yours faithfully'.

10. The writer's signature is inappropriate – there is no job title under the name and the e-mail address provided is not a work e-mail address.

Test your understanding 11

First	Introduction (c)
Second	Recommendations (a)
Third	Conclusion (b)
Fourth	Appendix (d)

Test your understanding 12

Statement	True	False
It is quicker and easier to communicate with colleagues using e-mail than to do so via telephone.		✓
Mobile telephones have no place in the workplace as they are only for personal use.		✓

Test your understanding 13

Options	✓
With all due respect, that cannot be right. This clown is one of our finest entertainers and has been doing parties for over thirty years. Maybe you should check your facts and call us back?	
I am really sorry to hear that there were issues with the clown at the party, but there is nothing we can do about it now that the party is over. Maybe if you are not happy you should use another supplier next time?	
I am really sorry to hear that there were issues at the party, we take these matters very seriously. We could give you all of your money back if you promise not to ask us any more questions about this.	
I am really sorry to hear that there you were not happy with the clown at the party; we will look into the specific circumstances as we take quality very seriously. We can offer a 10% refund if we find that there was an issue.	✓

Test your understanding 14

Options	✓
A telephone call	
A face-to-face meeting	✓
A presentation by Otto	
An e-mail	

Case study activity 13

Jessica needs to communicate a lot of information to internal and external customers	Report
Jessica has received a serious complaint in the post and needs to respond to it	Letter
Jessica has been asked to provide the latest figures from the system for the management to see	Spreadsheet
Jessica has been asked to contact a customer and speak to them urgently	Telephone
Jessica needs to see a colleague to tell them about some sensitive information	Face-to-face
Jessica has a query that anyone in the department may be able to help with – she needs to contact them all without leaving her desk	Instant messaging

📖 Case study activity 14

1		Hi Dawn-Marie	
2	Further to your recent communications with Otto, I am pleased to confirm some of the new arrangements for your account with us.		
3	I am pleased to confirm that NB Solutions Ltd's credit limit will be increased to £30,000 and we will offer a 10% early payment discount if you pay within 14 days of the invoice dates.		
4			You will also receive a weekly statement via e-mail to keep you informed.
5		Moving forward I am also pleased to confirm that you will not be charged for UK deliveries.	
6		Please contact me with any queries regarding this.	
7	Kind regards, Jessica		

Case study activity 15

Jessica needs to send a newsletters, adding attachments such as data files and photographs	E-mail
Jessica is doing her reports and wants to work out formulas and other figures	Spreadsheet
Jessica wants to write a letter and needs help with punctuation, grammar and spelling	Word processing
Jessica needs to show what the company does and how it can benefit the customer, to a group of people.	Presentation

Case study activity 16

Options	✓
See you later, Jessica	
Kind regards, Jessica	✓
Yours faithfully, Jessica	
Yours sincerely, Jessica	
Cheers, Jessica	

The principles of sales and purchases

Introduction

The purpose of accounting is to be able to provide financial information about an organisation. For example, managers will want to keep track of the profit made by the organisation in a certain period, and they will also want to see how much the organisation is worth at a specific point in time.

To be able to provide this information it is important to understand the principles of sales and purchases and how these contribute to the profit or loss of a company.

This chapter will introduce you to the accounting terminology used in relation to this.

KNOWLEDGE	CONTENTS
Working in the business environment	1 Income and expenditure
	2 Profit and loss
3 Understand how sales and purchases support business	3 Cash and credit transactions
3.1 Purposes of sales and purchases	4 Summary and further questions
3.2 Principles of sales	
3.3 Principles of purchases	
3.4 Payment terms	

1 Income and expenditure

1.1 Case study: an introduction

 Case study

Jessica is due to start her first week in the Sales and Purchasing department at How Two Ltd. She is really looking forward to learning how sales and purchases support businesses by monitoring income and expenditure.

Jessica is aware that How Two Ltd is a profit-making organisation. She is therefore keen to learn the principles of sales and purchasing and to be able to identify how they can assist a business to generate more income by means of saving on expenditure.

The purpose of most organisations is to make a profit or to raise funds so that they can continue supplying goods and services to customers. In order to calculate profit, an understanding of income and expenditure is needed.

1.2 What is income?

Any money received from the supply of goods and services to customers is known as income.

1.3 What is expenditure?

Any money paid for purchasing the goods and services and day to day expenses is known as expenditure.

 Definitions

Income is the money received by an organisation from selling its goods and services.

Expenditure is the money paid by an organisation to purchase goods and services.

Test your understanding 1

Jessica has been asked to decide which of the following are examples of income and which are examples of expenditure. Tick the correct box.

	Income	Expenditure
Payments to suppliers		✓
Electricity bill		✓
The cost of goods and services		✓
Cash sales	✓	
Sales of services	✓	
Telephone bill		✓
Water bill		✓

2 Profit and loss

2.1 What is a profit or loss?

A business needs to make money in order to operate. By selling goods or services they generate income, from this they need to deduct their expenses for buying in those goods and services. This is called the 'profit' or 'loss'.

As discussed in the earlier chapter, businesses in the voluntary sector operate to provide services and do not make money for their members. Therefore when deducting expenses from their income, they will make either a 'surplus' or a 'deficit'.

In order for a business to generate a 'profit' (or a surplus), their income needs to be more than their expenses. If their expenses are more than their income, they would make a loss which could make the business fail.

Definitions

Profit is the amount of money an organisation earns after expenditure has been deducted from income.

Loss is when an organisation has spent more money than it has earned from income.

Surplus is where the amount of income generated by a not-for-profit organisation exceeds the amount of money spent.

Deficit is where the expenses of a not-for-profit organisation exceeds the amount of income generated.

2.2 What happens when a business makes a profit?

An organisations main goal should be to make a profit. No business can survive long-term if they don't make a profit.

Profit is paid to the owners of a company or its shareholders. Alternatively, it can be used as a saving opportunity to enable the organisation to re-invest and therefore grow the business. Growing a business means expanding it; making it bigger. This may be through investing in research or new technology, opening new offices, operating in new markets or obtaining other businesses. A bigger company means a bigger part of the market share and therefore increased profitability.

2.3 What happens when a business makes a loss?

If a business is spending more on expenses than they are making from the sales of goods or services, they will be making a loss.

If an organisation is making a loss then the chances are that their bank account may become overdrawn. Ultimately, they will be charged high amounts of interest for this which only increases their expenditure even more. If this were to happen, the business may not have enough money to pay their suppliers which could result in the suppliers putting their account on hold, or even withdrawing their credit agreement.

As a result, the business would find it difficult to purchase goods or services for resale, meaning that they would struggle to meet their customer's demands. If this is the case, it can cause problems and the business could fail.

2.4 What happens when a not-for-profit organisation makes a surplus?

A not-for-profit organisation can make a surplus, providing it is used to further fund its purposes. Any surplus cannot go directly back to its members but could be used to repay any loans taken out to fund activities.

Generating a surplus is generally considered good practice and is important for the financial viability of the organisation and can help account for expected and unexpected expenses in the future.

2.5 What happens when a not-for-profit organisation makes a deficit?

Deficits can be difficult for not-for-profit organisations to overcome because they are heavily dependent upon the generosity of donors to stay afloat.

Sometimes they may need to cut costs in order to remain stable enough to continue but by communicating with members, often a solution can be found i.e. fundraising activities carried out to boost income.

Test your understanding 2

Jessica has been asked to identify which of the following are indicators of a business making a profit or a loss. Put a tick in the correct box.

	Profit	Loss
The business could fail		✓
The bank account is overdrawn		✓
A saving opportunity	✓	
There is an opportunity for growth	✓	
There is a high volume of sales	✓	
Money has been invested in new ventures	✓	
Not enough money to pay for purchases		✓
Suppliers withdraw their credit agreement		✓

Example

JBU Wines has recorded all sales income and expenditure for the previous month.

Alan, the Accounts Assistant, has been asked to calculate the profit for the month.

	£
Sales income	125,000
Cost of sales	75,000
Wages	15,000
Premises expenses	3,000
Vehicle expenses	2,500

Solution:

To calculate **profit (or loss)** the cost of sales are deducted from the sales income.

	Sales income:	£125,000
−	Cost of sales	- £75,000
−	Wages	- £15,000
−	Premises expenses	- £3,000
−	Vehicle expenses	- £2,500
=	**Total Profit**	**£29,500**

Therefore, Alan can report a profit of £29,500 for the month.

Note: If Alan had ended up with a minus figure at the end of her calculation, she would know that the company had made a loss i.e. JBU Wines' expenses were more than the company's income.

 Case study

In September, How Two Ltd's Liverpool office had recorded income from sales of £82,000. The cost of those sales was £66,000 and the other expenses were £25,000. Jessica is asked whether the Liverpool office made a profit or a loss.

Solution:

	Sales income:	£82,000
−	Cost of sales	- £66,000
−	Other expenses	- £25,000
=		**-£9,000**

Their expenses are more than their income so the Liverpool office of How Two Ltd made a loss of £9,000 in September.

Test your understanding 3

To assess the performance of How Two Ltd's Liverpool office in September, Jessica looks at the figures from the previous month. In August, the Liverpool office recorded income of £85,000. The cost of those sales was £69,000 and the other expenses were £18,000.

Did they make a profit or a loss? How do the two months compare?

 Test your understanding 4

Jessica has been asked to see if the performance of the Liverpool office is similar to the nearest office, in Manchester. The Manchester office of How Two Ltd has recorded all sales income and expenditure for the previous month.

Jessica needs to calculate the profit or loss for the month given the following information:

	£
Sales income from cash and credit sales	78,000
Cost of sales	50,700
Wages	7,500
Premises expenses	1,750
Vehicle expenses	2,000

Profit £16,050

 Test your understanding 5

Jessica is asked to summarise her findings via e-mail. One of the senior managers asks her a question: If How Two Ltd has total income lower than costs of sales plus expenses, have we made a profit or a loss?

Write a sentence for Jessica to e-mail to the manager to explain the answer to his question.

Understanding 3

$\begin{array}{r} 69 \\ +\ 18 \\ \hline 87 \end{array}$ $\begin{array}{r} -87 \\ -85 \\ \hline -2 \end{array}$

August   *September*

Income	£85,000	-£9,000
Cost of sales	£69,000	-£2,000 =
Other expenses	£18,000	-£7000
Total	-£2,000	

U4

Costs:	Income:
50,700	£78,000
7,500	£61,950
1,750	£16,050
2,000	
61,950	Profit

U5

As their sales income is lower than cost of sales plus expenses, the business has made a loss.

3 Cash and Credit Transactions

3.1 Customers and clients

Throughout this section, we will refer to customers and clients of a company and the types of transactions in which they are involved.

The term **'customer'** often refers to someone who purchases goods or services from a shop or online. The term **'client'** often refers to someone who is receiving professional services or advice, for example, accountancy services or legal services.

3.2 Recording cash and credit transactions

Income is the amount of money received by an organisation from the sale of its goods or services. Returning to our case study, How Two Ltd sell computers and accessories to their customers; these would be classified as their sales of goods. They also have a help desk that offer advice on technical issues or who deal with broken computers that customers bring into store to be fixed; this would be classified as their sales of services.

Sometimes money from sales is received immediately; this is classified as **cash sales**. At other times, the money is received later; this is classified as **credit sales**. It is important that these cash and credit transactions are recorded separately so that the organisation knows how much money it is owed by customers.

3.3 Cash and credit sales

 Definitions

Sales is the exchange of goods or services to an individual or organisation in exchange for money.

A **customer** is an individual or organisation to whom the goods or services have been sold. The organisation supplying the goods or services will then receive money in exchange.

A **receivable (also known as a debtor)** is a customer who has been sold goods on credit and who owes the business the money in respect of the sale.

Cash Sales is the term used to describe a payment at point of sale. The payment itself can be made by cash (currency), cheque, debit or credit card, or bank transfer. An example of a cash sale is when you go into a shop, choose the items you want to buy, and pay for them immediately.

Credit Sales are sales made where the goods or services will be paid later than the point of sale. Many organisations give credit to their regular trade customers so that one payment can be made for all the transactions made in each month. Credit sales are usually recorded by way of an invoice which will be covered in a later chapter.

3.4 Cash and credit customers

With cash sales the organisation gets the money immediately from the customer and the relationship ends there. With credit customers, there is a risk to the organisation that the customer may not pay for the goods.

Therefore, before allowing customers to pay on credit the organisation will make certain checks to ensure that the customer can pay. If these checks identify that the customer has the ability to pay its debts, payment terms will be agreed with the customer and a credit account set up.

Payment terms usually state the length of time a customer has to pay for their goods and also a maximum amount that they are allowed to owe the business at any one time. The amounts outstanding from customers can be analysed so that a business can see at what point they can expect the money to come into their bank account.

If customers are taking longer to pay than expected, a business should chase for the outstanding monies to ensure a continual flow of cash moving through the organisation.

It is assumed that the money owed by credit customers will be paid and therefore they are classed as **receivables** or **debtors** of the organisation.

Test your understanding 6

Jessica has been asked to identify whether the following would be classified as a cash or credit transaction?

Put a tick in the correct box.

	Cash	Credit
A customer purchases a computer and pays by credit card	✓	✓
A customer buys a mouse mat, a mouse and a printer and pays by debit card	✓	
A customer buys 5 tablet computers, and pays in 30 days		✓

3.5 Cash and credit purchases

Definition

Purchases – to buy goods or services from an organisation in exchange for money.

Cash Purchases are when goods or services are paid for at the time of purchase.

Case study

How Two Ltd may purchase some stock and pay by 'cash'. Although the payment could be by cash (currency), credit card or debit card or bank transfer, if the payment is made immediately it is classed as a cash purchase.

Credit Purchases are when an organisation pays for the goods or services sometime after making the purchase. The money will be sent to the supplier after an agreed amount of time, for example, thirty days.

The supplier is now a payable of the organisation and as money is owed to the supplier in respect of the transaction.

KAPLAN PUBLISHING

Definition

A **supplier** is an individual or organisation providing goods or services to another in exchange for money.

A **trade payable** is a supplier who is owed money for goods purchased on credit.

 Test your understanding 7

Jessica has been asked to identify whether the following would be classified as a cash or credit transaction?

Put a tick in the correct box.

	Cash	Credit
The Liverpool office purchases some inventory online and pays by bank transfer	✓	
The London office purchases some inventory and is issued an invoice from the supplier		✓
The Manchester office purchases a computer and pays by credit card	✓	

Test your understanding 8

Fill in the gaps below to complete the sentences. Choose from the Pick list provided.

When an organisation pays for items of expenditure at the time of purchase this is known as a _Cash purchase_.

When an organisation allows a customer to pay the amount they owe at a later date this is known as a _credit sale_.

Pick List

credit sale   cash sale   cash purchase   credit purchase.

Test your understanding 9

C Froome's Cycle World

Mr Froome has a small shop selling and repairing bicycles for individual customers.

He buys the spare parts that he needs from a large wholesaler.

Do you think that Mr Froome's income comes from cash sales or credit sales? *likely cash*

Do you think that the expenditure for spare parts is cash purchases or credit purchases? *credit*

4 Summary and further questions

This chapter has introduced you to some important accounting terminology. You can distinguish between income and expenditure and should also understand that a business needs more income than expenses in order to operate profitably.

We have also looked at the difference between credit sales and purchases and cash sales and purchases. Finally, the chapter looked at how the profit or loss of an organisation is calculated.

Let us now return to the case study for some further practice questions to test your knowledge of this key terminology.

 Case study activity 17

Jessica has been asked to define some key accounts terms to help explain her e-mail to the senior managers. Choose the correct option in each of these statements:

a.   The sum of money spent in making sales is known as [sales/cost of sales]

b.   If total income is greater than the cost of sales plus other expenses the organisation has made a [profit/loss]

c.   If total income is less than the cost of sales plus other expenses the organisation has made a [profit/loss]

Case study activity 18

Jessica needs to decide whether the following How Two Ltd transactions are cash or credit sales, or cash or credit purchases? Put a tick in the correct box.

	Cash Sale	Credit Sale	Cash Purchase	Credit Purchase
Printer paper bought from a supplier and paid for immediately.	✓		✓	
Cables delivered to a customer who will pay at the end of the month.		✓		✓
Laptop components bought from a supplier on credit.				✓
A payment received from a customer for goods purchased online and paid for at the checkout.	✓			✓

 Case study activity 19

Jessica has been given a list of terms which are commonly used every day in her department. She needs to decide if they are assets, liabilities, income or expenditure? Put a tick in the correct box.

	Asset	Liability	Income	Expenditure
Creditors		✓		✓
Electricity bill		✓		✓
Money in the bank	✓			
Sales to customers			✓	
Debtors	✓			✓
Office computers	✓			

Asset – ativo
Liability – passivo

Case study activity 20

Last month How Two Ltd's Head Office recorded income and expenditure in the table below:

Income and Expenditure	£
Sales	156,000
Cost of Sales	93,600
Wages	21,060
Administration Expenses	18,720
Selling Expenses	12,844

Jessica needs to use the income and expenditure figures to calculate the profit or loss and state underneath whether this would be a profit or loss.

Profit / Loss: £ 9,776.00 Profit

 Case study activity 21

The following month's recorded income and expenditure is shown in the table below:

Income and Expenditure	£
Sales	152,880
Cost of Sales	91,728
Wages	20,640
Administration Expenses	18,350
Selling Expenses	12,590

Jessica needs to use the income and expenditure figures to calculate the profit or loss and state underneath whether this would be a profit or loss.

Profit / Loss: £ 9,572.00 Profit

Answers to chapter activities

Test your understanding 1

	Income	Expenditure
Payments to suppliers		✓
Electricity bill		✓
The cost of goods and services		✓
Cash sales	✓	
Sales of services	✓	
Telephone bill		✓
Water bill		✓

Test your understanding 2

	Profit	Loss
The business could fail		✓
The bank account is overdrawn		✓
A saving opportunity	✓	
There is an opportunity for growth	✓	
There is a high volume of sales	✓	
Money has been invested in new ventures	✓	
Not enough money to pay for purchases		✓
Suppliers withdraw their credit agreement		✓

Test your understanding 3

	£
Sales income	85,000
Cost of sales	-69,000
Other expenses	-18,000
	-2,000

This means that their sales income is lower than their expenses and therefore they have made **a loss of £2,000**.

Although this is a loss, it is £7,000 less than the loss in September.

Test your understanding 4

	£
Sales income	78,000
Cost of sales	-50,700
Wages	-7,500
Premises expenses	-1,750
Vehicle expenses	-2,000
	16,050

The company have made **a profit of £16,050** because their sales income is more than the total of their expenditure.

Test your understanding 5

As their sales income is lower than cost of sales plus expenses, the business has made a loss.

Test your understanding 6

	Cash	Credit
A customer purchases a computer and pays by credit card	✓	
A customer buys a mouse mat, a mouse and a printer and pays by debit card	✓	
A customer buys 5 tablet computers, and pays in 30 days		✓

Test your understanding 7

	Cash	Credit
The Liverpool office purchases some inventory online and pays by bank transfer	✓	
The London office purchases some inventory and is issued an invoice from the supplier		✓
The Manchester office purchases a computer and pays by credit card	✓	

Test your understanding 8

When an organisation pays for items of expenditure at the time of purchase this is known as a **cash purchase.**

When an organisation allows a customer to pay the amount they owe at a later date this is known as a **credit sale.**

Test your understanding 9

Mr Froome's income is most likely to be from cash sales. His customers are individuals who will probably pay when they come to pick up their bicycles. They are unlikely to be very regular customers.

His expenditure for the spare parts is likely to be a credit purchase. As Mr Froome will buy regularly from the supplier he may have been given credit so that he can make daily or weekly purchases and then pay for all he owes at a later date.

Case study activity 17

a. The sum of money spent in making sales is known as **cost of sales**

b. If total income is greater than the cost of sales plus other expenses the organisation has made a **profit**

c. If total income is less than the cost of sales plus other expenses the organisation has made a **loss**

 Case study activity 18

	Cash Sale	Credit Sale	Cash Purchase	Credit Purchase
Printer paper bought from a supplier and paid for immediately.			✓	
Cables delivered to a customer who will pay at the end of the month.		✓		
Laptop components bought from a supplier on credit.				✓
A payment received from a customer for goods purchased online and paid for at the checkout.	✓			

 Case study activity 19

	Asset	**Liability**	**Income**	**Expenditure**
Creditors		✓		
Electricity bill				✓
Money in the bank	✓			
Sales to customers			✓	
Debtors	✓			
Office computers	✓			

Case study activity 20

	£
Sales	156,000
Cost of Sales	-93,600
Wages	-21,060
Administration Expenses	-18,720
Selling Expenses	-12,844
	9,776

Profit / Loss: £ 9,776 Profit

Case study activity 21

	£
Sales	152,880
Cost of Sales	-91,728
Wages	-20,640
Administration Expenses	-18,350
Selling Expenses	-12,590
	9,572

Profit / Loss: £9,572 Profit

Business documentation and procedures

7

Introduction

As stated in the previous chapter, customer and supplier transactions are recorded so that organisations know how much money they are owed by customers, and how much they owe to suppliers.

Business documents are used to record these transactions and the documents are exchanged between the supplier and the customer so that both parties have a record. It is important that both the supplier and the customer keep a copy of each of these documents. Mistakes can happen and each document is proof of a stage of the transaction.

The name of a document will depend on whether we look at it from the point of view of the seller or the purchaser. Thus an invoice may be called a 'sales invoice' for the seller but a 'purchase invoice' for the purchaser, although it is the same document.

KNOWLEDGE	CONTENTS
Working in the business environment	1 Sales documentation
	2 Purchases documentation
3 Understand how sales and purchases support business	3 Receipts and payments
	4 Summary and further questions
3.2 Principles of sales	
3.3 Principles of purchases	
3.4 Payment terms	
4 Apply business procedures to sales and purchases	
4.1 Importance of business procedures	
4.2 Business procedures for sales	
4.3 Business procedures for purchases and expenses	
4.4 Procedures	

1 Sales documentation

1.1 Case study: an introduction

 Case study

Jessica has really enjoyed her induction and feels like she is getting used to the terminology used within her department. She understands the principles behind sales and purchases and has now been tasked with looking through the different types of business documentation that she will come across on a day to day basis.

She is going to be shown what information is required on each document and then she will then be given the opportunity of completing some of these herself to be checked by her manager.

1.2 Offering credit and price quotations

Most transactions between business organisations will be on credit terms and this involves an element of risk. The goods are being taken away or delivered to the customer now with the promise of payment in the future. Therefore, suppliers must be confident that payment will be received.

In some organisations it is common practice to quote prices to customers over the telephone particularly if there is a catalogue or price list from which there are no deviations in price. However, some businesses will be prepared to offer certain customers goods at different prices and discounts may be offered and/or given to customers. Therefore, it is often the case that a price quotation is sent to a customer showing the price at which the goods that they want can be bought. The customer can then decide whether or not to buy the goods at that price. If they decide to purchase the goods upon receipt of the quotation, this can be used to generate the sales invoice later on in the sales process.

1.3 Purchase Order

If the customer is happy with the price quotation that they have received from the supplier then they will complete a purchase order for the goods or services required and send it to their supplier.

This document will state the details of the goods required, including:

* the quantity and description of the goods
* the price and other terms
* the supplier's code number for the items
* the date the order was placed.

When the supplier receives a purchase order, it is important for them to check all of the details carefully as it forms part of the sales contract.

* Is the price the same as the one which was quoted to the customer?
* Are the delivery terms acceptable?
* Are any discounts applicable?

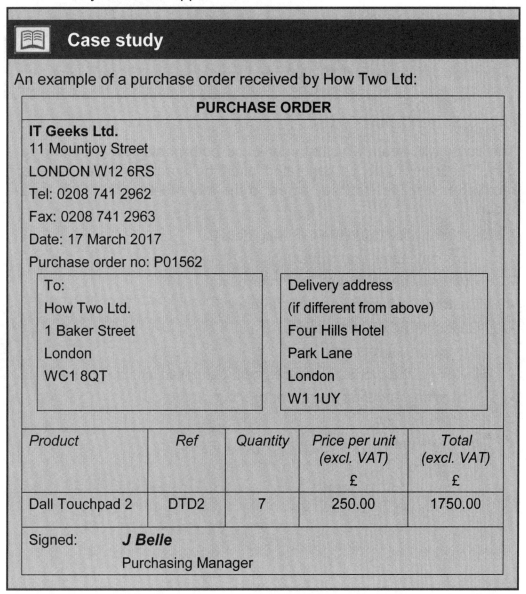

Case study

An example of a purchase order received by How Two Ltd:

PURCHASE ORDER

IT Geeks Ltd.
11 Mountjoy Street
LONDON W12 6RS
Tel: 0208 741 2962
Fax: 0208 741 2963
Date: 17 March 2017
Purchase order no: P01562

To:	Delivery address
How Two Ltd.	(if different from above)
1 Baker Street	Four Hills Hotel
London	Park Lane
WC1 8QT	London
	W1 1UY

Product	Ref	Quantity	Price per unit (excl. VAT) £	Total (excl. VAT) £
Dall Touchpad 2	DTD2	7	250.00	1750.00

Signed: *J Belle*
Purchasing Manager

Notes:

a) The customer, IT Geeks Ltd. has placed an order with the supplier of computers, How Two Ltd.

b) The purchase order clearly states that the customer wants to purchase 7 Dall Touch Pad 2's at a price of £250.00 each.

c) The total amount that the customer wants to pay for the tablet computers is £1,750.00 (7 touchpads x £250.00 = £1,750.00).

d) If How Two Ltd. do not agree with any of these details, they will need to contact IT Geeks Ltd. immediately. The purchase order has been signed by J Belle, the authorised signatory. This is important to demonstrate that the process has been completed as required by the business.

 Definition

An **authorised signatory** is an individual who has been given permission to sign an official document on behalf of an organisation.

1.4 Sales Order

The seller will create a sales order once both parties have agreed to a deal. The sales order is generated after the purchase order has been received to confirm that they agree to the terms set out in the purchase order.

A sales order will include the following details:

- Company name and contact information
- Customer name and contact information
- Customer reference/account number
- Customer billing information.
- Customer delivery address.
- Details of the products/services being supplied including quantities.
- Unit prices and total prices per product
- Total net price
- VAT amount
- Total price

1.5   Delivery note

When the goods or services are supplied, the supplier will prepare a delivery note to give to the customer. This document will show:

- The name and contact details of the seller
- Name and contact details of the customer
- Date of issue
- Date of delivery of the goods
- Delivery note number
- Purchase order number
- A description of the goods contained in the order
- The quantity of each type of goods

The delivery note will be signed by the customer upon receipt of the goods or services, so that the supplier has proof that the customer received them. This also ensures that there is a clear audit trail in case of any later queries.

1.6   The sales invoice

After the goods have been delivered, the supplier will request payment from the customer by sending an invoice. The invoice will state the code, quantity, description and price of the goods.

The invoice will also have a sequential number so that it can be filed in order.

The documentation used in order to generate this would include the quotation if there is one, a price list if it's a standard invoice and the delivery note.

An example from our case study is on the following page.

Case study

An example of a sales invoice provided by How Two Ltd:

INVOICE

How Two Ltd.

1 Baker Street
London
WC1 8QT
Tel: 020 7890 1234
Fax: 020 7890 1235

Invoice no: 005673
Tax point: 25 March 2017
VAT reg no: 618 2201 63
Delivery note: DN00673
Account no: BEL65

To:

IT Geeks Ltd.
11 Mountjoy St
London W12 6RS

Delivery:

Four Hills Hotel
Park Lane
London W1 1UY

Delivery date:

25 March 2017

Date: 25 March 2017

Sales order number: 41161

Product	Quantity	Price per unit (£)	Total (£)
Dall Touchpad 2	7	250.00	1,750.00
		VAT 20%	350.00
		Total	2,100.00

Payment terms: 14 days net

Notes:

This invoice confirms the price of the goods supplied to the customer

a) 7 Dall Touchpad 2's which have been supplied to the IT Geeks Ltd.

b) The price for the goods is £1,750.00

c) Value Added Tax (VAT) of 20%, £350.00 has been added to the cost of the goods.

d) The amount of £2,100.00 is now due from the customer.

e) The payment is due in 14 days from the date of the invoice.

1.7   Goods returned note

Upon receipt of goods, the customer may find that incorrect items have been delivered, some items are damaged, or they do not meet the required standard. In this case, the customer has the right to return the goods to the supplier. When a customer returns goods to a supplier, they complete a goods returned note.

A goods returned note is an important document as it will be used by the supplier to refund the customer or provide a replacement, depending on the circumstances surrounding the return.

The goods returned note will include the following details:

* Customer name, reference and contact details
* Contact details of the supplier
* Quantities, description and price of goods returned
* The reason for returning the goods
* Condition of the goods returned
* Date of the return
* Name and signature of the person who received the goods.

1.8   Pricing and discounts

Unit prices for goods or services are kept in master files which must be updated regularly. If a price quotation has been sent to a customer then this must be used to determine the price to use on the invoice.

Trade discounts are a definite amount that is deducted from the list price of the goods for the supplies to some customers, with the intention of encouraging and rewarding customer loyalty. As well as checking the actual calculation of the trade discount on the face of the invoice, the supplier's file or the price quotation should be checked to ensure that the correct percentage of trade discount has been deducted.

Even if no trade discount appears on the purchase invoice, the supplier's file or price quotation must still be checked as it may be that a trade discount should have been deducted.

A **bulk discount** is similar to a trade discount in that it is deducted from the list price on the invoice. However, a bulk discount is given by a supplier for orders above a certain size.

A **prompt payment discount** is offered to customers if they settle the invoice within a certain time period. The discount is expressed as a percentage of the invoice total but is not deducted from the invoice total as it is not certain whether or not it will be accepted. Instead the details of the settlement discount will be noted at the bottom of the invoice.

Test your understanding 1

Match the transaction to the relevant document:

Transaction	Document
A document sent by the supplier to the customer listing the goods or services supplied and requesting payment	Purchase Order
A document sent to a supplier detailing the goods that the customer wants to purchase.	Invoice
A document sent to a customer to accompany the goods. The customer signs this upon receipt of their items.	Delivery Note

1.9 VAT (sales tax)

VAT (Value Added Tax) also known as Sales Tax, is collected on behalf of HMRC (Her Majesty's Revenue and Customs) by companies in the UK. VAT registered companies charge VAT on the supply of goods and services to their customers. They can claim back any VAT paid on their purchases. The amount that gets paid to HMRC is the total amount of VAT charged to their customers minus the total amount of VAT that they can claim back on their purchases.

Definitions

Sales tax (VAT) is charged on the **taxable supply of goods and services** in the United Kingdom by a **taxable person** in the course of a business carried on by him.

Output tax is the tax charged on the sale of goods and services.

Input tax is the tax paid on the purchase of goods and services.

1.10 Rates of VAT (sales tax)

Taxable supply is the supply of all items except those which are **exempt.** Examples of exempt items are as follows:

- certain land and buildings, where sold, leased or hired
- insurance
- postal services

Input tax cannot be reclaimed where the trader's supplies are all exempt.

There are three rates of sales tax (VAT in the UK) on taxable supplies:

1. Some items are 'zero-rated' (similar to exempt except that input tax can be reclaimed), examples of which include:

    - water and most types of food
    - books and newspapers
    - drugs and medicines
    - children's clothing and footwear.

2. There is a special rate of 5% for domestic fuel and power

3. All other items are rated at the standard rate of 20%.

For the purpose of this assessment, you will normally be dealing with taxable supplies at the standard rate of 20%.

Therefore, if you are given the net price of goods, the price excluding VAT, then the amount of VAT is 20% or 20/100 of this price.

Note: VAT is always rounded down to the nearest penny.

 Example

A sale is made for £360.48 plus VAT. What is the amount of VAT to be charged on this sale?

Solution

VAT = £360.48 × 20/100 = £72.09

Remember to round down to the nearest penny.

An alternative way of calculating this would to be to multiply the net amount of £360.48 by 20% = £72.09.

If a price is given that already includes the VAT then calculating the VAT requires an understanding of the price structure where VAT is concerned.

	%
Selling price excl. VAT (net)	100
VAT	20
	───
Selling price incl. VAT (gross)	120
	───

Example

How Two Ltd offer a small office starter pack, with a selling price of £3,000 **inclusive** of VAT. What is the VAT on the goods and the net price of these goods?

Solution

	£
Net price (£3,000 ÷ 120 x 100)	2,500
VAT (£3,000 ÷ 120 x 20)	500
Gross price	3,000

 Test your understanding 2

Calculate the net, VAT and gross figures for the following transactions:

a) A credit sale for £3,600 inclusive of VAT

b) A cash sale for £2,800 exclusive of VAT

	a) Credit Sale	b) Cash Sale
Net		
VAT		
Gross		

 Test your understanding 3

Alba works in the accounts office at NB Solutions Ltd. She has been asked to check three invoices relating to office supplies.

Invoice 1 – NB Solutions purchased 24 boxes of paper towels at £12.45 for each box. What is the total cost of the paper towels?

Invoice 2 – NB Solutions spent £250 excluding (or net of) VAT on stationery. How much VAT would be charged?

Invoice 3 – NB Solutions bought two new dishwashers for the staff kitchens, at a total cost of £480 including VAT. How much VAT would have been included in the cost?

1.11 Preparing a sales invoice

 Case study

Dave Woody is the sales invoicing clerk for How Two Ltd, a VAT registered IT and Computer Consumables company.

Dave prepares the sales invoices to be sent to the customer from the price list and a copy of the delivery note sent up to him by the sales department.

Today he has received the following delivery note from the sales department:

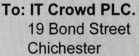 

Delivery note: 1036
Date of issue: 30th October 20X7
Purchase order number: PO1612

To: IT Crowd PLC.
19 Bond Street
Chichester
CH1 6MT

From: How Two Ltd.
1 Baker Street
London
WC1 8QT

Delivery Address:
As Above

Delivery date: 31st October 20X7

Quantity	Code	DESCRIPTION	Size
10	CJA 991	Codie Laptop	12"
15	CJA 992	Codie Laptop	14"
5	CJA 994	Codie Laptop	15.7"

Received by: ....

Signature: .... Date: ....

Code	Description	Screen Size	Unit price	VAT rate
CJA 991	Codie Laptop	12"	249.00	Standard
CJA 992	Codie Laptop	14"	279.00	Standard
CJA 993	Codie Laptop	15"	319.00	Standard
CJA 994	Codie Laptop	15.7"	349.00	Standard

The customer file shows that IT Crowd PLC's account number is ITC 4125 and that a trade discount of 10% is offered to this customer.

Dave must now prepare the sales invoice. Today's date is 2nd November 20X7 and the last invoice issued was numbered 95123.

Solution

INVOICE

How Two Ltd.

Invoice to:
IT Crowd PLC.
19 Bond Street
Chichester
CH1 6MT

Deliver to:

As above

How Two Ltd
1 Baker Street
London
WC1 8QT

Tel: 0207 890 1234
Fax: 0207 890 1235

Invoice no: 95124
Tax point: 2nd November 17
VAT reg no: 618 2201 63
Delivery note no: 1036
Account no: ICT 4125

Code	Description	Quantity	VAT rate	Unit price	Amount net of VAT
			%	£	£
CJA 991	**Codie Laptop**	10	20	249.00	2,490.00
CJA 992	**Codie Laptop**	15	20	279.00	4,185.00
CJA 994	**Codie Laptop**	5	20	349.00	1,745.00
					8,420.00
Trade discount 10%					(842.00)
					7,578.00
VAT					1,515.60
Total amount payable					9,093.60

How did Dave do it?

Step 1   Enter today's date on the invoice and the invoice number which should be the next number after the last sales invoice number.

Step 2   Enter the customer details – name, address and account number.

Step 3   Refer now to the delivery note copy and enter the delivery note number and the quantities, codes and descriptions of the goods.

Step 4   Refer to the price list and enter the unit prices of the goods and the rate of VAT

Step 5   Now for the calculations – firstly multiply the number of each item by the unit price to find the VAT exclusive price – then total these total prices – finally calculate the trade discount as 10% of this total, £8,420.00 × 10% = £842.00 and deduct it.

Step 6   Calculate the VAT – in this case there is only standard rate VAT on the laptops but you must remember to deduct the trade discount (£8,420 – £842) before calculating the VAT amount £7,578 × 20% = £1,515.60 – add the VAT to the invoice total after deducting the trade discount.

Test your understanding 4

As part of her role at How Two Ltd, Jessica is required to generate sales invoices.

Today she has received the following delivery note from the sales department.

Delivery Note

How Two Ltd.

To: St Peter's Secondary School
191 St. Petersgate
Manchester
M2 6KS

From: How Two Ltd.
1 Baker Street
London
WC1 8QT

Delivery Address:
As Above

Delivery note: 1114
Date of issue: 30th October 20X7
Purchase order number: P6486

Delivery date: 31st October 20X7

Quantity	Code	DESCRIPTION	Size
5	SMG 121	Samsong HD Monitor	17"
12	SMG 123	Samsong HD Monitor	24"
8	SMG 124	Samsong HD Monitor	28"

Received by: ....

Signature: .... Date: ....

Code	Description	Screen Size	Unit price	VAT rate
SMG 121	Samsong HD Monitor	17"	69.99	Standard
SMG 122	Samsong HD Monitor	19"	99.99	Standard
SMG 123	Samsong HD Monitor	24"	129.99	Standard
SMG 124	Samsong HD Monitor	28"	149.99	Standard

The customer file shows that St. Peter's Secondary School's account number is SPS 1124 and that a bulk discount of 15% is offered to this customer.

She must now prepare the sales invoice and pass it back to Dave Woody to be checked. Today's date is 3rd November 20X7 and the last invoice issued was numbered 95156.

Solution

INVOICE

How Two Ltd.

Invoice to:

Deliver to:

How Two Ltd
1 Baker Street
London
WC1 8QT

Tel: 0207 890 1234
Fax: 0207 890 1235

Invoice no:
Tax point:
VAT reg no:
Delivery note no:
Account no:

Code	Description	Quantity	VAT rate %	Unit price £	Amount net of VAT £
SMG 121					
SMG 123					
SMG 124					
Bulk discount					
VAT					
Total amount payable					

Test your understanding 5

You work for Cavalier Beds as a sales invoicing clerk. Your task is to prepare a sales invoice for each customer using the information below.

Today is 28 October, 20X6 and you have received the following delivery note from the sales department.

Use the information from the delivery note, the information from the customer file and the price list below to prepare an invoice for KP Furniture Ltd.

The last invoice issued was Invoice No. 67894.

Delivery Note:

Delivery note: 6785

To: KP Furniture Ltd
9 Paris Street
COLCHESTER
CF25 1XY

Cavalier Beds
3 Brussels Road
County Road
Gloucester
GL6 6TH
Tel: 01456 698271
Fax: 01456 698272

Delivery date: 27 October 20X6

Quantity	Code	DESCRIPTION	Size
5	MAT15K	Deluxe Mattress	King Size

Received by: ....

Signature: .... Date: ....

Customer File:

The customer file shows that KP Furniture Ltd's account number is KP12 and a trade discount of 10% is offered to this customer.

Price List:

Code	Description	Size	Unit price	VAT rate
MAT15S	Deluxe Mattress	Single	58.00	Standard
MAT15D	Deluxe Mattress	Double	74.00	Standard
MAT15K	Deluxe Mattress	King	98.00	Standard

Cavalier Beds
3 Brussels Road
County Road
Gloucester
GL6 6TH
Tel: 01456 698271   Fax: 01456 698272

Invoice to:

Invoice no:

Date:

VAT reg no: 488 7922 26

Delivery note no:

Account no:

Code		Quantity	VAT rate	Unit price £	Amount excl of VAT £
			20%	£	
Trade discount 10%					
Subtotal					
VAT					
Total amount payable					

1.12   The sales day book (SDB)

The sales day book records individual invoices issued to credit customers within one day, week or month. It is basically a list which is totalled at the end of the specified period to indicate how much a company has made in sales, how much VAT they owe to HMRC in respect of those sales and how much they are owed in total by their customers. It will then be used to perform double entry bookkeeping, which you will learn about in the AAT Foundation Certificate.

Example

SALES DAY BOOK

Date	Customer	Reference	Invoice number	Total £	VAT £	Sales £
1 July	Althams Ltd	ALT01	45787	120.00	20.00	100.00
2 July	Broadhurst plc	BRO02	45788	240.00	40.00	200.00
			TOTALS	360.00	60.00	300.00

Notes

- The reference number is the code number of the customer's account in the sales ledger this information can be found on the invoice.
- The invoice number is the number of the invoice issued for each sale.
- The Sales column is the total value of the goods sold as shown on the invoice after deducting trade discount, i.e. net of VAT.
- The amount of VAT is recorded in a separate column to show the amount owing to HMRC for these invoices.
- The Total column shows the total amount due from credit customers (Receivables).

2   Purchases documentation

2.1   Payment terms

As mentioned previously, the majority of business transactions nowadays are conducted on credit terms. This applies to both sales and purchases.

When a credit account is set up with a supplier an agreement is put in place which states the point at which payment is to be made for goods and services, any conditions of payment and any discounts that may be applicable. This helps to ensure that suppliers are paid on time and to give them an idea of cash flows within the business i.e. at what point they can expect the money to come into their bank account.

Payment in advance

A payment in advance is where a payment for goods or services is made ahead of schedule. This is not uncommon when dealing with larger orders as it helps the supplier to cover any 'out of pocket' expenses or to pay for the materials required to produce the order if they don't have enough capital to fund the purchase.

A payment in advance also helps safeguard the supplier against customers who don't pay or those that cancel a large order at the last minute.

 Example – payment in advance

Where a supplier requests a 50% upfront payment from the buyer.

Payment on delivery

Payment on delivery is where the supplier will distribute goods to the customer and take payment for the goods upon delivery. If the customer does not pay for the goods, they are returned to the supplier.

Payment after invoice date

A payment after the invoice date gives the customer a certain number of calendar days to make payment 'after' the date of the invoice. The supplier can specify how many days this would be but quite commonly this is 10, 14, 30 or 60 days after the invoice date. This arrangement would be put in place as part of the supplier agreement.

Payment at the end of the month of invoice

A payment at the end of the month of invoice means that the supplier is expecting the money at the end of the month in which they have issued the invoice.

 Example – payment at the end of month

Where an invoice is issued on the 15th September, the supplier will be expecting payment by the 30th September.

2.2 The Purchasing Process

The flow chart on the following page demonstrates the process that How Two Ltd would follow when making a purchase.

Case study

How Two Ltd select a supplier

Some businesses will have an **approved supplier list**. This is a list of suppliers who are reliable and have the capacity to meet their customers needs. An approved supplier usually provides a consistent high level of service along with excellent quality standards of their products.

They then raise a purchase order and send to the supplier

The purchase order in the purchasing process is exactly the same as that in the sales process. The only difference is that we are effectively the customer and therefore we are the ones completing the document and sending it to the supplier.

How Two Ltd receive the goods or services from the supplier

How Two Ltd check the delivery note against the goods received and sign the delivery note to say that they agree that it matches

The delivery note contains details as stated in the Sales section above. If there are any differences between the delivery note and the goods received, How Two Ltd. makes a note of any differences and queries them with the supplier. This would be noted before the delivery note was signed because otherwise How Two Ltd. could be invoiced for goods that they have never actually received.

How Two Ltd complete a goods received note (GRN)

A **goods received note** is an internal document used to identify proof of goods actually received. See below for further explanation.

How Two Ltd receive an invoice from the supplier in respect of the purchase

How Two Ltd check the invoice received from the supplier against the purchase order, delivery note/goods received note to ensure that they have been invoice correctly

Once satisfied that they have been invoiced accurately for their purchase, How Two Ltd make a payment to the supplier and record the expenditure.

2.3   The Goods received note (GRN)

A goods received note is an internal document that is used to document the receipt of goods or services. Upon delivery, the goods received will be checked against the delivery note sent from the supplier. If everything is present and correct, the customer will sign the delivery note to be returned to the supplier and will generate a GRN as proof of what has been received. This is then compared to the purchase order and the supplier invoice before payment is made.

 Case study

You work for How Two Ltd. and have been asked to prepare a goods received note using the following information:

Today is 31st October 20X7, there has been a delivery of goods into the warehouse. Yacob Solvez has checked the goods received and agrees that the details on the following delivery note are correct.

Using the information in the delivery note below, prepare the goods received note as requested, ensuring all of the relevant details are entered.

Delivery Note

To: How Two Ltd.
  1 Baker Street
  London
  WC1 8QT

From: PC's R Us Ltd.
  212 Wellington Street
  London
  WC12 8RD

Delivery Address:
1 Baker Street
London
WC1 8QT

Delivery note: 1056
Date of issue: 30th October 20X7
Purchase order number: PO5571

Delivery date: 31st October 20X7

Quantity	Code	DESCRIPTION
20	DKT476	Dall Laptop Model SKW665
25	ESMJA2	Epsan MJA2 projectors

Received by: ....

Signature: .... Date: ....

Goods Received Note

Goods Received Note

Received From:
PC's R Us
212 Wellington Street
London
WC12 8RD

GRN number: 102

Date goods received: 31st October 20X7

Delivery note number: 1056

Quantity	Code	DESCRIPTION
20	DKT476	Dall Laptop Model SKW665
25	ESMJA2	Epsan MJA2 projectors

Received by: *YACOB SOLVEZ* ....

Signature: *Y. Solvez*............... Date: *31st October 2017* ....

Note:

The details entered include the dates that the goods have been received, a goods received note number, the delivery note number from the supplier (so that it can be matched up later), the supplier details, quantities, descriptions and codes of the goods received and then details of the person who has received the goods into store.

 Test your understanding 6

Jessica has been asked to prepare a goods received note using the following information:

Today is 31st October 20X7, there has been a delivery of goods into the warehouse.

Jessica has checked the goods received and agree that the details on the following delivery note are correct.

The last GRN created was number 123.

Delivery Note:

Delivery Note		
Delivery note: 2212		
Date of issue: 30th October 20X7		
Purchase order number: PO5589		
To: How Two Ltd.	**From: Tablet World**	
1 Baker Street	477 High Street	
London	Oxford	
WC1 8QT	OX10 5WD	

Delivery Address:
1 Baker Street
London
WC1 8QT

Delivery date: 31st October 20X7

Quantity	Code	DESCRIPTION
15	SSX52	Samsong SX52 9" Tablet computers
15	DL656	Dall MC656 8" Tablet computers

Received by: ....

Signature: .... Date: ....

Goods Received Note:

Goods Received Note		
Received From:		
GRN number:		
Date goods received:		
Delivery note number:		

Quantity	Code	DESCRIPTION

Received by: ....

Signature: .... Date:................................

2.4   The purchases day book

As seen earlier in the chapter, credit sales are recorded in the 'sales day book'. In the case of credit purchases, we have the 'purchases day book'.

The purchases day book is simply a list of the purchases invoices that are to be processed for a given period (e.g. a week). In its simplest form, the purchases day book will comprise just the names of the suppliers and the amount of the invoices received in the week.

Example

PURCHASES DAY BOOK

Date	Supplier	Reference	Invoice number	Total £	VAT £	Purchases £
1 Sept 17	W E L Ltd	Q73243	56712	1,800	300	1,500
3 Sept 17	Vivalitee plc	L73244	AV942	402	67	335
			TOTALS	**2,202**	**367**	**1,835**

Example

You work in the accounts department of R Porte Manufacturing Ltd and have received the following:

R Moore Fashions

12 Dutch Corner
High Wycombe
HG4 7NQ

Invoice no: 005673
Tax point:14 July 2016

INVOICE

To: R Porte Manufacturing Ltd
   5 Ventoux Crescent, Cardiff, CA2 3HU

Product	Quantity	Price per unit	Total
		£	£
Cargo pants	5	25.00	125.00
T-shirts	10	15.00	150.00
			275.00
		VAT 20%	55.00
		Total	330.00
Payment terms: 30 days net			

As you are dealing with documents for R Porte Manufacturing and this invoice is sent to you at R Porte Manufacturing, R Moore Fashions must be the supplier Therefore, this is a supplier invoice and should be entered into the **purchases day book.**

The entry would appear as follows:

Date	Supplier	Reference	Invoice number	Total £	VAT £	Purchases £
14 July 16	R Moore Fashions	MORS78	005673	330	55	275
			TOTALS	**330**	**55**	**275**

3 Receipts and payments

3.1 Case study: an introduction

 Case study

Having looked at the variety of documents which are issued in the sales and purchasing processes, and considered the procedures to follow, Jessica is keen to see the whole process through. She has asked her manager whether she can therefore have an insight into how the receipts and payments relating to these documents are recorded.

Her manager is really pleased that she is showing initiative and is keen to learn. Jessica will learn the process for recording the payments and have a go herself but has been told her not to process anything until it has been checked by a supervisor.

3.2 Cash receipts and payments

There are many different ways a business can make and receive payments. A lot of businesses make electronic payments; however, many customers still pay in cash or by writing a cheque. When physical payments are received by an organisation, the monies will need to be paid into the business's bank account.

In a cash sale or purchase, the transaction is much simpler. The customer will probably place an order verbally and payment is always made as soon as the customer receives the goods or services. Payment for cash sales or purchases are usually made by cash, credit or debit card.

The customer will need a copy of the sales receipt in case they need to return them to the supplier.

 Definition

Monies – A term used to describe all types of payments and receipts including cash, cheques and direct bank transfers.

3.3   Paying-in slips

All business organisations are provided with a paying-in book by the bank. Each paying-in book contains paying-in slips. When money is received from customers in cash or by cheque, it is paid into the bank and is accompanied by one of the completed paying-in slips.

If your job is to pay money into the bank, you will need to complete and sign the bank paying-in slip taken from the paying-in book. The paying-in slip is then given to the bank cashier who will check it against the monies being paid in to the bank.

You only need to enter the number of cheques being paid in and the total amount on the front of the paying in slip. On the back of the paying in slip you should write a list of the cheques being paid in.

The paying-in stub is the part of the paying-in slip which stays in the paying-in book and is a record for the organisation of the amounts paid into the bank. Sometimes a business may keep a separate list of monies received so that they can cross reference it the bank statement to ensure the correct amount has been paid in, or with the paying in slip should issues arise further on down the line.

KAPLAN PUBLISHING

3.4 Example of a paying-in slip

Today's date

Cash and Cheques sums

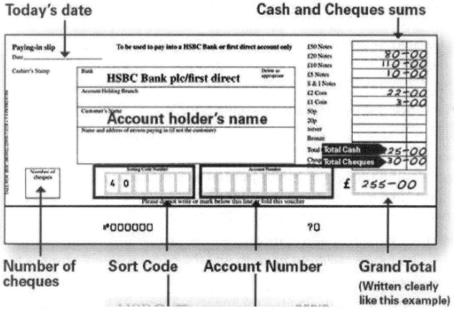

HSBC Bank plc/first direct

Account holder's name

£50 Notes		80-00
£20 Notes		110-00
£10 Notes		10-00
£5 Notes		
£2 Coin		22-00
£1 Coin		3-00
Total Cash		25-00
Total Cheques		30-00

£ 255-00

Number of cheques

Sort Code

Account Number

Grand Total
(Written clearly like this example)

(Source: www.hsbc.co.uk)

 Test your understanding 7

Today's date is 19 November 2017.

Jessica has been asked to complete a bank paying-in slip for the money received today, which is as follows:

Notes	Coins	Cheques	
3 x £20 notes	25 x £1 coins	Thomas	£1,500.00
15 x £10 notes	8 x 50p coins	Friebe	£ 750.00
20 x £5 notes	20 x 10p coins		

Complete the paying-in slip below:

Date:	ABC Bank plc	£50 notes	
	Manchester	£20 notes	
		£10 notes	
	Account	£5 notes	
	How Two Ltd	£2 coin	
		£1 coin	
No of cheques	Paid in by	Other coin	
	Jessica Howard	Total cash	
	Sort Code Account No	Cheques	
	25-22-78 30087251	Total £	

Test your understanding 8

When Jessica asked her manager to check over the paying in slip to ensure that she had completed it correctly before taking it to the bank, she was asked why it is important that the paying-in slip is signed and dated.

What would Jessica's response have been?

3.5   The use of cheques

When a person (or organisation) writes a cheque they are instructing their bank to transfer a specified amount of money from their bank account to the bank account of the recipient of the cheque – the payee.

If the cheque hasn't been completed correctly the bank may return it to the payee. The payee will then have to ask for a replacement cheque from the organisation.

As this causes delays in the payment process, it is important that the cheque is completed correctly in the first place.

3.6   Cheque requirements

For a cheque to be valid it should include:

- **Payee name** The payee is the person or organisation to whom the cheque is written. The payee's name should exactly match the name on their bank account.

- **Date** The date that the cheque is written must include the day, month and the year. A cheque that is more than 6 months old is invalid and the bank will not accept the cheque.

- **Words** The pounds part of the amount being paid must be written in words but the pence part can be written in numbers. If the amount is a whole number of pounds then you should write 'ONLY' after the amount to prevent someone changing the figure.

- **Numbers** The amount being paid should be written in numbers in the box on the right hand side of the cheque. The amount in numbers should exactly match the amount written in words.

- **Signature** The cheque should be signed by an authorised signatory of the organisation.

 Definition

Signatories – a person or persons who are authorised to sign cheques on behalf of an organisation.

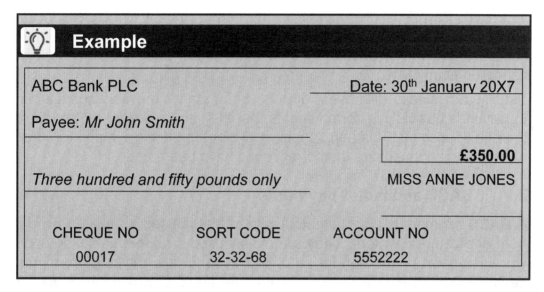

Example

ABC Bank PLC	Date: 30th January 20X7
Payee: *Mr John Smith*	
	£350.00
Three hundred and fifty pounds only	MISS ANNE JONES

CHEQUE NO	SORT CODE	ACCOUNT NO
00017	32-32-68	5552222

3.7 Cheque stubs

When cheques are paid out, the person who writes the cheque will fill in the cheque book stub. This contains details of the date the cheque was written out, who the cheque was sent to and the amount paid.

The bookkeeper uses the cheque book stub to update the accounting records, to show the payments made.

They will then cross reference the cheque number to the bank statement to ensure the correct amount of money has been paid out of the bank. This will be covered in more detail in the next chapter.

3.8 Direct debits and standing orders

A **direct debit** is an electronic payment set up by you. You instruct your bank or building society to allow a third party to take money from your bank account at a specified time.

The amounts paid could vary in amount but you will have been informed of how much this will be and when the money will be taken, by the company you are making payment to.

An example of this might be when you are paying your gas or electric bill. The total of the bill will vary from month on month depending on how much gas and electric you use; however, you will have been sent the bill in advance of the money being taken from your bank and this will advise you of the date on which the money will be taken.

A **standing order** is where you set up a regular automated payment to be taken from your bank at a specified time in the month e.g. the 1st of every month. With a standing order, the amounts to be paid are fixed for a certain amount of time. An example of this might be when you are paying your rent. Payments of rent will be the same amount to be paid at the same time each month, in this case, a standing order would be the most suitable method of payment. Standing orders can be amended or cancelled at any time.

Usually, a business will have a direct debit or standing order schedule set up which is basically list of payments that they are expecting to go out of their bank account. This helps them to cross reference payments on their bank statement to ensure the correct ones have been made.

3.9   BACS and faster payments

A **BACS** payment is an automated system that is used to make payment from one bank to another. They are mainly used for direct debits so once you have given permission for an organisation to take payment from your bank account, they will usually do this via the BACS system. A BACS payment takes 3 days to clear in a bank account so if payment was made on Monday, it wouldn't appear in the recipient's bank until Wednesday.

A **faster payment** is an electronic payment that can be made online via internet banking or over the phone. A faster payment is usually made within two hours of making the payment meaning that the money will clear in the recipient's bank account the same day. Both banks have to be part of the faster payments service for this method of payment to be an option however nowadays this is a common service used by businesses to make quick payments to suppliers of goods or services.

Bank Statements are sent from the bank in paper format or can be downloaded from the online banking system. Bank statements show the monies paid in or out of the business bank account and can be used to identify transactions that have not been processed in the accounting software.

As a bookkeeper, it is important that an amount showing on the bank statement that has not been recorded in the accounting software are fully investigated and evidence of the transaction is located to ensure there is an audit trail. For example, a director may have paid for a meal out with a client using the business debit card but may not have provided a receipt for the transaction. The bookkeeper has a duty to investigate this and locate a copy of the receipt for the accounting records before processing the transaction on the system. Bank statements will be covered in more detail in a later chapter.

Automatic Bank Feeds are where the accounting software is directly linked to the business bank account. The technology surrounding automatic bank feeds allows the software to automatically allocate amounts to the relevant accounting records within the system. These are then reviewed and agreed to ensure the information has been transferred accurately.

Automating large proportions of manual bookkeeping transactions, saves time manually entering transactions which helps to increase efficiency and productivity. It also helps reduce the risk of human error and in turn increases the accuracy of financial data.

 Test your understanding 9

Match the definitions with the correct words used in banking

A person who is authorised to sign documents on behalf of an organisation	payee
The person or organisation to whom the cheque is written	stub
A written instruction to transfer a specified sum of money from one bank account to another.	monies
The part of a cheque or paying-in slip kept as a record of the transaction	signatory
The term used to describe different forms of payments and receipts including cash, cheques and direct bank transfers.	cheque

3.10 The cash book

Definition

The Cash Book records receipts and payment made by cash, cheque, credit or debit card, or bank transfer.

One of the most important books used within a business is the cash book. There are various forms of cash book, a 'two column' and a 'three column' cash book.

A two column cash book records details of cash and bank transactions separately as shown here:

CASH BOOK							
Date	Details	Bank	Cash	Date	Details	Bank	Cash
		£	£			£	£
		Receipts				Payments	

Notes

- The left hand side of the cash book represents the debit side – money received. Often the paying in slips, remittance advices received from customer and lists of receipts will be used to update this side of the cash book.

- The right hand side of the cash book represents the credit side – money paid out. Often the list of payments, direct debit/standing order schedules and cheque book stubs are used to update this side of the cash book.

- In practice, there is usually a column on both the debit and the credit side for the date.

- The details column describes the transactions – typically the name of the customer or supplier.

- The bank column on the debit side represents money received (by cheque or other bank payment) whereas the bank column on the credit side represents money paid (by cheque or other bank payment).

- The cash column on the debit side represents cash received whereas the cash column on the credit side represents cash paid out in respect of purchases or other expenses.

Some organisations keep separate cash books to record receipts and payments. These are known as the cash receipts book and cash payments book, respectively.

Test your understanding 10

Alba works in the accounts department at NB Solutions Ltd. She has been asked to complete a two column cash book by recording transactions from today.

For each of the following, indicate whether they should be on the left or right hand side of the Cash Book.

	Left / right
Money received	
Money paid out	
Credit	
Debit	
£220 cash to pay for catering at NB Solutions event	
Bank transfer from a one-off customer for £150	
Cheque from Miss B Craven for £232	
Cheque payable to How Two Ltd for £459	

4 Summary and further questions

In this chapter we have looked in detail at the documents used to record transactions for credit and cash customers and suppliers. You should now know what information is required for each of these documents and you should be able to accurately generate them from given information.

Let us return to the case study to see how Jessica uses some of the documents to record sales and purchases at How Two Ltd.

 Case study activity 22

Jessica has been given three pieces of paper:
- A delivery note
- A sales invoice
- A purchase order

Match the document with the correct description to help Jessica understand how they relate to sales or purchases.

	Document
Sent by the customer (How Two Ltd) to state which goods they want to purchase	
Sent by the supplier to How Two Ltd with the goods when despatched	
Sent by the supplier to How Two Ltd to inform them of how much the goods cost	

Case study activity 23

Jessica has been asked to prepare a delivery note using the information below:

Today is 29th October 20X7 and the following purchase order has been processed with the goods ready to be despatched to the customer. The last delivery note issued was number 1026 and the goods are due to be delivered tomorrow.

Using the information above along with the purchase order below, prepare the delivery note as requested, ensuring all of the relevant details are entered.

PURCHASE ORDER

Redshaw Cables
17 High Street
Manchester M1 6RS
Tel: 0161 741 2962
Fax: 0161 741 2963
Date: 23rd October 20X7
Purchase order no: P01562

To:	Delivery address
How Two Ltd.	(if different from above)
1 Baker Street	Four Lane Ends
London	New Mills
WC1 8QT	SK22 4LG

Product	Ref	Quantity	Price per unit (excl. VAT) £	Total (excl. VAT) £
HDMI Cables	HDMI62	20	15.00	300.00
Epsan SXA projectors	ESXA14	5	300.00	1,500.00

Signed: *J Johnson*
              Purchasing Manager

Delivery Note:

Delivery Note		
To:		**From:**

Delivery Address:

Delivery note:
Date of issue:
Purchase order number:

Delivery date:

Quantity	Code	DESCRIPTION

Received by: ....

Signature: .... Date: ....

Case study activity 24

Jessica has been asked to enter the invoice below into the sales day book.

How Two Ltd	
1 Baker Street London WC1 8QT	Invoice no: 5698 Tax point: 22 Nov 20X7

INVOICE

To: G Thomas (A/C Ref TH02)
5 Holland Crescent, Chesham CA2 3HU

Product	Quantity	Price per unit	Total
Goods (Deluxe Laptop Case)	5	£50.12	£250.60
		VAT 20%	£50.12
		Total	£300.72
Payment terms: 30 days net			

Complete the Sales Day Book below with the correct information:

Date	Customer	Reference	Invoice No	Total £	VAT £	Net £

 Case study activity 25

Given the document below should Jessica record it in the sales day book or the purchases day book or both?

King & Co	
Highbrow HI4 3SQ	Invoice no: 2867 Tax point: 18 June 20X7

Invoice

To: How Two Ltd
1 Baker Street, London WC1 8QT

Product	Quantity	Price per unit	Total
Item 5	10	£35.50	£355.00
		VAT 20%	£71.00
		Total	£426.00
Payment terms: 14 days net			

Case study activity 26

Jessica is considering the payment terms offered by How Two Ltd and those they are given by their suppliers.

Using the documents from the previous two activities and the invoice below, complete the table to show when the payments for these invoices were due.

Customer	Reference	Amount	Payment Due Date
G Thomas	5698	£300.72	
How Two Ltd (from King & Co)	2867	£426.00	
Boujee Beauty UK Ltd			

How Two Ltd

1 Baker Street
London
WC1 8QT

Invoice no: 7124
Tax point: 4 Dec 20X7

INVOICE

To: Boujee Beauty UK Ltd
27 The Promenade
Fraikle Street
Boltown BL98 7YZ

Product	Quantity	Price per unit	Total
Power station LEB22	6	£34.00	£204.00
		VAT 20%	£40.80
		Total	£244.80
Payment terms: End of month of invoice			

Case study activity 27

Jessica has been asked to set up the following payments. For each one indicate the best method of payment from the pick list provided.

Payment	Payment method
The telephone bill for calls and line rental for the Manchester office, for which the statement is paid in full on 15th of each month.	
A fixed monthly fee of £3,750, paid on 1st of each month, to Platinum Property Management for rent of the Liverpool offices.	
An urgent payment for £75 to a local contractor who is performing decorating and maintenance work in Reading, but will not work until paid.	
A refund to a small business who placed an order in error and do not have account terms with How Two Ltd. They have written to request the refund.	

Pick list

Cheque

Faster payment bank transfer

Direct debit

Standing order

 Case study activity 28

Jessica has been asked to send a cheque to a supplier (MMC Direct) for the payment of recent orders.

Which day book should the amount be listed in?

Answers to chapter activities

Test your understanding 1

Transaction	Document
A document sent by the supplier to the customer listing the goods or services supplied and requesting payment	Purchase Order
A document sent to a supplier detailing the goods that the customer wants to purchase.	Invoice
A document sent to a customer to accompany the goods. The customer signs this upon receipt of their items.	Delivery Note

(A document sent by the supplier to the customer listing the goods or services supplied and requesting payment → Invoice)

(A document sent to a supplier detailing the goods that the customer wants to purchase → Purchase Order)

(A document sent to a customer to accompany the goods → Delivery Note)

Test your understanding 2

	a) Credit Sale	b) Cash Sale
Net	£3,000	£2,800
VAT	£600	£560
Gross	£3,600	£3,360

Workings:

a) $3,600 \div 120 \times 100 = 3,000$

   $3,600 \div 120 \times 20 = 600$

b) $2,800 \div 100 \times 20 = 560$

   $2,800 \div 100 \times 120 = 3,360$

Test your understanding 3

Invoice 1 – The cost of the paper towels is £298.88.

Invoice 2 – £250.00 × 20/100 = £50.00. Therefore the VAT would be £50.

Invoice 3 – £480.00/1.2 = £400. £480 - £400 = £80.00. Therefore the VAT would be £80.

 Test your understanding 4

INVOICE

Invoice to:
St Peter's Secondary School
141 St Petersgate
Manchester
M2 6KS

Deliver to:

As above

How Two Ltd
1 Baker Street
London
WC1 8QT

Tel: 0207 890 1234
Fax: 0207 890 1235

Invoice no: 95157
Tax point: 3rd November 17
VAT reg no: 618 2201 63
Delivery note no: 1114
Account no: SPS 1124

Code	Description	Quantity	VAT rate	Unit price	Amount net of VAT
			%	£	£
SMG 121	Samsung HD Monitor	5	20	69.99	349.95
SMG 123	Samsung HD Monitor	12	20	129.99	1,559.88
SMG 124	Samsung HD Monitor	8	20	149.99	1,199.92
					3,109.75
Bulk discount 15%					(466.46)
					2,643.29
VAT					528.65
Total amount payable					3,171.94

Test your understanding 5

Cavalier Beds
3 Brussels Road
County Road
Gloucester
GL6 6TH
Tel: 01456 698271   Fax: 01456 698272

Invoice to:		Invoice no:	67895
		Date:	28/10/X6
KP Furniture Ltd 9 Paris Street COLCHESTER CF25 1XY		VAT reg no:	488 7922 26
		Delivery note no:	6785
		Account no:	KP12

Code		Quantity	VAT rate	Unit price £	Amount excl of VAT £
MAT15K	Deluxe Mattress	5	20%	98.00	490.00

Trade discount 10%	49.00
Subtotal	441.00
VAT	88.20
Total amount payable	529.20

Test your understanding 6

Goods Received Note

Goods Received Note		
GRN number: 124		
Date goods received: 31ˢᵗ October 20X7		
Delivery note number: 2212		
Received From:		
Tablet World		
477 High Street		
Oxford		
OX10 5WD		

Quantity	Code	DESCRIPTION
15	**SSX52**	**Samsong SX52 9" Tablet computers**
15	**DL656**	**Dall MC656 8" Tablet computers**

Received by: *JESSICA HOWARD* ....

Signature: *J. Howard*............ Date: *31ˢᵗ October 2017*..........

 Test your understanding 7

Date:	ABC Bank plc	£50 notes	
19/11/17	Manchester	£20 notes	60.00
		£10 notes	150.00
	Account	£5 notes	100.00
	How Two Ltd	£2 coin	
		£1 coin	25.00
No of cheques:	Paid in by *J Howard*	Other coin	6.00
		Total cash	341.00
2	Sort Code Account No	Cheques	2250.00
	25-22-78 30087251	Total £	2591.00

 Test your understanding 8

The paying-in slip must be dated and signed so that the bank cashier can contact the person who paid in the money in to the bank, in case there are any queries.

Test your understanding 9

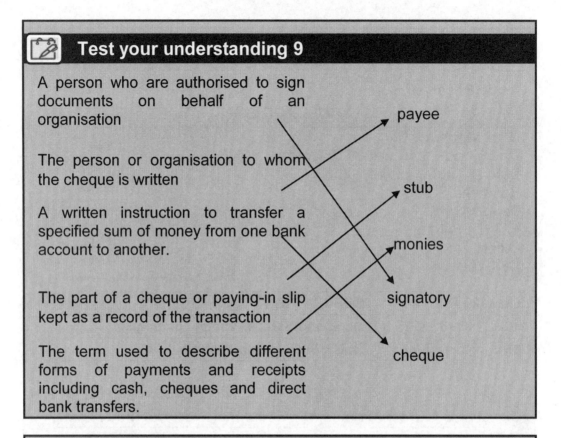

A person who are authorised to sign documents on behalf of an organisation

The person or organisation to whom the cheque is written

A written instruction to transfer a specified sum of money from one bank account to another.

The part of a cheque or paying-in slip kept as a record of the transaction

The term used to describe different forms of payments and receipts including cash, cheques and direct bank transfers.

payee

stub

monies

signatory

cheque

Test your understanding 10

	Left / right
Money received	Left
Money paid out	Right
Credit	Right
Debit	Left
£220 cash to pay for catering at NB Solutions event	Right
Bank transfer from a one-off customer for £150	Left
Cheque from Miss B Craven for £232	Left
Cheque payable to How Two Ltd for £459	Right

Case study activity 22

	Document
Sent by the customer (How Two Ltd) to state which goods they want to purchase	**A purchase order**
Sent by the supplier to How Two Ltd with the goods when despatched	**A delivery note**
Sent by the supplier to How Two Ltd to inform them of how much the goods cost	**A sales invoice**

 Case study activity 23

Delivery Note

To: Redshaw Cables
17 High Street
Manchester
M1 6RS

From: How Two Ltd.
1 Baker Street
London
WC1 8QT

Delivery Address:
Four Lane Ends
New Mills
SK22 4LG

Delivery note: 1027
Date of issue: 29th October 20X7
Purchase order number: PO1562

Delivery date: 30th October 20X7

Quantity	Code	DESCRIPTION
20	HDMI62	HDMI Cables
5	ESXA14	Epsan SXA projectors

Received by: ....

Signature: .... Date: ....

Case study activity 24

Date	Customer	Reference	Invoice No	Total £	VAT £	Net £
22 Nov 20X7	G Thomas	TH02	5698	300.72	50.12	250.60

Case study activity 25

This invoice is sent from King and Co who must be the supplier of the goods. Therefore, this is an invoice received by How Two Ltd from a supplier and should be entered into the **purchases day book.**

 Case study activity 26

Customer	Reference	Amount	Payment Due Date
G Thomas	5698	£300.72	22 Dec 20X7
How Two Ltd (from King & Co)	2867	£426.00	2 July 20X7
Boujee Beauty UK Ltd	7124	£244.80	31 Dec 20X7

 Case study activity 27

Payment	Payment method
The telephone bill for calls and line rental for the Manchester office, for which the statement is paid in full on 15th of each month.	**Direct debit**
A fixed monthly fee of £3,750, paid on 1st of each month, to Platinum Property Management for rent of the Liverpool offices.	**Standing order**
An urgent payment for £75 to a local contractor who is performing decorating and maintenance work in Reading, but will not work until paid.	**Faster payment bank transfer**
A refund to a small business who placed an order in error and do not have account terms with How Two Ltd. They have written to request the refund.	**Cheque**

 Case study activity 28

This is a payment from How Two Ltd and should therefore be listed in the **cash payments book.**

Checking documentation

Introduction

In the previous chapter we looked at the different types of business documentation and the purposes for each. Here, we will look at the importance of ensuring that these documents are accurate. We will compare documents in the purchasing process to ensure that they are accurate.

We will also look at the different types of errors that could occur and what action should be taken should this happen.

KNOWLEDGE	CONTENTS
Working in the business environment	1 Business procedures
1 Develop skills for the workplace	2 Checking documents
1.4 Professional behaviour	3 Summary and further questions
4 Apply business procedures to sales and purchases	
4.1 Importance of business procedures	
4.4 Procedures	

1 Business procedures

1.1 Case study: an introduction

 Case study

Jessica is now feeling very confident about her bookkeeping skills and has been working on processing sales and purchasing documentation for a few days now. She feels as though she is really starting to understand the systems and processes around this.

Jessica is keen to continue looking at How Two Ltd's finances and helping to balance the books. Her manager makes Jessica aware of the impact it could have on the organisation if these documents are not accurate and the consequences as a result of them being incorrect.

Therefore it is vital that Jessica understands the importance of checking all business documentation before processing it. As a result, Jessica is now going to explore in more detail how to check business documents for accuracy and what to do if she discovers discrepancies or errors.

1.2 The need to follow business procedures

It is essential to follow business procedures when dealing with sales and purchases. This will ensure that the processes are completed fully and accurately as required by the organisation. Failure to do so could result in deadlines being missed, which ultimately causes issues for the business.

For example, if goods are not checked properly upon receipt this could lead to the company creating a goods received note for incorrect items of stock and they could be charged incorrectly for items that they have never received.

If there are many queries raised in relation to goods received, this could lead to further complications when it comes to the payment run, and could result in the internal deadline being missed. If this was the case, the supplier may not receive their payment on time which could damage the business relationship with the supplier.

It is important to follow the correct procedures for the following reasons:

- It helps to avoid errors – if the process of completing business documents is followed properly, the number of errors made will be minimal. Examples of such errors are provided below.

- It helps to avoid missing internal or external deadlines – this is key to the smooth operation of the sales and purchasing departments. If deadlines are missed, a backlog of work will be created. If you get behind with your work, you could rush to try to get back on top of it which creates a risk of errors being made.

- It ensures processes are completed as required by the business – every business has different needs and requirements from business documents. Invoices, credit notes, purchase orders, delivery notes, goods returned notes and goods received notes will look different depending on the company that has created them. The basic information within these documents however, will remain the same.

- It maintains good business relationships with customers and suppliers – if procedures are followed accurately then the number of errors or queries will be minimal, payments will be made on time and therefore business relationships will remain positive.

 Example

When processing sales invoices, it is important to ensure the figures processed are a true reflection of the customer's order.

If the figures are overstated, this could lead to customers being chased for more money than they actually owe. As a result, the customer would dispute the amount owed and it would take time for the discrepancy to be investigated and corrected.

Not only could this damage the businesses reputation with the customer, but the receipt of money owed would be delayed which could result in cash flow issues.

 Example

When processing purchase invoices or making payments to suppliers, it is important to review the accounting records for accuracy. Failure to do so could result in an overpayment/underpayment, ultimately leading to further errors in the accounting records.

If the business overpays them or makes duplicate payments to the supplier, this could lead to cash flow problems for the business.

As a result, the business may find that they don't have enough money to pay other suppliers and could therefore either face operational/ production delays or have to source money from elsewhere (e.g. a loan or overdraft). This is an expensive option for the business and could have a negative effect on the overall profit or loss.

Example

Likewise, if an underpayment is made, this could lead to a lack of trust between the supplier and the business, making future the partnership between the organisations, and any future commercial arrangements, more difficult.

It could also result in the supplier putting the account on hold and refusing to process any further orders of inventory. This would cause delays in supplies, leading to problems with business operations and fulfilling customer orders in a timely fashion, therefore having a negative impact on both the customer and supplier relationship.

1.3   Ensuring procedures are followed correctly

Following procedures correctly is of paramount importance to the smooth operation of an organisation.

The following steps give you an idea of how to ensure that you are performing work-related tasks correctly to prevent wasting time tracing and correcting errors.

- Ensure that business documentation is completed fully and accurately – make sure that all quantities, prices and discounts are cross checked for accuracy and that all item codes, customer or supplier codes and document reference number e.g. PO numbers or delivery note numbers are correct too.

- Complete all documents on time – within the sales and purchasing departments there will be deadlines that need to be met. It is highly likely that someone else within the department is relying on the completion of your work before they can complete theirs. Failure to meet deadlines will cause delays in sales invoices being sent out to the customer and therefore will delay the payment coming in from the customer. It could also create delays in payments to suppliers which could cause issues in terms of receiving stock to fulfil customer orders. This will have a negative effect of business relationships with both customers and suppliers.

- Ensure that the correct authorisation has been obtained – not having the correct authorisation before sending out documents or processing documentation can lead to errors being made within the system. Obtaining authorisation means that your work has been checked and it has been agreed with someone more senior who has the ability to make business decisions. Failure to do so could lead to incorrect information being entered into the accounts.

- An overstatement or understatement of figures within the accounting records could lead to incorrect profit or loss figures being recorded. It is imperative that this is accurate for accurate business decisions to be made. For example, if a profit figure is overstated, the director could start thinking about expansion plans for the business. If the business doesn't have the correct resource to be able to put this into place then this could lead the business to fail.

📝 Test your understanding 1

Which ONE of the following is a likely outcome of procedures NOT being followed correctly?

Options	✓
Deadlines being met	
Greater customer satisfaction	
Increased profits	
Errors when completing documentation and/or payments	

---

2 Checking documents

2.1 Dealing with common errors and discrepancies

If there are errors when checking purchasing documentation, it depends on what the error is as to how it should be dealt with.

There are many different errors or discrepancies that may be found when checking documents but the main ones that you will come across on an invoice might include:

- calculation errors
- incorrect VAT calculations
- incorrect type/quantity of goods
- incorrect prices being charged for the goods.

If this is the case then the invoice should be rejected and a dispute raised with the supplier.

Another common example of discrepancies involves the goods themselves. If the goods are damaged or the incorrect goods have been delivered then the buyer will return the goods to the supplier with a goods returned note, requesting a credit note to be issued from the supplier. Upon receipt of the credit note, the buyer would need to check the goods returned note against the credit note to make sure that there are no discrepancies.

The following information should be checked:

- Do the purchase order numbers match?

- Do the details of the goods returned match, including, the quantity, price and description?

- Have the same % of discounts been applied to the credit note?

- Has the VAT been calculated correctly?

If an error or discrepancy is discovered on a credit note or goods returned note, the issue should be raised and the credit note should not be recorded or processed in the accounts.

Test your understanding 2

Which of the following should be checked on documentation relating to sales and purchases to identify potential errors? (Tick ALL correct answers).

Options	✓
Purchase Order number	
Quantity of goods supplied	
Prices of goods supplied	
VAT calculation on goods supplied	
Registered charity no of supplier	
Company logo of supplier	
Discount given by supplier	

2.2   Case study: an example of checking documents

 Case study

Jessica has been asked to check the following documentation to see whether there are any discrepancies.

PURCHASE ORDER				

How Two Ltd.
1 Baker Street
London
WC1 8QT
Tel: 0207 3972 226

Date: 25th October 20X7
Purchase order no: P01671

To: MMC Direct 12 Saunders Street London, WC4 VCV Tel: 0207 3972 226	Delivery address (if different from above) **As above**

Product	Ref	Quantity	Price per unit (excl. VAT) £	Total (excl. VAT) £
Koduk SNS200 Printer	SNS200	10	99.99	999.99
Koduk SNS400 Printer	SNS400	15	149.99	2,249.85
Epsan EPS500 Printer	EPS500	20	109.00	2,810.00

Signed: ***A Khan***
                 Purchasing Manager

Delivery Note:

Delivery Note		
To: How Two Ltd. 1 Baker Street London WC1 8QT	**From:** MMC Direct 12 Saunders Street London WC4 VCV	

Delivery note: 2331   **Date of issue:** 30th October 20X7
Purchase order number: PO1671

Delivery Address:
12 Saunders Street
London
WC4 VCV

Delivery date: 31st October 20X7

Quantity	Code	DESCRIPTION
15	SNS201	Koduk SNS201 Printer
10	SNS400	Koduk SNS400 Printer
15	EPS500	Epsan EPS500 Printer

Received by: ....

Signature: .... Date: ....

Goods Received Note:

Good Received Note
Received From: MMC Direct 12 Saunders Street London WC4 VCV

Delivery note number: 2333
Purchase order number: PO1671

Quantity	Code	DESCRIPTION
15	SNS200	Koduk SNS200 Printer
10	SNS400	Koduk SNS400 Printer
15	EPS500	Epsan EPS500 Printer

Received by: *YACOB SOLVEZ* ....

Signature: *Y. Solvez* .... Date: *31st October 20X7* ....

When checking the documents for accuracy the following errors have been identified:

- When checking the calculations of prices on the PO the total price for the Epsan EPS500 Printer is incorrect. The order states 20 @ £109.00 which equals £2,180.00. The total price on the order has been entered as £2,810. This has been signed by A Khan (Purchasing Manager) to say that it is correct.

- The incorrect quantities have been delivered.

  The PO states:

  - 10 x Koduk SNS200 Printers
  - 15 x Koduk SNS400 Printers
  - 20 x Epsan EPS500 Printers

  The delivery note states:

  - 15 x Koduk SNS201 Printers
  - 10 x Koduk SNS400 Printers
  - 15 x Epsan EPS500 Printers

- Some incorrect items have also been delivered. How Two Ltd. ordered 10 x Koduk SNS200 Printers but 15 x Koduk SNS201 Printers have been delivered.

- The supplier address has been entered as the delivery address on the delivery note. This should be the address of How Two Ltd.

- Yacob Solvez has completed a GRN even though the items delivered do not match the PO.

- Yacob has entered the delivery note number incorrectly on the GRN which will cause issues when dealing with the queries.

- On the GRN Yacob states that 15 x Koduk SNS200 Printers have been received when in actual fact it was 15 x Koduk SNS201 Printers. This is the wrong item and therefore should not be accepted. If he has signed to say that the correct item has been received this could cause issues when raising a query with the supplier.

As all of the above is incorrect, this should be referred back to the Purchasing Manager to resolve.

3 Summary and further questions

In this chapter we have looked at how invoices and credit notes should be checked in business. You should now be able to check the relevant purchasing documentation for errors and you should understand why this is important. You should know what to do if you discover any discrepancies within a place of work and how these should be dealt with.

We will return to the How Two Ltd case study to further practice checking documentation.

Case study activity 29

Jessica has been asked to review the following price list and check whether the Purchase Order has been completed correctly.

She has then been asked to check the additional documentation to see whether there are any discrepancies between the PO, delivery note and GRN.

Price List

Item description	Item Code	Price (excluding VAT)
HT Notebook	HT477	345.00
Dall Notepad	DL90X	350.00
Tashibo Note Perfect	TNP450	295.00
Micrasaft Touch Pro	MTP225	399.00

PURCHASE ORDER

How Two Ltd.
1 Baker Street
London
WC1 8QT
Tel: 0207 890 1234

Date: 29ᵗʰ October 20X7
Purchase order no: P01682

To: Tech Unlimited 427 Lever Street Manchester, M1 2LF Tel: 0161 484 7711	Delivery address (if different from above) **As above**

Product	Ref	Quantity	Price per unit (excl. VAT) £	Total (excl. VAT) £
HT Notebook	HT477	5	354.00	1,770.00
Micrasaft Touch Pro	MTP225	7	399.00	2,793.00
Dall Notepad	DL90X	8	350.00	2,400.00

Signed: **A Khan**
Purchasing Manager

Delivery Note:

Delivery Note	
To: How Two Ltd. 1 Baker Street London WC1 8QT	**From:** Tech Unlimited 427 Lever Street Manchester M1 2LF

Delivery note: 2401　　　　　　　　**Date of issue:** 31st Oct 20X7
Purchase order number: PO1682

Delivery Address:
1 Baker Street
London
WC1 8QT

Delivery date: 1st November 20X7

Quantity	Code	DESCRIPTION
5	HT478	HT Notebook
8	MTP225	Micrasaft Touch Pro
7	DL90X	Dall Notepad

Received by: ....

Signature: ....　　Date: ....

Goods Received Note:

Good Received Note
Received From: MMC Direct 12 Saunders Street London WC4 VCV

Delivery note number: 2401
Purchase order number: PO1682

Quantity	Code	DESCRIPTION
5	HT477	HT Notebook
7	MTP225	Micrasaft Touch Pro
8	DL90X	Dall Notepad

Received by: *YACOB SOLVEZ* ....

Signature: *Y. Solvez*...............　　Date: *31st October 2017*

Case study activity 30

Jessica has been asked to review the following goods returned note and check whether the credit note has been completed correctly.

Good Returned Note			
MMC Direct 12 Saunders Street London WC4 VCV VAT Number: 231 7787 543			**To: How Two Ltd.** 1 Baker Street London WC1 8QT

Goods returned note number: 1023
Purchase order number: PO193

Date: 31st October 2017

Quantity	Code	DESCRIPTION	£
1	HT477	HT Notebook	225.00
2	MTP225	Micrasaft Touch Pro	500.00
1	DL90X	Dall Notepad	200.00

Received by: *YACOB SOLVEZ*..

Signature: *Y. Solvez*............... Date: *31st October 2017*.........

Credit Note		
How Two Ltd. 1 Baker Street London WC1 8QT	MMC Direct 12 Saunders Street London WC4 VCV	

Date: 5th November 2017
Credit note number: CN440
Purchase order number: PO182

Quantity	Code	DESCRIPTION	£
1	HP499	HP Notebook	225.00
1	MTP225	Micrasaft Touch Pro	500.00
1	DL90X	Dall Notepad	200.00
		Net	925.00
		VAT	155.00
		Total	1,080.00

Answers to chapter activities

Test your understanding 1

Options	✓
Deadlines being met	
Greater customer satisfaction	
Increased profits	
Errors when completing documentation and/or payments	✓

Test your understanding 2

Options	✓
Purchase Order number	✓
Quantity of goods supplied	✓
Prices of goods supplied	✓
VAT calculation on goods supplied	✓
Registered charity no of supplier	
Company logo of supplier	
Discount given by supplier	✓

Case study activity 29

The following errors and discrepancies can be identified:

- The HT Notebook has been priced at £354 on the purchase order instead of £345.

- The total of the HT Notebooks should be £1,725 if the correct price of £345 had been stated however £1,770 has been entered on the PO.

- The total of the Dall notepads should be £2,800 but £2,400 has been entered on the PO.

- The incorrect product code has been entered on the delivery note for the HT Notebook.

- The incorrect quantities have been entered on the delivery note for the Micrasaft Touch Pro and the Dall Notepad, 7 Micrasaft Touch Pros had been ordered but the delivery note states 8 have been delivered and 8 Dall Notepads had been ordered but the delivery note states that 7 have been delivered.

- The goods received note matches the purchase order but due to the discrepancies on the delivery note this does not match the goods received note.

 Case study activity 30

The following errors and discrepancies can be identified:

- The incorrect purchase order number has been stated on the credit note

- The incorrect product code has been stated on the credit note for the HP Notebook, this should be HT477 not HP499

- The goods returned note states that 2 Micrasaft Touch Pros have been returned but only one has been credited

- 2 Micrasaft Touch Pros have been returned which in total come to £500. Only 1 has been entered on the credit note but the price state is still £500

- The VAT has been calculated on the credit note. It should be £185 not £155.

- The total of the credit note is incorrect, this should be £1,110 not £1,080.

Mock Assessment 1 – Level 1 Award in Business Skills

Introduction

The following is a Mock Assessment to be attempted in exam conditions.

You should attempt and aim to complete EVERY task.

Read every task carefully to make sure you understand what is required.

Where the date is relevant, it is given in the task.

Both minus signs and brackets can be used to indicate negative numbers UNLESS task instructions say otherwise.

You must use a full stop to indicate a decimal point.

You may use a comma to indicate a number in the thousands, but you don't have to.

The assessment includes 6 tasks.

The total number of marks available for this assessment is 80.

Time allowed: 90 minutes

1 Mock Assessment Questions

Task 1 (12 marks)

There are different types of organisation.

a)   Complete the following sentences by selecting the most appropriate option from the list of items below each sentence. **(2 marks)**

An animal welfare organisation is a _*charitable*_ organisation.

The fire service is a _*public sector*_ organisation.

Pick list

- private sector

- public sector

- charitable

b)   Show whether these statements are true or false by ticking the correct box. **(3 marks)**

Statement	True	False
The primary aim of an organisation in the private sector is to make a profit.	✓	
The public sector is funded by private individuals or organisations.		✓
A Community Interest Company is a not for profit organisation.	✓	

It is important to understand the role of the accounting department within an organisation.

c) Show whether the following statements are true or false. **(3 marks)**

Statement	True	False
Information provided by the accounting department is used by external customers only.		✓
An example of an internal customer of the accounting department is a close friend of one of the managers of the organisation.		✓
The Human Resources department are responsible for dealing with employee relations and personnel and their payroll.	✓	

d) Refer to the following organisation chart:

Top Level	Directors
Middle Level	Department managers
Lower Level	Department staff

Enter the following options into the table above, as they would appear within a three-level organisation chart. **(3 marks)**

Options

- Department managers

- Directors

- Department staff

e) Which of the following statements regarding Public Limited Companies (PLCs) is correct? Tick the correct statement. **(1 mark)**

Statement	✓
A Public Limited Company (PLC) provides services that are essential to the population, like health care.	
The shares of a Public Limited Company (PLC) are made available to the public.	✓
A Public Limited Company (PLC) is a not for profit organisation.	

Task 2 (14 marks)

At the end of every year, a sole trade organisation calculates the profit or loss for the year.

a) Complete the sentence below by selecting the most appropriate option from the following list: **(1 mark)**

- equals
- is more than
- is less than

When income _is less than_ expenditure this results in a loss.

b) State whether the following statement is true or false. **(1 mark)**

Statement	True	False
When a sole trader makes a loss, they have the ability to repay loans to help them pay their bills.		✓

c) Last year your organisation recorded income and expenditure as shown in the table below:

Income and expenditure	£
Sales	192,000
Cost of sales	115,200
Premises expenses	25,920
Heat and light	23,040
Administration and wages	15,808

Use the income and expenditure figures to calculate the profit or loss and complete the statement below to show whether this is a profit or loss. **(2 marks)**

Statement

This would be a

profit	✓
loss	

of £ _12,032_ .

d)   Complete the following sentence, selecting the correct option from the pick list. **(1 mark)**

When a charity records less income than expenses, this results in a

_____deficit_____.

Pick list

Profit   Loss   Surplus   Deficit

It is important to understand the terminology used when buying and selling goods for cash and on credit.

e)   Insert an item from the following pick list into the right hand column of the table below to identify the term described. You will not need to use all of the items. **(2 marks)**

Description	Term described
A person or organisation who is owed money by the company for purchases made.	creditor/ payable
A transaction to sell goods when the payment is made one month later.	a credit sale

Pick list

A cash sale   A cash purchase   A credit sale

A credit purchase   A debtor/receivable   A creditor/payable

f)   Your organisation purchased 12 packs of printer cartridges at £28.65 per box from MG Stationers.

What is the total cost of the printer paper? **(1 mark)**

Answer: £   343.80

g)   MG Stationers have asked for immediate payment.

Is the purchase of the printer paper a cash transaction or a credit transaction?

Tick the correct answer below. **(1 mark)**

Type of transaction	✔
Cash transaction	✓
Credit transaction	

h) From the pick list below, enter the correct payment term next to the most appropriate statement. **(2 marks)**

Statement	Payment term
To help the supplier with out of pocket expenses for large orders is a………..	*payment in advance*
When a customer pays upon receipt of the goods or services is a……………	*payment on delivery*

Pick list

- Payment after invoice date
- Payment at the end of the month of invoice
- Payment in advance
- Payment on delivery

i) You have been given the following details of amounts due to credit suppliers:

Supplier	Amount	Payment Terms	Invoice Date
Parker Products Ltd.	£225.80	14 days after the date of invoice	3rd June
Pencil Case Supplies	£198.27	10 days after the date of invoice	26th June
Prestige Ltd.	£1,264.67	At the end of the month of invoice	28th June

Identify the date that payment will be due to each credit supplier and complete the table below. **(3 marks)**

Supplier	Date by which payment should be made to each credit supplier
Parker Products Ltd.	
Pencil Case Supplies	
Prestige Ltd.	

KAPLAN PUBLISHING

Task 3 (12 marks)

a) You have received an invoice from a credit supplier whose credit terms are payment within 14 days.

There is no supporting documentation to refer to in order to check the invoice for accuracy, but the payment is due today.

You have never encountered this issue before, what should you do?

Select the most appropriate action from the following options.
(1 mark)

Options	✓
Pay the invoice to prevent missing the deadline	
Take no action to avoid making a mistake	
Seek advice from your manager	

b) The company you work for has recently changed the process for sales invoices. An update to the system forced these changes. What internal changes need to be made?

Select the most appropriate answer from the following options:
(1 mark)

Options	✓
The sales invoicing procedure needs to be updated and all changes communicated to the relevant staff	
The sales manager should process all sales invoices following the system update	
The IT department should review the update and process the sales invoices as per any amendments	

c) Identify the correct document that would be used in each of the following circumstances. **(3 marks)**

Description	Document
A customer sends this as proof of payment to a supplier	
Issued following the return of faulty goods	
Accompanies the shipment of goods	

Documents

Credit note	Purchase Order	Remittance Advice
Sales invoice	Delivery note	Statement of Account

d) Refer to the following Purchase Order and Delivery Note.

ABC Ltd.

123 High Street

Manchester

M23 1RD

VAT Reg No. 441 3898 00

Telephone Number: 0161 838 9921

To: XYZ Ltd

Sunnyside

Beach Business Park

LN1 5NQ

Date: 27/11/202X

P.O. Number: PO12457

Quantity	Description	Unit Price	Price
10	Product S123	10.99	109.90
15	Product RC557	12.50	187.50
		Net	297.40
		VAT	59.48
		Total	356.88

Delivery Date: 30th November 202X

Delivery Note

XYZ Ltd.

Sunnyside

Beach Business Park

LN1 5NQ

To: ABC Ltd. 132 High Street Manchester M23 1RD	Date: 2nd December 202X Delivery Note Number:1001
10 x Product S123 @ £10.99 each 15 x Product RE557 @ £15.20 each	
Received by: *A Parker*	Date: *3rd December 202X*

Comparing the above delivery note to the relevant purchase order, identify whether the following statements are true or false. **(5 marks)**

Statement	True	False
The goods were delivered to the correct address.		
There were errors in the quantities delivered.		
There were errors in the products delivered.		
The product pricing was incorrect.		
The goods were delivered on time.		

e) Show whether the following statements are true or false by ticking the appropriate box. **(2 marks)**

Statement	True	False
A sales invoice is always issued for cash sales.		
Purchases are always made from an approved supplier list.		

Task 4 (10 marks)

Your organisation maintains records of sales by store.

Monday's sales for each region are shown in the spreadsheet below.

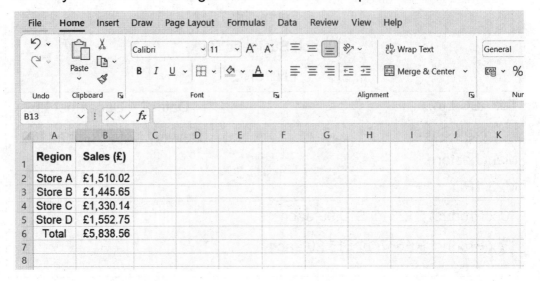

	Region	Sales (£)
1	Region	Sales (£)
2	Store A	£1,510.02
3	Store B	£1,445.65
4	Store C	£1,330.14
5	Store D	£1,552.75
6	Total	£5,838.56
7		
8		

a) Select the correct option from the list below to show which icon would be used to change the colour of the font within a cell. **(1 mark)**

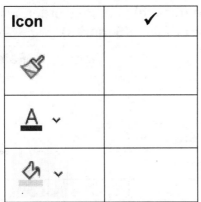

Icon	✓
🖌	
A ⌄	
🪣 ⌄	

b) Which store made the highest amount of sales? **(1 mark)**

c) Which store made the lowest amount of sales? **(1 mark)**

d) What is the range of sales made? **(1 mark)**

e) Which of the following formula options would perform the same role as the AutoSum button for Cell B6 with the sales data? **(1 mark)**

Formula	✓
=B2+C2+D2+E2	
=B2*B3*D2*E2	
=B2+B3+B4+B5	
=B2/B5	

Motor fuel expenses for each of four delivery vehicles are shown in the table below.

f) Complete the table to show the motor fuel expense for Vehicle 1. **(1 mark)**

Delivery vehicles	Motor fuel expense £
Vehicle 1	
Vehicle 2	241.12
Vehicle 3	221.90
Vehicle 4	259.58
Total	974.20

g) Calculate the average motor fuel expense per vehicle. **(1 mark)**

Answer: £ [ ]

Expenses relating to items of stationery purchased within the first quarter of the year are shown in the spreadsheet below:

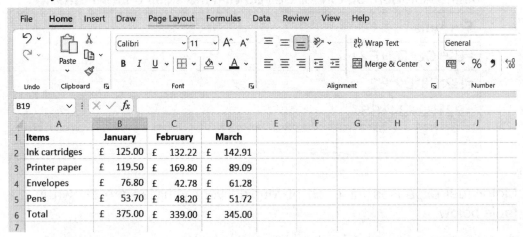

h) Select the correct option from the list below to show which icon would be used to amend the totals to italic text. **(1 mark)**

Icon	✓
B	
A^	
I	

i) Select the correct cell range that would be highlighted to amend the totals to italics. **(1 mark)**

Formula	✓
B2:B5	
A1:D1	
A6:D6	

j) In which cell has the total been added up incorrectly? **(1 mark)**

Cell	✓
B6	
C6	
D6	

Task 5 (16 marks)

Your organisation records of wages by store in each region.

Wages for each of the stores for Monday are shown in the table below.

Region	Wages (£)
Store A	116.77
Store B	119.68
Store C	106.41
Store D	124.22
Total	467.08

a) Which of the following is the ratio of the total wages to wages for Store A? **(1 mark)**

Ratio	✓
2:1	
3:1	
4:1	

You have been asked to calculate the annual bonuses for three of the sales staff.

b) Using the information in the table below, calculate the bonuses for employees B and C. **(4 marks)**

Employee	Annual Salary	Bonus calculated as a % of salary	Bonus Payment	Total Pay for the year
A	£25,000	5%	£1,250	£26,250
B	£19,500	10%		
C	£28,000	7.5%		

c) Employee B has performed really well this year and as a result has been awarded a pay increase equivalent to 1/5 of her current salary.

How much will Employee B receive in respect of her pay increase? **(1 mark)**

d) What will Employee B's total salary be for next year before any bonus calculations? **(1 mark)**

e) Based on her new wage, how much should Employee B expect to be paid per month before any tax or national insurance deductions? **(1 mark)**

You have been given the following information relating to the wages of three employees in another department.

	A	B	C	D	E	F
1	Employee	Annual Salary	Monthly Salary	Bonus calculated as a 5% of monthly salary	Total Monthly Pay	
2	A	£25,200		£ 105.00	£2,205	
3	B	£18,720	£1,560		£1,638	
4	C	£23,820	£1,985	£ 99.25		
5	Total	£67,740.00				
6						

You are using spreadsheet software to perform the above wages calculations, to ensure accuracy within the payroll figures.

f) What formula would be used in cell C2, to calculate the monthly salary of employee A? **(1 mark)**

g) What figure would be displayed in cell C2 after entering the formula? **(1 mark)**

h) What formula would be used in cell D3, to calculate the bonus due to employee B? **(1 mark)**

i) What figure would be displayed in cell D3 after entering the formula? **(1 mark)**

k) What formula would be used in cell E4, to calculate the total pay for employee C? **(1 mark)**

k) What figure would be displayed in cell E4 after entering the formula? **(1 mark)**

l) What formula would be used in cell E5, to calculate the total monthly pay for all 3 employees? **(1 mark)**

m) What figure would be displayed in cell E5 after entering the formula? **(1 mark)**

Task 6 (16 marks)

a) Identify the most appropriate software to use in each of the situations below. **(4 marks)**

Situation	Type of software to use			
	Presentation ✓	Word processing ✓	Email ✓	Spreadsheet ✓
Listing the mileage of the sales staff paid at 45p per mile				
Communicating training on the new system to your team				
Communicating a request to take some annual leave				
Communicating with a customer to chase an outstanding debt				

It is important to observe confidentiality.

b) Complete the following sentence by selecting the most appropriate option from the pick list below. **(1 mark)**

The addresses of all staff should be accessible to _____.

Pick list

all staff

accounts department staff only

authorised staff only

c) Identify whether the following statements are true or false **(2 marks)**

Statement	True	False
A virus will damage files on your computer but will not affect its performance.		
Encrypting data is effective against hackers.		

d) You receive an invoice attached to an email which contains a payment link. The email address looks strange and you suspect the email may be suspicious.

i) What would you do? **(1 mark)**

Options	✓
Open the invoice and seek advice from your manager as to whether to pay it or not	
Delete the email unopened and report it to your IT department	
Do not open the invoice but click on the payment link and pay the invoice	

ii) Which of the following threats is this is an example of? **(1 mark)**

Options	✓
Hacking	
Employee fraud	
Phishing	

e) You are struggling to meet a deadline at work. Rather than tell anyone about this, you pretend you are sick and leave work early.

Is this acceptable behaviour? **(1 mark)**

Yes	No

f) It is month end, and you are particularly busy as you have numerous tasks to complete for different stakeholders within the business.

In addition to this, a request has been made for you to attend a number of departmental meetings and you are also due to attend college for half a day on Wednesday.

Whilst you know the deadlines are achievable, you want to plan your week appropriately and be able to keep track of the tasks that have been completed and set yourself reminders to ensure deadlines are met.

Which planning aids would you use? Select two from the following options. **(2 marks)**

Options	✓
A paper-based to-do list	
An online calendar	
A digital to-do list	
An online collaboration tool	

g) You work in the accounts department at KHJ Properties Ltd.

Your colleague has asked you to check the following business letter for him.

Your manager asked him to write to a supplier to express disappointment in the level of service received from them and the quality of the goods received.

KHJ Properties Ltd.

Unit 14 Dunlin Trading Estate

Manchester

M4 2LW

23rd July 202X

Livingstone Ltd.

Maythorpe Mill

Maythorpe

MY16 4LE

Dear Sir/Madam

I am writing to tell you that we wont be using u anymore to supply hour goods. You're service is terrible and the goods are rubbish therefore we cant sell them. Please close hour account as of today.

Yours Faithfully

Wayne Bradley (Purchase Ledger Clerk)

Check the letter for accuracy and state whether the following are true are false. **(4 marks)**

Statement	True	False
There is effective use of spelling and grammar		
The correct opening and closing salutations have been used		
There is effective use of punctuation		
The content of the business letter is appropriate for the message being communicated		

Mock Assessment 2 – Level 1 Award in Business Skills

Introduction

The following is a Mock Assessment to be attempted in exam conditions.

You should attempt and aim to complete EVERY task.

Read every task carefully to make sure you understand what is required.

Where the date is relevant, it is given in the task.

Both minus signs and brackets can be used to indicate negative numbers UNLESS task instructions say otherwise.

You must use a full stop to indicate a decimal point.

You may use a comma to indicate a number in the thousands, but you don't have to.

The assessment includes 6 tasks.

The total number of marks available for this assessment is 80.

Time allowed: 90 minutes

1 Mock Assessment Questions

Task 1 (12 marks)

There are different types of organisation.

a) Place a tick in the appropriate column below to show whether each of the organisations listed are in the public sector, private sector, charitable sector, service sector or manufacturing sector. **(4 marks)**

Organisation	Public Sector	Private Sector	Charitable Sector	Service Sector	Manufact-uring Sector
A retail supermarket					
The local library					
An organisation generating income to support its purpose					
An organisation that makes products to sell					

It is important to understand the role of the accounting department within an organisation.

b) Show whether the following statements are true or false. **(2 marks)**

Statement	True	False
Information provided by the accounting department is of no interest to anybody else in the organisation		
Customers of the accounting department can be from inside or outside the organisation.		

c)   Identify whether the following statements are true or false. **(4 marks)**

Statement	True	False
Sustainable businesses are more profitable than private organisations.		
A social enterprise is a profit making organisation.		
A Community Interest Company is funded by the government.		
Professional ethics is important in all types of organisations.		

d)   Complete the following sentence using the pick list below. **(1 mark)**

A partnership is owned and managed by _____.

Pick list

one person

exactly two people

between two and twenty people

public shareholders

e)   The following statements refer to responsibilities within an organisation. Tick the correct statement from the list of options. **(1 mark)**

Statement	✓
Directors are responsible for the induction and training of new staff.	
Keeping data secure is solely the responsibility of the IT department.	
Payroll issues would be dealt with by the Human Resources department.	
Departmental managers have overall responsibility for the running of an organisation and all high level decisions.	

Task 2 (14 marks)

At the end of every year your organisation calculates the profit or loss for the year.

a) Complete the sentence below by selecting the most appropriate option from the following list:

- equals
- is more than
- is less than

When expenditure _____ income this results in a loss. **(1 mark)**

Last year your organisation recorded income and expenditure as shown in the table below:

Income and expenditure	£
Sales	163,200
Cost of sales	119,760
Premises expenses	22,032
Heat and light	19,584
Administration and wages	13,437

b) Use the income and expenditure figures to calculate whether you have made a profit or loss and state whether this is a profit or loss. Complete the statement below to show your answer. **(2 marks)**

Statement

This would be a

profit	
loss	

of £ _____.

c) Tick the appropriate box below to indicate whether the following statement is true or false. **(1 mark)**

When a business makes a loss, the bank balance will be overdrawn.

True	
False	

d) Show whether the following situations would affect the bank account immediately or not by ticking the relevant boxes. **(2 marks)**

Transaction	Will affect the bank immediately	Will not affect the bank immediately
Cash received into the bank today from a credit customer		
An invoice received from a credit supplier with 14 day credit terms		

You have been given the following details of amounts owed to credit suppliers and the date by which the payment should be received.

Supplier	Payment to be received by supplier	Invoices to be paid	
		Invoice Amount	Invoice date
ABC Ltd.	10 days from invoice date	£1,245.75	30/09/2X
DEF Ltd.	At the end of the month of invoice date	£543.82	17/09/2X
		£746.69	28/09/2X
KLM Ltd.	30 days after the invoice date	£986.41	26/09/2X
		£742.53	26/09/2X

e) Complete the table below by inserting the total amount to be paid to DEF Ltd and the date by which the supplier should receive their payment. **(4 marks)**

Supplier	Amount to be paid (£)	Date supplier should receive payment
ABC Ltd.	£1,245.75	
DEF Ltd.		
KLM Ltd.	£1,728.94	

f) Identify whether the following statements are true or false. **(4 marks)**

Statement	True	False
When expenses are higher than income, a business can provide a return to its owners		
Saving opportunities arise when a business generates more income than expenses		
When a business has more expenditure than the income it generates, suppliers may withdraw credit		
When a not-for-profit organisation has more income than expenditure, they make a profit		

Task 3 (12 marks)

a) Match each of the following descriptions to the correct business document. **(4 marks)**

A document used in the sales process when an order is placed	Sales Invoice
A document used to place an order with a supplier	Delivery Note
The document which accompanies goods purchased from a supplier	Customer order
A document sent to a customer detailing amounts due for goods/services	Purchase Order

b) A business receives a delivery of goods purchased from a credit supplier.

Use the Pick list below to complete the following table to show the process that should be followed. **(2 marks)**

Order	Action
1	Business checks the delivery note against the goods received
2	
3	Business completes a goods received note
4	
5	Business makes payment and records the expenditure

Pick list

- Business checks the purchase invoice against the purchase order and delivery note/goods received note

- Business makes a note of any differences and queries them with the supplier

c) Identify whether the following statements are true or false. **(2 marks)**

Statement	True	False
Paying invoices received straight away is good for cash flow and helps maintain positive relationships with credit suppliers		
Following the correct business procedures and planning work effectively helps to avoid missing internal and external deadlines		

d) Refer to the following delivery note and goods received note (GRN) relating to goods received from XYZ Ltd. You have been asked to check the documents.

Delivery Note
XYZ Ltd. Sunnyside Beach Business Park LN1 5NQ

To: ABC Ltd. 123 High Street Manchester M23 1RD	Date: 2nd July 202X Delivery Note Number: 549
10 x Ink Cartridges Product Code AJ5544 @ £8.45 each 25 x Ink Cartridges Product Code MM9980 @ £12.90 each 15 x Ink Cartridges Product Code HAJ512 @ £9.80 each	
Received by: *A Parker*	Date: *3rd July 202X*

Goods Received Note
Received From: XYZ Ltd. Sunnyside Beach Business Park LN1 5NQ

Good Received Note Number: 2244 Delivery Note Number: 459	

Quantity	Product Code	Description
10	AJ5854	Toners
25	MM9980	Ink Cartridges
15	HAJ512	Ink Cartridges
Received by:	Date:

Having checked the documentation, identify whether the following statements are true or false. **(4 marks)**

Statement	True	False
The correct quantity of goods has been delivered.		
The product codes noted on the goods received note match those on the delivery note.		
The goods received note has not been signed.		
The delivery note number has been noted correctly on the GRN		

Task 4 (10 marks)

You work in the accounts team of a retail business with a number of branches in different areas of the UK.

You have been asked to produce some calculations in relation to the number of customers that have visited the stores over the last 4 weeks.

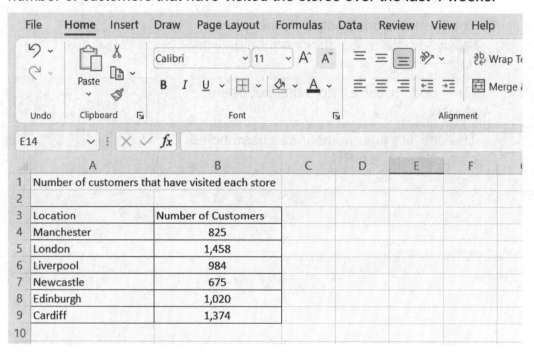

a) Select the correct option from the list below to show which icon would be used to make the text within the title bold. **(1 mark)**

Icon	✔
B	
<u>U</u>	
I	

b) How many customers visited the Cardiff store to the nearest 100? **(1 mark)**

c) Select the correct option from the list below to show which icon would be used to centralise the text in the 'Location' column. **(1 mark)**

Icon	✔
⇤☰	
☰	
☰	

d) Calculate the range for the number of customers visiting the stores. **(1 mark)**

e) What is the average number of customers visiting the stores during this period? **(1 mark)**

f) From the following options, select the icon which matches the description of how it is used to format data in a spreadsheet. Place a tick in the relevant box. **(3 marks)**

Icon	Used to format data within a spreadsheet to 'accounting'	Used to format data with a thousands separator	Used to show fewer decimal places in a spreadsheet
%			
,			
⌷⌖ ⌄			
←0 .00			
.00 →0			

g) An organisation is reviewing the selling price of some of its products.

The current selling price of product number AB3 is £89.00. This is to be increased by 8%.

Calculate the increase in selling price for product number AB3.
(1 mark)

h) The current selling price of product number BA8 is £146.00. This is to be increased by 3/8 (three eighths).

Calculate the increase in selling price for product number 74.
(1 mark)

Task 5 (16 marks)

a) Complete the following table to express the figures as fractions, decimals and percentages. **(4 marks)**

Fraction	Decimal	Percentage
	0.20	20%
¼		25%
	0.1	

b) Complete the following calculations. Where necessary, present your answers to 2 decimal places. **(4 marks)**

Question	Answer
A manufacturer produces one vase every 6 minutes on a production line. Express 6 minutes as a percentage of an hour.	
In one week, there were 50 hours available on the production line. The total number of vases produced was 500. 25 vases were damaged. What percentage of vases were damaged?	
475 vases were available to sell. The selling price was £6.80 per vase. Calculate the total sales revenue.	
¼ of the sales revenue would be distributed to the production workers in bonus payments. Calculate the total bonus amount.	

You have been provided a partially completed spreadsheet showing the sales, cost of sales and profits related to product X, for the first 6 months of the year.

	A	B	C	D	E
1	Month	Product X	Sales Revenue	Cost of Sales	Profit
2	January	300		£ 840.00	
3	February	320	£ 1,728.00	£ 896.00	£ 832.00
4	March	340	£ 1,836.00	£ 952.00	£ 884.00
5	April	380	£ 2,052.00		
6	May	365	£ 1,971.00	£ 1,022.00	£ 949.00
7	June	350	£ 1,890.00	£ 980.00	
8	Totals	2,055			
9					
10	Average profit per unit				
11					

c)   You sell product X for £5.40 per unit. What formula would be used in cell C2, to calculate the sales revenue generated by product X in January? **(1 mark)**

d)   What figure would be displayed in cell C2 after entering the formula? **(1 mark)**

e)   The cost of sales related to one unit of product X is £2.80. What formula would be used in cell D5, to show the cost of sales related to product X in April? **(1 mark)**

f)   What figure would be displayed in cell D5 after entering the formula? **(1 mark)**

g)   What formula would be used in cell E7, to calculate the profit generated by product X in June? **(1 mark)**

h)   What figure would be displayed in cell E7 after entering the formula?
     (1 mark)

i)   What formula would be used in cell E8, to calculate the total profit
     generated by product X in the first 6 months of the year? **(1 mark)**

j)   What formula would be used in cell B10, to calculate the average
     profit per month generated by product X? **(1 mark)**

Task 6 (16 marks)

You work for Markham Products and have been asked to send an email to Martin Dale, your manager, to confirm that you have arranged refreshments for a director's board meeting on 8 August. You should point out that the refreshments will be served at 10.30am.

Using the items at the bottom of the page, compose an appropriate e-mail in the template below. You will not need to use all of the items. **(6 marks)**

From: AATstudent@markhamproducts.com	
To:	1.
Subject:	2.

3.

4.

5.

6.

I've ordered refreshments.	Board meeting: Refreshments	Please accept this email as confirmation that refreshments for the board meeting on 8 August will be served at 10.30am. .	
AAT student	Attendance	The refreshments will be at the meeting on 10 August and served at 8.30am.	
Cheers	Hey M	Kind regards,	Hi Martin
mdale@markhamproducts.com		janettebones@kazeekrafts.com	

KAPLAN PUBLISHING

b) Identify whether the following statements are true or false. **(2 marks)**

Statement	True	False
The use of a spell check is not required when proof reading your own work.		
When addressing a business letter to an unknown recipient, the correct opening salutation is 'Dear Sir/Madam' and the correct closing salutation is 'Yours Faithfully'.		

c) Complete the following sentence using the options from the picklist below. **(1 mark)**

You received your induction a while ago and since then, the offices have moved. It is the responsibility of the _____ to ensure the working environment is safe.

Pick list

- the employee

- the employer

e) Since moving into the new offices, you notice that there are lots of archive boxes that have not yet been unpacked. There are also a number of computers stored in the corner of the room and multiple wires are causing a trip hazard.

What should you do? Select the correct option below. **(1 mark)**

Options	✓
Nothing, it is your employer's responsibility	
Tidy the cables up and ensure the boxes are stacked neatly	
Unpack the boxes in their new location and set the computers up in the spare office	
Report the issues as they pose a health and safety risk	

It is important to observe confidentiality.

f)   Complete the following sentence by selecting the most appropriate option from the pick list below. **(1 mark)**

Confidential information should be _____ if you have to leave your desk.

Pick list

- kept in a locked drawer
- hidden under the computer keyboard
- given to a colleague for safekeeping

g)   Effective team work is essential to the smooth operations of a business. Identify whether the following statements are true or false. **(3 marks)**

Statement	True	False
Work within a team will be allocated in order of when it comes in, regardless of how important or urgent it is.		
Meeting deadlines helps to promote effective team working.		
Online meetings are particularly effective when employees work from remote settings.		

h)   Select the most appropriate password from the options below. **(1 mark)**

Options	✓
Password1	
Jenny24041985	
#J3nNy4520*!	
MyPassword123	

i) Complete the following sentence by selecting the correct option.
(1 mark)

A piece of software which helps multiple people work on a project at the same time is known as _____.

Options	✓
A digital to-do list	
A database	
Accounting software	
An online collaboration tool	

Mock Assessment Answers

1 Mock Assessment 1 Answers

Task 1 (12 marks)

a) An animal welfare organisation is a **charitable** organisation.

The fire service is a **public sector** organisation. **(2 marks)**

b) Show whether these statements are true or false by ticking the correct box. **(3 marks)**

Statement	True	False
The primary aim of an organisation in the private sector is to make a profit.	✓	
The public sector is funded by private individuals or organisations.		✓
A Community Interest Company is a not for profit organisation.	✓	

c) Show whether the following statements are true or false. **(3 marks)**

Statement	True	False
Information provided by the accounting department is used by external customers only.		✓
An example of an internal customer of the accounting department is a close friend of one of the managers of the organisation.		✓
The Human Resources department are responsible for dealing with employee relations and personnel and their payroll.	✓	

d) Enter the following options into the table above, as they would appear within a three-level organisation chart. **(3 marks)**

Top Level	• Directors
Middle Level	• Department managers
Lower Level	• Department staff

e) Which of the following statements regarding Public Limited Companies (PLCs) is correct? **(1 mark)**

Statement	✔
A Public Limited Company (PLC) provides services that are essential to the population, like health care.	
The shares of a Public Limited Company (PLC) are made available to the public.	✔
A Public Limited Company (PLC) is a not for profit organisation.	

Task 2 (14 marks)

a) When income **is less than** expenditure this results in a loss. **(1 mark)**

a) State whether the following statement is true or false. **(1 mark)**

Statement	True	False
When a sole trader makes a loss, they have the ability to repay loans to help them pay their bills.		✔

b) **Statement**

This would be a

profit	✔
loss	

of **£12,032**. **(2 marks)**

c) When a charity records less income than expenses, this results in a **Deficit**. **(1 mark)**

d) Insert an item from the following pick list into the right hand column of the table below to identify the term described. **(2 marks)**

Description	Term described
A person or organisation who is owed money by the company for purchases made.	**A creditor/ payable**
A transaction to sell goods when the payment is made one month later.	**A credit sale**

e) What is the total cost of the printer paper? **(1 mark)**

Answer: £ 343.80

f) Is the purchase of the printer paper a cash transaction or a credit transaction? **(1 mark)**

Type of transaction	✓
Cash transaction	✓
Credit transaction	

g) From the pick list below, enter the correct payment term next to the most appropriate statement. **(2 marks)**

Statement	Payment term
To help the supplier with out of pocket expenses for large orders is a………..	**Payment in advance**
When a customer pays upon receipt of the goods or services is a……………	**Payment on delivery**

h) Identify the date that payment will be due to each credit supplier and complete the table below. **(3 marks)**

Supplier	Date by which payment should be made to each credit supplier
Parker Products Ltd.	**17th June**
Pencil Case Supplies	**6th July**
Prestige Ltd.	**30th June**

Task 3 (12 marks)

a) There is no supporting documentation to refer to in order to check the invoice for accuracy, but the payment is due today.

You have never encountered this issue before, what should you do? **(1 mark)**

Options	✓
Pay the invoice to prevent missing the deadline	
Take no action to avoid making a mistake	
Seek advice from your manager	✓

b) The company you work for has recently changed the process for sales invoices. An update to the system forced these changes. What internal changes need to be made? **(1 mark)**

Options	✓
The sales invoicing procedure needs to be updated and all changes communicated to the relevant staff	
The sales manager should process all sales invoices following the system update	
The IT department should review the update and process the sales invoices as per any amendments	✓

c) Identify the correct document that would be used in each of the following circumstances. **(3 marks)**

Description	Document
A customer sends this as proof of payment to a supplier	**Remittance Advice**
Issued following the return of faulty goods	**Credit note**
Accompanies the shipment of goods	**Delivery note**

d) Comparing the above delivery note to the relevant purchase order, identify whether the following statements are true or false. **(5 marks)**

Statement	True	False
The goods were delivered to the correct address.		✓
There were errors in the quantities delivered.		✓
There were errors in the products delivered.	✓	
The product pricing was incorrect.	✓	
The goods were delivered on time.		✓

e) Show whether the following statements are true or false by ticking the appropriate box. **(2 marks)**

Statement	True	False
A sales invoice is always issued for cash sales.		✓
Purchases are always made from an approved supplier list.		✓

Task 4 (10 marks)

a) Select the correct option from the list below to show which icon would be used to change the colour of the font within a cell. **(1 mark)**

Icon	✓
🖌	
A ⌄	✓
🪣 ⌄	

b) Which store made the highest amount of sales? **(1 mark)**

Store D

c) Which store made the lowest amount of sales? **(1 mark)**

Store C

d) What is the range of sales made? **(1 mark)**

£222.61

e) Which of the following formula options would perform the same role as the AutoSum button with the sales data? **(1 mark)**

Formula	✓
=B2+C2+D2+E2	
=B2*B3*D2*E2	
=B2+B3+B4+B5	✓
=B2/B5	

f) Complete the table to show the motor fuel expense for Vehicle 1. **(1 mark)**

Vehicle 1	**251.60**

g) Calculate the average motor fuel expense per vehicle. **(1 mark)**

Answer: £ | 243.55 |

h) Select the correct option from the list below to show which icon would be used to amend the totals to italic text. **(1 mark)**

Icon	✓
B	
A^	
I	✓

i) Select the correct cell range that would be highlighted to amend the totals to italics. **(1 mark)**

Formula	✓
B2:B5	
A1:D1	
A6:D6	✓

i) In which cell has the total been added up incorrectly? **(1 mark)**

Cell	✓
B6	
C6	✓
D6	

Task 5 (16 marks)

a) Which of the following is the ratio of the total wages to wages for Store A? **(1 mark)**

Ratio	✓
2:1	
3:1	
4:1	✓

b) Using the information in the table below, calculate the bonuses for employees B and C. **(4 marks)**

Employee	Annual Salary	Bonus calculated as a % of salary	Bonus Payment	Total Pay for the year
A	£25,000	5%	£1,250	£26,250
B	£19,500	10%	**£1,950**	**£21,450**
C	£28,000	7.5%	**£2,100**	**£30,100**

c) How much will Employee B receive in respect of her pay increase? **(1 mark)**

£3,900

d)   What will Employee B's total salary be for next year before any
     bonus calculations? **(1 mark)**

     £23,400

e)   Based on her new wage, how much should Employee B expect to be
     paid per month before any tax or national insurance deductions?
     (1 mark)

     £1,950

f)   What formula would be used in cell C2, to calculate the monthly
     salary of employee A? **(1 mark)**

     =B2/12

g)   What figure would be displayed in cell C2 after entering the formula?
     (1 mark)

     £2,100

h)   What formula would be used in cell D3, to calculate the bonus due to
     employee B? **(1 mark)**

     =C3*5%

i)   What figure would be displayed in cell D3 after entering the formula?
     (1 mark)

     £78

j)   What formula would be used in cell E4, to calculate the total pay for
     employee C? **(1 mark)**

     =C4+D4

k)   What figure would be displayed in cell E4 after entering the formula?
     (1 mark)

     £2,084.25

l)   What formula would be used in cell E5, to calculate the total monthly
     pay for all 3 employees? **(1 mark)**

     =SUM(E2:E4)

m) What figure would be displayed in cell E5 after entering the formula? **(1 mark)**

£5,927.25

Task 6 (16 marks)

a) Identify the most appropriate software to use in each of the situations below. **(4 marks)**

Situation	Type of software to use			
	Presentation ✓	Word processing ✓	Email ✓	Spreadsheet ✓
Listing the mileage of the sales staff paid at 45p per mile				✓
Communicating training on the new system to your team	✓			
Communicating a request to take some annual leave			✓	
Communicating with a customer to chase an outstanding debt		✓		

b) The addresses of all staff should be accessible to **authorised staff only. (1 mark)**

c) Identify whether the following statements are true or false **(2 marks)**

Statement	True	False
A virus will damage files on your computer but will not affect its performance.		✓
Encrypting data is effective against hackers.	✓	

d) You receive an invoice attached to an email which contains a payment link. The email address looks strange and you suspect the email may be suspicious.

i) What would you do? **(1 mark)**

Options	✓
Open the invoice and seek advice from your manager as to whether to pay it or not	
Delete the email unopened and report it to your IT department	✓
Do not open the invoice but click on the payment link and pay the invoice	

ii) Which of the following threats is this is an example of? **(1 mark)**

Options	✓
Hacking	
Employee fraud	
Phishing	✓

e) Is this acceptable behaviour? **(1 mark)**

Yes	No
	✓

f) Which planning aids would you use? Select two from the following options. **(2 marks)**

Options	✓
A paper-based to-do list	
An online calendar	✓
A digital to-do list	✓
An online collaboration tool	

g) Check the letter for accuracy and state whether the following are true are false. **(4 marks)**

Statement	True	False
There is effective use of spelling and grammar		✓
The correct opening and closing salutations have been used	✓	
There is effective use of punctuation		✓
The content of the business letter is appropriate for the message being communicated		✓

2 Mock Assessment 2 Answers

Task 1 (12 marks)

a) Place a tick in the appropriate column below to show whether each of the organisations listed are in the public sector, private sector, charitable sector, service sector or manufacturing sector. **(4 marks)**

Organisation	Public Sector	Private Sector	Charitable Sector	Service Sector	Manufact-uring Sector
A retail supermarket		✓			
The local library	✓				
An organisation generating income to support its purpose			✓		
An organisation that makes products to sell					✓

b) Show whether the following statements are true or false. **(2 marks)**

Statement	True	False
Information provided by the accounting department is of no interest to anybody else in the organisation		✓
Customers of the accounting department can be from inside or outside the organisation.	✓	

c) Identify whether the following statements are true or false. **(4 marks)**

Statement	True	False
Sustainable businesses are more profitable than private organisations.		✔
A social enterprise is a profit making organisation.		✔
A Community Interest Company is funded by the government.		✔
Professional ethics is important in all types of organisations.	✔	

d) A partnership is owned and managed by **between two and twenty people. (1 mark)**

e) Tick the correct statement from the list of options. **(1 mark)**

Statement	✔
Directors are responsible for the induction and training of new staff.	
Keeping data secure is solely the responsibility of the IT department.	
Payroll issues would be dealt with by the Human Resources department.	✔
Departmental managers have overall responsibility for the running of an organisation and all high level decisions.	

Task 2 (14 marks)

a) When expenditure **is more than** income this results in a loss. **(1 mark)**

b) **Statement**

This would be a

profit	
loss	✔

of £ **11,613**.

(2 marks)

c) When a business makes a loss, the bank balance will be overdrawn. **(1 mark)**

True	
False	✓

d) Show whether the following situations would affect the bank account immediately or not by ticking the relevant boxes. **(2 marks)**

Transaction	Will affect the bank immediately	Will not affect the bank immediately
Cash received into the bank today from a credit customer	✓	
An invoice received from a credit supplier with 14 day credit terms		✓

e) Complete the table below by inserting the total amount to be paid to DEF Ltd and the date by which the supplier should receive their payment. **(4 marks)**

Supplier	Amount to be paid (£)	Date supplier should receive payment
ABC Ltd.	£1,245.75	10th October 20X7
DEF Ltd.	**£1,290.51**	30th September 20X7
KLM Ltd.	£1,728.94	26th October 20X7

f) Identify whether the following statements are true or false. **(4 marks)**

Statement	True	False
When expenses are higher than income, a business can provide a return to its owners		✓
Saving opportunities arise when a business generates more income than expenses	✓	
When a business has more expenditure than the income it generates, suppliers may withdraw credit	✓	
When a not-for-profit organisation has more income than expenditure, they make a profit		✓

Task 3 (12 marks)

a) Match each of the following descriptions to the correct business document. **(4 marks)**

A document used in the sales process when an order is placed	Customer order
A document used to place an order with a supplier	Purchase Order
The document which accompanies goods purchased from a supplier	Delivery Note
A document sent to a customer detailing amounts due for goods/services	Sales Invoice

b) Use the Pick list below to complete the following table to show the process that should be followed. **(2 marks)**

Order	Action
1	Business checks the delivery note against the goods received
2	**Business makes a note of any differences and queries them with the supplier**
3	Business completes a goods received note
4	**Business checks the purchase invoice against the purchase order and delivery note/goods received note**
5	Business makes payment and records the expenditure

c)   Identify whether the following statements are true or false. **(2 marks)**

Statement	True	False
Paying invoices received straight away is good for cash flow and helps maintain positive relationships with credit suppliers		✓
Following the correct business procedures and planning work effectively helps to avoid missing internal and external deadlines	✓	

d)   Having checked the documentation, identify whether the following statements are true or false. **(4 marks)**

Statement	True	False
The correct quantity of goods has been delivered.	✓	
The product codes noted on the goods received note match those on the delivery note.		✓
The goods received note has not been signed.	✓	
The delivery note number has been noted correctly on the GRN		✓

Task 4 (10 marks)

a)   Select the correct option from the list below to show which icon would be used to make the text within the title bold. **(1 mark)**

Icon	✓
B	✓
U	
I	

b) How many customers visited the Cardiff store to the nearest 100? **(1 mark)**

> 1,400

c) Select the correct option from the list below to show which icon would be used to centralise the text in the 'Location' column. **(1 mark)**

Icon	✓
⭰	
☰	✓
☰	

d) Calculate the range for the number of customers visiting the stores. **(1 mark)**

> 783

e) What is the average number of customers visiting the stores during this period? **(1 mark)**

> 1,056

f) From the following options, select the icon which matches the description of how it is used to format data in a spreadsheet. Place a tick in the relevant box. **(3 marks)**

Icon	Used to format data within a spreadsheet to 'accounting'	Used to format data with a thousands separator	Used to show fewer decimal places in a spreadsheet
%			
,		✓	
🖳 ˅	✓		
←0 .00			
.00 →0			✓

g) Calculate the increase in selling price for product number AB3. **(1 mark)**

£7.12

h) Calculate the increase in selling price for product number 74. **(1 mark)**

£54.75

Task 5 (16 marks)

a) Complete the following table to express the figures as fractions, decimals and percentages. **(4 marks)**

Fraction	Decimal	Percentage
1/5	0.20	20%
¼	**0.25**	25%
1/10	0.1	**10%**

b) Complete the following calculations. Where necessary, present your answers to 2 decimal places. **(4 marks)**

Question	Answer
A manufacturer produces one vase every 6 minutes on a production line. Express 6 minutes as a percentage of an hour.	**10%**
In one week, there were 50 hours available on the production line. The total number of vases produced was 500. 25 vases were damaged. What percentage of vases were damaged?	**5%**
475 vases were available to sell. The selling price was £6.80 per vase. Calculate the total sales revenue.	**£3,230**
¼ of the sales revenue would be distributed to the production workers in bonus payments. Calculate the total bonus amount.	**£807.50**

c) You sell product X for £5.40 per unit. What formula would be used in cell C2, to calculate the sales revenue generated by product X in January? **(1 mark)**

=B2*5.4

d) What figure would be displayed in cell C2 after entering the formula? **(1 mark)**

£1,620

e) The cost of sales related to one unit of product X is £2.80. What formula would be used in cell D5, to show the cost of sales related to product X in April? **(1 mark)**

=B5*2.8

f) What figure would be displayed in cell D5 after entering the formula? **(1 mark)**

£1,064

g) What formula would be used in cell E7, to calculate the profit generated by product X in June? **(1 mark)**

=C7-D7

h) What figure would be displayed in cell E7 after entering the formula? **(1 mark)**

£910

i) What formula would be used in cell E8, to calculate the total profit generated by product X in the first 6 months of the year? **(1 mark)**

=SUM(E2:E7)

j) What formula would be used in cell B10, to calculate the average profit per month generated by product X? **(1 mark)**

=E8/6

Task 6 (16 marks)

Using the items at the bottom of the page, compose an appropriate e-mail in the template below. You will not need to use all of the items. **(6 marks)**

From: AATstudent@markhamproducts.com	
To:	**1.** mdale@markhamproducts.com
Subject:	**2.** Board meeting: Refreshments

3. Hi Martin

4. Please accept this email as confirmation that refreshments for the board meeting on 8 August will be served at 10.30am.

5. Kind regards,

6. AAT student

b) Identify whether the following statements are true or false. **(2 marks)**

Statement	True	False
The use of a spell check is not required when proof reading your own work.		✓
When addressing a business letter to an unknown recipient, the correct opening salutation is 'Dear Sir/Madam' and the correct closing salutation is 'Yours Faithfully'.	✓	

c) You received your induction a while ago and since then, the offices have moved. It is the responsibility of the **the employer** to ensure the working environment is safe. **(1 mark)**

e) Select the correct option below. **(1 mark)**

Options	✓
Nothing, it is your employer's responsibility	
Tidy the cables up and ensure the boxes are stacked neatly	
Unpack the boxes in their new location and set the computers up in the spare office	
Report the issues as they pose a health and safety risk	✓

f) Confidential information should be **kept in a locked drawer** if you have to leave your desk. **(1 mark)**

g) Effective team work is essential to the smooth operations of a business. Identify whether the following statements are true or false. **(3 marks)**

Statement	True	False
Work within a team will be allocated in order of when it comes in, regardless of how important or urgent it is.		✓
Meeting deadlines helps to promote effective team working.	✓	
Online meetings are particularly effective when employees work from remote settings.	✓	

h) Select the most appropriate password from the options below.
(1 mark)

Options	✓
Password1	
Jenny24041985	
#J3nNy4520*!	✓
MyPassword123	

i) A piece of software which helps multiple people work on a project at the same time is known as _____. **(1 mark)**

Options	✓
A digital to-do list	
A database	
Accounting software	
An online collaboration tool	✓

INDEX

KAPLAN PUBLISHING